D1569945

Anne Sexton's Confessional Poetics

UNIVERSITY PRESS OF FLORIDA

Florida A&M University, Tallahassee
Florida Atlantic University, Boca Raton
Florida Gulf Coast University, Ft. Myers
Florida International University, Miami
Florida State University, Tallahassee
New College of Florida, Sarasota
University of Central Florida, Orlando
University of Florida, Gainesville
University of North Florida, Jacksonville
University of South Florida, Tampa
University of West Florida, Pensacola

Anne Sexton's Confessional Poetics

ॐ

JO GILL

University Press of Florida
Gainesville/Tallahassee/Tampa/Boca Raton
Pensacola/Orlando/Miami/Jacksonville/Ft. Myers/Sarasota

Copyright 2007 by Jo Gill
Printed in the United States of America on acid-free paper

12 11 10 09 08 07   6 5 4 3 2 1

Library of Congress Cataloging-in-Publication Data
Gill, Jo, 1965–
Anne Sexton's confessional poetics / Jo Gill.
p. cm.
Includes bibliographical references and index.
ISBN 978-0-8130-3175-0 (acid-free paper)
1. Sexton, Anne, 1928–1974—Criticism and interpretation. I. Sexton,
Anne, 1928–1974. II. Title.
PS3537.E915Z685 2007
811.'54—dc22   2007027530

The University Press of Florida is the scholarly publishing agency
for the State University System of Florida, comprising Florida A&M
University, Florida Atlantic University, Florida Gulf Coast University,
Florida International University, Florida State University, New College
of Florida, University of Central Florida, University of Florida,
University of North Florida, University of South Florida, and
University of West Florida.

University Press of Florida
15 Northwest 15th Street
Gainesville, FL 32611-2079
http://www.upf.com

Contents

Acknowledgments

Thanks are due to Shelley Saguaro and Peter Widdowson and others in the School of English at the University of Gloucestershire; to Stan Smith of Nottingham Trent University; to past and present colleagues at Kingston University, Bath Spa University, and the University of Exeter. I owe gratitude to the staff of the Harry Ransom Humanities Research Center at the University of Texas in Austin and to the Schlesinger Library, Radcliffe College, Harvard University for facilitating access to their collections. I also gratefully acknowledge the cooperation of Anne Sexton's daughter, Linda Gray Sexton, and I am indebted to the scholarship of Sexton's biographer, Diane Wood Middlebrook. The patient guidance of Amy Gorelick and others at the University Press of Florida has been appreciated, as have the insights of their anonymous reviewers. Personal thanks to Jeannette Gill, George and Margaret Gill, Sheena and Ray Hennessy, Ian Stevens, Frances Hollingdale, Mark Whalan, and Alice Entwistle. The biggest debt is to Jacob, Freya, Keziah and, above all, to Neil.

Excerpts from *The Complete Poems* by Anne Sexton. Copyright © 1981 by Linda G. Sexton. Reprinted by permission of Houghton Mifflin Company. All rights reserved. Excerpts from *Anne Sexton: A Self-Portrait in Letters* edited by Linda Gray Sexton and Lois Ames. Copyright © 1977 by Linda Gray Sexton and Loring Conant Jr., executors of the will of Anne Sexton. Reprinted by permission of Houghton Mifflin Company. All rights reserved. Excerpts from "An Obsessive Combination of Ontological Inscape, Trickery and Love" from *Selected Poems of Anne Sexton*. Copyright © 1988 by Linda G. Sexton. Reprinted by permission of Houghton Mifflin Company. All rights reserved. Published material reprinted by permission of Sll/sterling Lord

Literistic, Inc. Copyright © 1981 by Anne Sexton. Unpublished material from the Anne Sexton archive is used with the permission of Linda Gray Sexton and the Harry Ransom Humanities Research Center, University of Texas at Austin. Excerpts from an unpublished letter of John Holmes are used with the permission of Doris Holmes Eyges and the Harry Ransom Humanities Research Center, University of Texas at Austin.

Earlier versions of parts of chapters 2 and 3 appeared in *Twentieth-Century Literature* 50.1 (2004) and in Mark Jackson, ed., *Health and the Modern Home* (Routledge 2007) respectively. My thanks to the editors of both volumes for their valuable comments. Finally, I am grateful to the British Association for American Studies and the British Academy for research support.

Sources and abbreviations

Unless otherwise indicated, the text used for Sexton's poems is *Anne Sexton: The Complete Poems* (Boston: Houghton Mifflin, 1981). The sources of Sexton's published prose and uncollected poetry are indicated in parenthetical references and listed in the bibliography. Published letters are quoted from *Anne Sexton: A Self-Portrait in Letters*, ed. by Linda Gray Sexton and Lois Ames (Boston: Houghton Mifflin, 1979) and indicated parenthetically by the shortened title *Letters* followed by the page number. Published interviews with Anne Sexton are listed parenthetically by the name of the interviewer and the page number; full references are given in the bibliography.

Unpublished materials (principally journal entries, lecture notes, poem drafts and worksheets) are, unless otherwise indicated, from the Harry Ransom Humanities Research Center, University of Texas at Austin (referenced parenthetically by the abbreviation HRHRC). Original material obtained from other sources is identified in the endnotes. Unpublished letters are cited within the text and referenced parenthetically by the abbreviation HRHRC.

Unpublished lecture notes from Sexton's tenure as Crawshaw Chair in Literature at Colgate University are cited parenthetically by the short form "Crawshaw" followed by lecture and typescript page number. In all cases, unless otherwise indicated, these are original typescripts now held at the HRHRC. The draft of an unpublished poem, "The Thought Disease," is reproduced as an Appendix.

Unless otherwise specified, the dates cited for collections of poems are first U.S. publication and the dates cited for individual poems are dates of composition, as indicated by manuscript drafts held at the HRHRC.

Introduction

Anne Sexton, suburban housewife, mother, psychiatric patient, lover, Pulitzer Prize–winning poet, playwright, and professor, was one of the leading writers of her generation. Born in 1928 in Massachusetts, she experienced a fraught—if materially privileged—childhood. Inadequately educated and at odds with her family, she eloped at the age of twenty and, after one or two short-term moves with her then-naval husband, moved to the suburbs of Boston. She gave birth to two daughters, and in 1957, stimulated in part by her therapist (whom she had started seeing after a diagnosis of postpartum depression) and in part by seeing "new critic" I. A. Richards speaking about the sonnet, on public service television, Sexton began to write poetry.

Success as a writer came swiftly. Sexton enrolled in Robert Lowell's Boston University poetry class where she became acquainted with Sylvia Plath, amongst others, and she began to identify herself with the label "poet." As she explains, "I don't really believe the poem, but the name is surely mine so I must belong to the poem. So I must be real. . . . All I am is the trick of words writing themselves" (qtd. in Middlebrook *Biography* 82). Similarly, to her agent, Sexton writes: "Whatever I am I am because I wrote it" (*Letters* 288). For the next fifteen years or so, Sexton wrote, studied, taught, and performed. She produced ten volumes of poetry (two posthumously). She read other poets' work and corresponded voraciously with other writers, critics, editors, and fans. She participated in writing workshops and summer schools and taught on writing projects in mental institutions, at Boston University and at Colgate University where in 1972 she was awarded the Crawshaw Chair in Literature. She produced a play, *Tell Me Your Answer True*, off Broadway and she performed her own work on countless occasions at readings throughout the United States and in the United Kingdom, including, for a period, with her own chamber rock band, "Anne Sexton and Her Kind." During this time, as Diane Wood Middlebrook's biography of Sexton and Sexton's daughter's memoir—*Searching for Mercy Street*—reveals, Sexton grappled with the multiple problems of psychiatric illness, dependence on the medications prescribed for her condition, alcohol addiction, and a succession of difficult and mutually damaging relationships both within and outside the family. After repeated hospitalizations and several attempts on her own life, Sexton committed suicide in October 1974.

Sexton's work is hugely varied in form, style, tone, and voice. It ranges from the brilliantly executed and formally controlled poems evidenced in the early volumes *To Bedlam and Part Way Back* (1960) and *All My Pretty Ones* (1962) through the lyrical, elegiac, or contemplative work in *Live or Die* (1966) and *Love Poems* (1969) to the bold revisionist fairy tales of *Transformations* (1971) and the more abstract, surreal, and challenging poems of the late and posthumous collections. The present book discusses poetry from the whole repertoire. One of its aims is to demonstrate the diversity and richness of Sexton's writing and to show that the later poems, although sometimes disregarded because of their abstraction or apparent impenetrability, are both fascinating and fundamental to a full understanding of Sexton's poetics. The study which follows is necessarily selective in its choice of poems. It comprises rereadings of some of the well-known and by now canonical poems, appraisals of some of the apparently atypical and thus little-read poems, and an examination of some of the long poems and the late sequences—poems which are often overlooked because of their apparent diffuseness, surrealism, and opacity. However, my main aim is to suggest new ways of reading Anne Sexton. To this end, I propose a nexus of perspectives and concerns which are sustained by, but by no means limited to, the specific poems I have chosen. I hope that readers will feel galvanized to revisit the writing for themselves, and will find some value in looking at their own selection of poems from the new perspectives proffered here.

This study begins with a number of early poems (including "Her Kind," "For John Who Begs Me Not to Enquire Further," and "The Double Image") and closes with the long and rather later poems "Hurry Up Please It's Time" and "Is It True?" It thus follows a loosely chronological structure. I say "loosely" because Sexton's poetry in many ways resists reading according to such a trajectory. First, she often returns in poems of the middle and late periods to themes, styles, and voices first employed much earlier (so "Daddy

Warbucks," for instance, written in May 1974 and published in 1976, revisits the same scene as "The House" of March 1961). Second, many of the poems published late in Sexton's career were, as manuscript evidence at the Harry Ransom Humanities Research Center at the University of Texas at Austin reveals, drafted much earlier and subsequently revised (for example, "Self in 1958") or were long-term projects. The sequence of "Letters to Dr. Y.," for example, published posthumously in 1978, record the concerns of a whole decade. Nevertheless, throughout the study, I have attempted both to flag up key and persistent areas of interest in Sexton's work and to show how her poetry developed and changed in different periods.

It is not only Sexton's published poetry which is my subject in this book. I am interested too in the handful of prose essays and short stories which she produced (for example, "The Letting Down of the Hair" and "The Freak Show" discussed in chapter five) and in early drafts and manuscripts of un-published work, diaries, letters, interviews, and lecture notes—principally the extensive series of notes for the Crawshaw Lectures which Sexton deliv-ered while Chair in Literature at Colgate University. This rich, and as yet un-derscrutinized archive material, derives principally from the holdings of the Harry Ransom Humanities Research Center, although I have also drawn on other archives, for example, the Schlesinger Library of the Radcliffe Institute at Harvard University. In addition, I offer a reading of her visual representa-tions and self-representations in photographs, on book jackets, in the 1966 television documentary with which she cooperated, and in staged readings or performances of her work.

This is not a book about confessional writing, nor is it an account of post-war women's poetry. Nevertheless, questions of genre and gender emerge repeatedly. My intention is to read Sexton within her generic and gender contexts and to demonstrate the ways in which her work interrogates, resists and extends the limitations ascribed to both. My study differs from those of some earlier Sexton scholars in that it benefits from the practices and in-sights offered by recent principally poststructuralist approaches to writing. These approaches, although anticipated in Sexton's work, have only come to prominence in the decades since her death. The following chapters will dem-onstrate that new posthumanist understandings of the previously accepted givens of Sexton's poetry—of its relation to an unproblematized confessional impulse and to autobiographical self-representation, of its authenticity and referentiality—permit its radical reevaluation. As David Attwell proposes in an interview with the South Africa writer J .M. Coetzee, "It is logical that you should bring deconstruction to bear on the analysis of confession where the problem of the self's residence within language is so visible" (245).

Anne Sexton's Confessional Poetics seeks a way of reading Sexton that will do three key things. First, it will offer a close reading of the poetry, a reading which is attentive to its structure, voice, idiom, and style—or its "formal representations" as Marjorie Perloff terms them (*Poetic* 26). Second, it will bring a nuanced and critical eye to the questions of truth, authenticity, subjectivity, and reference which have so dominated orthodox readings of confessional writing in general and Sexton's work in particular. In what ways, I will ask, does Sexton's poetry undermine conventional expectations of agency, reliability, and transparency? Instead of reading Sexton's as a poetry of harrowing authenticity, I propose that it is characterized by self-conscious strategies of distortion, occlusion, and denial. Finally, this book seeks a reading strategy which will attend to the place of Sexton's work in specific historical, political, and ideological contexts.

This is a tall task, and one which may seem contradictory. We might inquire whether it is possible to integrate a close reading of the poetry with a sense of its historical and literary context, and to frame both of these with poststructuralist attentiveness to the indeterminacy of subjectivity and truth and the uncertainties of language and reference. Sexton's work demands a reading strategy commensurate with its own complexity, depth, and range. In meeting the challenge of explicating it, I draw on a number of reading strategies and resources, and I adopt a number of valuable models. For example, like Rachel Blau DuPlessis in *Genders, Races and Religious Cultures in Modern American Poetry*, I "propose a reactivation of close reading to examine in poetry the textual traces and discursive manifestations of a variety of ideological assumptions, subject positions, and social concepts." I adopt "reading strategies that can mediate between the historical terrain and the intimate poetic textures of a work" (1). We might think of *Anne Sexton's Confessional Poetics* in Leigh Gilmore's words (drawing, in turn, on Michel Foucault) as a "genealogy" of Sexton's poetry. A "genealogy" such as this "finds its subject in the act of seeking it . . . it is always a story of changed minds and catastrophe, of digressions that cannot predict or control their narrative ends." As Gilmore explains, "Genealogy proceeds through a diffusion of desire more interested in multiplying knowledges than in waiting for the right 'one'" (*Autobiograph-*

ics 5–6). In this respect my book, like Sexton's writing, represents not a search for truth but an open-ended process of engagement and enquiry.

Anne Sexton's Confessional Poetics is structured in three main parts. The first part of the book (chapters one through three) examines Sexton's place in its literary, cultural, and historical contexts. Chapter one begins by tracing the origins of the confessional mode of poetry which so dominated American literature in the 1960s and with which Sexton was typically, if problematically, identified. Chapter two considers the question of narcissism—a term which has often been used pejoratively as a synonym for confession. Here I draw on psychoanalytic and postmodern theories in order to restore some of the potential to the concept. I suggest that the apparent narcissism of Sexton's work (manifested in many ways, not least in her repeated use of metaphors of mirrors, glass, and other reflective surfaces) should be understood as a sophisticated and self-reflexive strategy. It is but one element of the larger questioning in her work of the confessional mode within which she operates. When Sexton begins, as she does in the early poems discussed in these chapters, to ask about the dynamics of confession, its authority, its referentiality and its efficacy, she is inevitably talking also about the ethics of confession, its place in the world, and its responsibility to a particular culture in a particular time and place. Chapter three, then, proceeds to inquire about the origins of Sexton's poetry in mid-century suburban America and its synthesis of the ideologies of gender dominant at the time. It asks what Sexton makes of these contexts and, drawing on the work of Deborah Nelson and others, suggests contiguities between Sexton's confessions, expectations of femininity and domesticity, and a Cold War climate of secrecy and mistrust. Finally, it explores Sexton's mediation of broader social, political, and ideological issues. Can it be true, as the 1963 poem "To Lose the Earth" avows, that history "means nothing to me"? The emphasis throughout part one, then, is on Sexton's negotiation first of the relationship between penitent and confessor, then of self and other, and finally of private and public. It is the notion of narcissism which is the key; when recuperated as a strategy which reconciles the inside and the out, the private and the public, the self and the other, it offers a strategy for reading both the detail of Sexton's writing and its engagement with larger contexts.

Part two of the book (chapters four and five) moves on to explore Sexton's appropriation and testing of broader autobiographical discourses and her self-conscious manipulation of audiences in performed and performative contexts. Part three (chapters six and seven) looks at Sexton's challenging examination of the reliability of language and her playful testing of the apparent "truth" of confession. For Sexton, truth and language alike are slippery, evasive, and unreliable. In this final section of the book, we look at what Sexton makes of these profound uncertainties. I argue that is in relation to debates about truth and its representation that Sexton stakes her claim to an idiosyncratic confessional poetics—a poetics which is paradoxically both profoundly knowing and deeply uncertain. It is this paradox—this desire to embrace the either/or, to inhabit that liminal space between inside and out, subject and other—that is Sexton's persistent inspiration and concern.

PART I

&

Confessional cultures

I

The confessional mode

Anne Sexton has been labeled the "high-priestess" and the "mother" of the confessional mode of poetry. It has been said that "No poet was more consistently and uniformly confessional than Anne Sexton. . . . Her name has almost become identified with the genre" (Phillips 6; George *Oedipus* 90; Lerner 52). Sexton herself commented, "At one time I hated being called confessional and denied it, but mea culpa. Now I say that I'm the only confessional poet" (*Letters* 372). Yet the evidence of Sexton's poems, and of comments which she makes in letters, interviews, and lectures, belies any such straightforward identification. Indeed, Sexton's own mea culpa may be read as a rueful and ironic sign of a label unwillingly tolerated, rather than as a wholehearted statement of affiliation.

This chapter examines the ways in which Sexton's writing negotiates a position for itself within this mode, testing, manipulating, subverting, and extending its boundaries as necessity requires. Confession for Sexton is never straightforward, it is never a solution to the personal problems which apparently precede and stimulate it. It is, rather, a ritual or a set of practices which preoccupies, constrains, and finally corrupts the subject. A number of poems from throughout Sexton's career seem to assimilate and then re-present some of the hostility with which the mode has been met. In "Cripples and Other Stories" and "The Death Baby," for example, the confessional subject depicts herself as waste, vomit, or food for other people's consumption. In many other poems, as we will see in the next chapter, it is confession itself which is Sexton's subject. In "For John Who Begs Me Not to Enquire Further," for example, it is the procedures, practices, and effects of confession as much (if not more than) the story of the suffering self which are laid bare. Confession, then, is a highly self-conscious and a highly rhetorical mode. At stake for Sexton in her use of the mode, as of any of the other autobiographical forms she chooses (memoir, letters, diaries, performance), is the viability of her own project. What are the parameters and conventions of these forms? How might they be read? Leigh Gilmore has identified certain "limit cases" in autobiography, cases which test the borders of the genre and productively "force difficult questions to the fore" (*Limits* 14). And Susanna Egan has spoken in terms of "autobiography in crisis" (4). Sexton, I suggest, proffers a limit case for confession, and, in the later poems in particular (the poems discussed in part three of this book), shows us the mode in crisis.

The confessional "school" of poetry with which Sexton has been associated was first delineated by M. L. Rosenthal in his 1959 review of Robert Lowell's *Life Studies* ("Poetry" 154). Here, Rosenthal isolates what were to become the defining features of confessional writing. The new poetry is understood to be primarily therapeutic in intent and effect, truthful (it features "uncompromising honesty"), and autobiographical (Lowell's speaker is "unequivocally himself"). According to Rosenthal, the author's "private humiliations, sufferings, and psychological problems" are central to the poem. This notion of the therapeutic or cathartic potential of this particular literary form underpins much subsequent writing about confessionalism, this notwithstanding Sexton's own ambivalence about such ends. In a 1970 interview, she pointedly dissociates personal experience from the process of writing and foregrounds the deceptive nature of the text: "You don't solve problems in writing. They're still there. I've heard psychiatrists say, 'See, you've forgiven your father. There it is in your poem.' But I haven't forgiven my father. I just wrote that I did" (Packard 46).

This "new poetry" (Rosenthal) seems to offer a decisive break from the formalist, impersonal poetics which preceded it. And although it is clear that mid-century American poets from the Beats and confessionals onwards were developing a radically different aesthetic, it would be a simplification to say that there was no common ground between the old and the new. It will be clear throughout this book that Sexton owes a significant debt to earlier generations of women poets, from Emily Dickinson and H. D. to her contemporaries Adrienne Rich and Sylvia Plath. Moreover, as part three will argue, Sexton's work engages in stimulating ways with T. S. Eliot's poetics, and, in particular, with his influential doctrine of the impersonality of the poet. Although Sexton frequently identified herself as a "personal" poet and thus, implicitly at least, positioned her writing in opposition to Eliot's, there is more contiguity between the two stances than might at first appear. For example, the critical and readerly tendency to identify confessional speaker with poet notwithstanding, Sexton insists on the importance of distinguishing between the two. Her assertion that "to really get to the truth of something is the poem, not the poet" (Marx 74) confirms Eliot's view that "honest criticism and sensitive appreciation is directed not upon the poet but upon the poetry" ("Tradition" 44). Further, it is possible to read the abjection of many of the voices of Sexton's poetry as exemplary of Eliot's imperative: "The progress of an artist is a continual self-sacrifice, a continual extinction of personality" ("Tradition" 44). Throughout her work, Sexton responds to the challenge of Eliot's statement, displaying a multitude of voices in various states of decline, attenuation, and fragmentation. The confessional poet, in accordance with the requirements of the poetics of impersonality, extinguishes or sacrifices herself again and again in her work.

M. L. Rosenthal's explanation of how he chose the term "confessional" ("The term 'confessional poetry' came naturally to my mind when I reviewed Robert Lowell's *Life Studies*") implies that the work arises irrepressibly and spontaneously from a fount of subjective experience and thence to the page (*New Poets* 25). Such rhetoric is pervasive in confessional criticism, where confession is typically figured as an inevitable reaction to extreme personal circumstances. Early commentators, taking their cue perhaps from Theodor Reik's well-known 1959 book *The Compulsion to Confess* (a study of the "unconscious forces that shape the destiny of us all" [xi]) perceive the mode as something both necessary and regrettable, as something to be tolerated and managed rather than, as Sexton's work indicates, to be employed as a deliberate literary strategy. Karen Jackson Ford implies a similar point when she asks whether the evidence of Sylvia Plath's poem "Words heard, by accident, over the phone" renders her "merely a confessional poet". As Ford explains, "The answer here and elsewhere is that she clearly employed that mode as one particularly rich and productive poetic vein" (127).

Early readings of confessional poetry favor the use of organic and geological metaphors such as those of tidal waves, volcanoes, earthquakes, and storms. Rosenthal describes the confessional poet as a "uniquely seismographic instrument" (*New Poets* 130). The figure emerges with an explicitly gendered inflection in Alicia Ostriker's *Stealing the Language*: "A moment arrives when the volcano erupts, the simmering blood boils over, the fire breaks out.... The imperative of this moment has almost become an axiom in feminist poetry and criticism" (a process which Ostriker calls "expressive-purgative") (126). Erica Wagner's recent description of Ted Hughes's *Birthday Letters* as "the artistic flowering of more than thirty years of pent-up emotion: this is the tidal force that gives the poems their power" uses a similar idiom (3).

There are precedents for these kinds of figures. Emily Dickinson, for instance, uses images of volcanoes in poems about creativity—particularly creativity emerging in unexpected circumstances (Poems 601 and 1705). Adrienne Rich draws on the latter in the title of her essay "Vesuvius at Home: The Power of Emily Dickinson" (*On Lies*). Interestingly, though, these are not metaphors which Sexton herself uses. Unlike Dickinson who, as Ford has shown, uses volcanic and thunderous imagery "as a spontaneous reaction to the forces that threaten to silence her" (41), Sexton eschews metaphors of large-scale geological faults. She is more likely, instead, to speak in terms of the fissured, broken, or eruptive human body. One might read these volcanic images as positive signifiers of power, heralding the potential to make a catastrophic impact, or one might see them as a reductive means of identifying female poets with nature and chaos and, by implication, male poets with culture and order. In both cases, the subject is figured as the passive victim of some unpredictable and irrepressible urge while the auditor or reader of the confessions (the "confessor") is seen as being vulnerable to harm by association.

Readings which are predicated on the compulsive intensity of confessional experience risk generating a judgmental, even authoritarian, critical practice such that the poems which are considered most successful are those which can best contain or assuage the fiercest of emotions. It is the subject's ability to control her material which is valued. Rosenthal finds in the epigraphs to Sexton's first two volumes ("the slogans of the confessional movement," as he labels them) "force of character," "a hard yet sensitive simplicity," and "clarity of line" (*New Poets* 131–32). However, it is arguable that the epigraphs emphasize uncertainty, indeterminacy, and disorientation rather than decisiveness and determination. When Sexton cites the story of Oedipus at the beginning of *To Bedlam and Part Way Back*, it is Jocasta's fear and indecision which interest her. When she quotes Franz Kafka at the beginning of *All My Pretty Ones* ("'a book should serve as the ax for the frozen sea within us'"), it is the condition of despair, isolation, and disorientation to which the "ax" (writing) gives access which she emphasizes: "the books we need are the kind that act upon us like a misfortune . . . that make us feel as though we were . . . lost in a forest."

Confessional poetry is met with a latent anxiety about the subject's possible failure to control her overwhelming emotions (failure to stem the flood, or cap the volcano), thereby placing the auditor at risk. In a letter, poet Louise Bogan complains of the risk of infection: "One poem, by Anne Sexton, made me positively ill" (375). James Dickey's notorious and vitriolic review of Sexton's *To Bedlam and Part Way Back* reveals his fear of contamination by her effusions:

> Anne Sexton's poems so obviously come out of deep, painful sections of the author's life that one's literary opinions scarcely seem to matter; one feels tempted to drop them furtively into the nearest ash can, rather than be caught with them in the presence of so much naked suffering. ("Five" 318)[1]

Of her next volume, he complains: "It would be hard to find a writer who deals more insistently on the pathetic and disgusting aspects of bodily experience" ("On All" 106). Dickey expresses many of the misgivings which characterize contemporary readings of confessional poetry: the sense of shame, the fear of becoming voyeuristic, the anxiety about taboo, the nervousness about being contaminated by the object of the gaze, and the uncertainty about how exactly to read (how to bring one's "literary opinions" to bear).

Patricia Meyer Spacks, too, reveals an anxiety about contamination. In her review of *45 Mercy Street*, she asks: "How, for instance, can one properly respond to lines as grotesquely uncontrolled as these?" What is the "proper" (the etymological connection with the French *propre*—neat, orderly, clean— should be noted) way to read? How can one witness somebody else's breakdown without being tarnished, defiled, or shamed by what one sees? Is it possible to read and respond to the text while retaining a *cordon sanitaire*? Spacks laments Sexton's "increasing slovenliness" before admonishing her to strengthen her control over her mental and physical excesses: "Art requires more than emotional indulgence, requires a saving respect for disciplines and realities beyond the crying needs, the unrelenting appetites, of the self" ("On 45" 186–89). Such anxieties, I will argue in the following chapters, are not only projected on to or experienced by Sexton's readers, but inform Sexton's own ambivalence about her work, reemerging in visceral and scatological metaphors and in images of self as poisoner.

As Judith Harris has shown, "confessional" continues to be used as a pejorative adjective and continues to be used disproportionately for poetry written by women. If it is perceived as volcanic, eruptive, leaky, somatic, natural, irrational, out of control, grotesque (Mary Russo defines the female grotesque as an "open, protruding, extended, secreting body" [62–63]) then it is implicitly or otherwise identified with the feminine. In her essay "Breaking the Code of Silence," Harris attempts to recuperate poets Sharon Olds and Linda McCarriston from the charge of narcissism and to demonstrate that theirs, like Sexton's and Plath's before them, is "a poetry of ideas, of acute political consciousness, that demonstrates through testimony, an individual's relationship to a community" (254).

Edward Brunner suggests that the literary culture of the 1950s, or the decade immediately before the rise of confessionalism, is characterized by anxieties about the democratization of poetry. A cultural elite which senses its power ebbing away posits a need for quarantine in order to avoid a potentially dangerous mingling of mass and high cultures. The rhetoric of contagion and poison which I have described was anticipated in the early 1950s by the response meted out to male homosexual poets whose work was also seen as posing a threat to the dominant ideology (12, 78). David Yezzi's scathing review of Ted Hughes's *Birthday Letters* assimilates the point: "With its built-in emotional firepower, *Birthday Letters* is poetry for people who ordinarily would never pick up the stuff—and no surprise, really. The whole narrative plays into the popular image of what a poet should be: tortured, beautiful, and famous" (2).

In Sexton's case, suspicion of the populist potential of the poetry sometimes translates into mockery of its readers. Shortly before the publication of *The Complete Poems*, William Pritchard predicted that "she is already being and will come to be read less and less, her main audience a few unhappy college students, probably female ones" (391). Janet Badia identifies a similar response to Sylvia Plath's readers who are typified as representatives of "young adult female angst" (126). In both cases, we might follow Brunner and Badia in arguing that the hostility towards the reader and particularly the paternalistic concern about who is reading, how they are reading, and why, speaks more about the anxieties of the dominant culture than it does about the poetry. Sexton herself consciously courted an unconventional audience, hence, for example, her innovative founding of her own chamber rock band, "Anne Sexton and Her Kind," which was conceived as a way of broadening the audience for poetry. However, as Diane Wood Middlebrook notes, this generated misgivings among some friends, readers, and critics who perceived the plan as an undermining of poetic standards (*Biography* 306). In time, Sexton began to find the attentions of a mass audience oppressive, even punitive. F. D. Reeve's recent indictment of confessional poetry's readers ("only the faint in heart and weak in intellect require literally to touch a poet's suffering as if it were a religious relic" [13]) strikes chords with aspects of Sexton's own experience.

The question of the relationship between subject and reader, penitent and confessor or more properly, as we will see in a moment, between subject, text, and reader, is an important one. In an early and influential essay, "After the Tranquillized Fifties," C. B. Cox and A. R. Jones, like a number of their contemporaries, assume a direct and productive relationship between individual experience and society as a whole. Wider society, we are told, both plays a part in generating overpowering feelings and benefits from their expression. Cox and Jones postulate an explicit relationship between individual and social breakdown ("in a deranged world, a deranged response is the only possible reaction of the sensitive mind"); personal breakthrough ("the poet moving into new and disturbingly unusual territories"); and generic breakout. They argue that poets are "traditionally" and "necessarily" mad, but are to be tolerated because they share their "vision of truth beyond the horizon of ordinary mental states" and their experience of "derangement" with, and for, the reader (108). There are some "sensitive" minds ("mad" poets) who experience the world as "deranged" and, by sharing their experience, cause the rest of us to appreciate the virtues of "normality."

These early and defining accounts of confessional poetry are now open to dispute. Developments in critical theory since the nascence of the confessional school in the early 1960s have cast terminal doubt on some of the certainties behind these readings. These certainties include the essentialist belief that there is a truth out there that the "sensitive" mind will retrieve, the normative distinction between "them" (the insightful or plain "mad" poet) and "us" (the "normal adjusted" masses who wait attentively for the insights to be brought back from the front line of insanity) and the naïve confidence in literature's mimetic qualities and in the transparency of language. To counter just one of these assertions, as Sexton's writing indicates, "mad" is a social construction not a fixed, determinate, and transhistorical identity. It is a role to be appropriated and discarded at will: "I have been given a dramatic role in that I am popularly known as the crazy poet. . . . It is my fault. I did write about it thoroughly, explored it so I made my own costume" (*Letters* 396).

The inevitable association between confession and psychoanalytic practice—or the "talking cure" as Sigmund Freud and his colleague Josef Breuer termed it in their "Case of Anna O" (83)—is also relevant to our understanding of confession's reception. As this book will make clear, my intention is neither to psychoanalyze Sexton nor to read confessional poetry as a succession of case notes. Nevertheless, psychoanalysis and other forms of psychotherapy do have a place in mid-century American culture, particularly for poets such as Sexton and Plath who were treated within some form of these regimes and who read fairly widely in the field. Psychoanalysis offers fruitful ways of thinking about the processes and relationships at stake in the confession; it is, above all, a method of interpretation which, like confession, strives to reveal the previously hidden by means of the productive engagement of speaker and listener. Freud himself points both to a similarity and a key difference between the two forms: "In confession the sinner tells what he knows; in analysis the neurotic has to tell more" (qtd. in Berman 4). Psychoanalysis, like confession, seems to offer a key to truth; in Toril Moi's words, it "discloses and unlocks secrets" (195). The metaphor of locks and keys, to which we will return in chapter six, speaks for a number of associated processes. In Freud's "Fragment of an Analysis of a Case of Hysteria ('Dora')," the key is used as a sexual image (102, 137) and as a figure for the mechanism by which secrets are exposed and released. "Sexuality," Freud says, is "the key to the problem of the psychoneuroses . . . no one who disdains the key will ever be able to unlock the door" (156). Sexton's poetry, as we will see later, draws on but also complicates this analogy.

In the light both of the complexity and transgressiveness of Sexton's work and of what J. Hillis Miller, Antony Easthope, and John Thompson have called a "paradigm shift" in literary studies (that is, the posthumanist development of a diverse and challenging range of critical theories and practices), the confessional framework proposed by Sexton's contemporaries and maintained by many since seems no longer adequate for explicating her work (*Theory Now* 205; *Contemporary* vii). It is necessary to find new perspectives, new reading strategies, which will be alert at one and the same time to the nuances of her language, to the sophistication and ambition of her poetics, and to the place of her work in multiple literary, gendered, and historical contexts.

As a first stage in reappraising the confessional process, I turn to the work of Michel Foucault. His understanding of confession offers a valuable means of rethinking the critiques discussed thus far and provides a source of insight into Sexton's own complex and sophisticated poetics. It is thus necessary to quote him at some length:

> The confession is a ritual of discourse in which the speaking subject is also the subject of the statement; it is also a ritual that unfolds within a power relationship, for one does not confess without the presence (or virtual presence) of a partner who is not simply the interlocutor but the authority who requires the confession, prescribes and appreciates it, and intervenes in order to judge, punish, forgive, console, and reconcile; a ritual in which the truth is corroborated by the obstacles and resistances it has had to surmount in order to be formulated; and finally, a ritual in which the expression alone, independently of its external consequences, produces intrinsic modifications in the person who articulates it: it exonerates, redeems, and purifies him; it unburdens him of his wrongs, liberates him, and promises him salvation. (*History* 61–62)

For Foucault, confession is not a means of expressing the irrepressible truth of prior lived experience, but a ritualized "technique . . . for producing truth" (*History* 61–62). It is not the product of free self-expression, but rather the effect of an ordered regime by which the self begins to conceive of itself as individual, responsible, culpable, and thereby confessional. Confession takes place in a context of power, prohibition, and surveillance. It is generated and sustained not by the troubled subject/confessant, but by the discursive relationship between speaker and reader (confessant and confessor) or, for Leigh Gilmore, developing Foucault's model, by a triangular relationship between "penitent/teller," "listener," and "tale" (speaker, reader, and text) (*Autobiographics* 121).

Sexton's early (February 1959) poem, "Kind Sir: These Woods," is a deceptively playful text which offers a suggestive engagement with some of the practices and problems of confession, thereby exemplifying Foucault's understanding of the field. In its emphasis on "games," "tricks," and voluntary participation, it indicates that the confession may be willed, sought out, and constructed, rather than spontaneous, reactive, and compulsive. The poem cites as its epigraph a line from Thoreau's *Walden*: "For a man needs only to be turned around once with his eyes shut in this world to be lost. . . . Not til we are lost . . . do we begin to find ourselves." The metaphor of being "lost"— the use of the passive mode is significant—represents psychological distur- bance and vulnerability. "Kind Sir" dramatizes this disorientation and, more importantly, renders the verb "to lose" in its active form, thus transforming being lost into the rather more purposive act of losing oneself. Becoming lost is a strategy, not an accident. Sexton's speaker, rather than seeking the way out of the wood of mental collapse, is looking for the way in. Jacqueline Rose explains (here confirming Thoreau's understanding): "You can only start seeing—this was Freud's basic insight—when you know that your vision is troubled, fallible, off-key. The only viable way of reading is not to find, but to disorientate, oneself" (*States* 144).

"Kind Sir" presents us with what is, in archetypal terms, a nightmare scene. Yet this literal and metaphorical loss of self is also, and paradoxically, a "tech- nique" for finding oneself. The poem emphasizes not the horror of being lost, nor the bravery of the search for the way out, but the process by which one might activate this crisis. The references to the literal or metaphorical loss of self as a "game" and a "trick," and the idiom of the nursery rhyme ("the forest between Dingley Dell / and grandfather's cottage") undermine the alleged inevitability and necessity of the trauma and show the speaker to be an active and willing participant in the performance.

"Kind Sir" moves from these recollections of a childhood game to a more insistent and self-reflexive commentary on the kinds of process and tech- nique which are central to Sexton's poetics. These include, first, the embrac- ing of excess and abundance that marks a disregard for rules and prohibitions. Sexton's speaker has gone one stage further than the epigraph from *Walden* advocates; she has "turned round twice with my eyes sealed." Such celebra- tion of excess is a productive technique for the woman writer. As Ford argues of the "poetics of excess"—which she identifies in Dickinson, Gertrude Stein, Plath, Sonia Sanchez, Nicki Giovanni and others—"excess is a rhetorical strategy adopted to overcome the prohibitions imposed by the application of a disabling concept of decorum" (13). Second, we see the process of introspec- tion. Although her eyes are sealed, the speaker has gained insight from the technique of looking inward. Sexton's figurative use of the woods again bears comparison with Emily Dickinson's work. Ford draws attention to an 1862 letter from Dickinson to her mentor Thomas Wentworth Higginson (letter 271) where Dickinson repeatedly describes her turn to the apparent "chaos and danger of the woods" as a counter to the authority and control Higginson seems to value: "What Dickinson discovers in the woods is authorization for her own waywardness, solitude, instincts, and impulses" (34).

In "Kind Sir," Sexton's speaker finally acknowledges—albeit only to belittle them—contemporary readings of the courage and bravery of the confessional search:

> And opening my eyes, I am afraid of course
> to look—this inward look that society scorns—
> Still, I search in these woods and find nothing worse
> than myself, caught between the grapes and the thorns.

This rhetoric of courage and bravery is typical of readings of confessionalism, even to this day.[2] "Courage" is the only quality which James Dickey concedes in his notorious review: "Mrs. Sexton's candor, her courage, and her story are worth anyone's three dollars" ("Five" 319). Again, we might compare Sexton's stance with Dickinson's. In both cases, we have women poets ostensibly acknowledging—but only in order the better to expose, exaggerate, or otherwise repudiate—the standards of judgment of their peers. Sexton's speaker claims to be "afraid," although the weakness of the adjective and the dismissive rider, "of course," belie any real sense of terror. "Of course" reads as a concession to the expectations of her audience rather than a credible statement of her own position. Indeed, she indicates (and this insight will inform my subsequent reading of a number of poems) that such fear as exists is not a consequence of her own encounter with the anticipated object of her search but a product of her anxiety about the audience's "scorn." If we are to understand the confessional text not as the compulsive expression of the prior experience of the author, but as a gesture which achieves its meaning and status as confession only in the process of being received or read, then it is arguable that it is the audience, and not the experience, which induces fear. For Foucault, it is precisely the barriers and difficulties to free expression which construct and validate what we take to be "courage" (or what we take to be truthful, a quality to which it is related, hence Dickey's yoking of "candor" and "courage"). As Foucault suggests in the comments cited earlier, in confession "the truth [or the subject's bravery] is corroborated by the obstacles and resistances it has had to surmount in order to be formulated."

Finally, to go back to the metaphor of the map and the technique of disorientation, "Kind Sir: These Woods" shows that the speaker is able to ascertain her place on the map—metaphorically to find herself—by a process of triangulation, by situating herself in relation to two other points (the grapes of salvation and the thorns of crucifixion). There are, thus, as Leigh Gilmore argues, three elements to the confessional relationship: the subject, the text (here signified by the fruitful and productive grapes), and the audience (signified by the "thorns" which represent suffering and condemnation).

Another early poem "With Mercy for the Greedy" (1960), one of the few in which Sexton explicitly names "confession," develops these thoughts further. The poem, which is prefaced with a dedication: "For my friend, Ruth, who urges me to make an appointment for the Sacrament of Confession," refuses the assumption that the confession is a symptom of the subject's compulsion or need to confess and shows that the auditor too places demands.[3] It is the desire to fulfill these which, at least in part, sustains the confession. It posits a form of exchange, exemplifying what J. Hillis Miller calls an "economy of equivalence, of giving and receiving, of equable translatioɪ and measure" (*Tropes* 141). In "With Mercy for the Greedy," the reciprocity of benefit (the merciful need to give and the greedy need to take) symbolizes the dialogue at the heart of confession. More importantly, the poem shows that the reader wields considerable power. Foucault proposes that although the "veracity" of the confession is "guaranteed" by "the bond, the basɪ⸱ intimacy in discourse, between the one who speaks and what he is speaking about," power in fact has a more specific origin:

> The agency of domination does not reside in the one who speaks . . . but in the one who listens and says nothing; not in the one who knows and answers, but in the one who questions and is not supposed to know. (*History* 62)

Thus critical attention must be redirected from the putative experience of the needy or "greedy" subject to the role of the potentially merciful and thus powerful auditor.

The mock formality of the opening lines of "With Mercy for the Greedy" (replicating the apostrophe in "Kind Sir: These Woods"), the legalistic repetitions, and the exaggerated dichotomy of "you" and "me" confirm the penitent's subservience to the authority of her listener:

> Concerning your letter in which you ask
> me to call a priest and in which you ask
> me to wear The Cross that you enclose.

The wooden cross which inspires the poem is posited as the means of mediation between the merciful and the greedy and as a symbol of potential salvation. It acts as a metaphor for the confessional text in that the transfer of the cross and the poem from one party to the other symbolizes confessional dialogue or the communication of needs between penitent subject and ideally merciful and responsive confessor. In the context of this poem, at least, the cross and the proposed confession hold out the hope of some kind of comfort or cure.

Yet such hopes are thwarted. The cross fails because of the inability of the recipient to understand or read it, or, more properly, because of its own refusal of signification. To quote Hillis Miller again, "A true gift can never be returned. . . . The final realm in which rational equivalence and exchange breaks down is . . . that of language itself" (*Tropes* 143). The meaning of the cross and, by extension, of the confessional poem as understood by its donor (the confessing subject) is always and already lost to the recipient/reader. Furthermore, the cross itself is only ever a sign of something which is not there. It is a metaphor for the absent Christ who is, in turn, perhaps a metonym for God. It delivers its message at one remove: "It tapped me lightly as a child's heart might, / tapping secondhand, softly waiting to be born." In like manner, the confessional text is only ever a sign of something absent: an unverifiable and unrepresentable subjectivity. In the last stanza of the poem, the speaker's final response to the gift of the cross reads:

My friend, my friend, I was born
doing reference work in sin, and born
confessing it. This is what poems are:
with mercy
for the greedy,
they are the tongue's wrangle,
the world's pottage, the rat's star.

Sexton's defense and manifesto encompasses all of the contradictions and complexities of the confessional situation: the appeal for understanding, the recognition of the importance of the personal past, the reference to the process of rendering textual account, and the give and take which characterizes confessional dialogue. Most importantly, it acknowledges the bitter discontent and the ugly, painful messiness of the act of confession. Like the aesthetically pleasing cross, it appears promising, but masks a more profound and troubling confusion. The cumbersome gutturals and plosives of "the tongue's wrangle, / the world's pottage" form an obstruction, denying any soothing resolution. The reference to "pottage" (the allusion is to the biblical story of Esau's poor exchange of his birthright for his brother Jacob's "pottage," or stew [Genesis 25:29–34]) signifies an early, but nevertheless persistent, doubt about the value of confessional poetry and its ability to achieve the kind of individual and social salvation which early practitioners and commentators may have expected of it. The final palindromic, and thus circular, image of the "rat's star" has a similar effect. As with Sexton's reference to the poem itself as simultaneously a cry for and sign of, sacrament, it forces the text back on itself, confirming its self-referentiality.

In one of her Crawshaw lectures, Sexton cites the final lines of "With Mercy for the Greedy" to support a crucial point about the fundamentally discursive nature of confession. There is no single meaning possessed by the author and symptomatic of her trauma or "need." Rather, there are multiple and diverse meanings (or, conversely, moments of aporia) produced in the process of reading:

> Rat's star, by the way, is a palindrome. It reads backwards the same way as it reads forwards. Rats is star spelled backwards. . . . It means something to me. My husband thinks it's crazy and has no meaning. (Crawshaw [9] 3)

Sexton makes the point more explicitly in her poem "Is It True?" (discussed in chapter seven): "To one shit is a feeder of plants / to another the evil that permeates them." The language of the confessional text, although often regarded as transparent and direct, may be nonreferential, opaque, and differential. The words which she uses, although clear and expressive to her, may bear a profoundly different meaning or indeed no meaning to the reader.

The difficult relationship between confessional speaker and reader is at the heart of one of Sexton's best-known works. In "Her Kind," the poem which she read at the beginning of every public performance of her work and which consequently became identified with her particular confessional poetics, Sexton explores the perceptions, or more properly misperceptions, held by her audience. Crucial to the poem and its depiction of "what kind of poet I am," is the line: "A woman like that is misunderstood. / I have been her kind." "Her Kind" opens flamboyantly, defiantly, with the "I" so disdained by critics of the mode: "I have gone out, a possessed witch / haunting the black air, braver at night." Typically accused of introspection, the speaker here explicitly reaches outwards ("I have gone out") and takes the wider view. She is proud of the madness or possession which seizes her, yet refuses to specify the source of her inspiration. Is she "possessed" by madness? Or by poetry? Or, in the context of the very public, and repeated, performance of the poem, is she "possessed" or controlled by the expectations of her audience?

The speaker of "Her Kind" explicitly claims the bravery so valorized in confessional poetry, yet her claim is undermined by the fact that she makes it only at night, under cover of darkness. Of course, the claim to be "braver at night, / dreaming evil" is a warning that Sexton and persona should be dissociated. The life of the imagination, the adoption of different personae, and the role of the witch belong to the realm of fantasy. They are to be played out at night and in dreams and should not be confused with the real life of the poet. The image of self as "twelve-fingered" (similar metonyms are used frequently in Sexton's work to connote the writing subject) shows the speaker embracing her distinctive role as poet of disorder, extremity, and excess.

Stanza two proffers a further defense of Sexton's idiosyncratic and specifically female poetics. She defiantly celebrates her place as an outsider who is ill at ease in the dominant poetic tradition. In this poem, as in "Kind Sir," her place is beyond civilization in the woods. Although literally outside, and figuratively beyond, the recognition or understanding of a conventional, tacitly formalist criticism, there is evidence in these "caves in the woods" of a different and distinctive kind of creative process. Sexton accepted the label "primitive" (in her interview with William Heyen and Al Poulin, she explains: "I was just what one would call a primitive" [141]). The list of "skillets" and "carvings" in the poem celebrates this particular kind of naïve, domestic, folk art:

I have found the warm caves in the woods,
filled them with skillets, carvings, shelves,
closets, silks, innumerable goods;
fixed the supper for the worms and the elves:
whining, rearranging the disaligned.

These lines concede the role played by the confessional audience (the "disaligned"). If there is a compulsion or imperative behind confessional poetry, might it not be the imperative to respond to, and alleviate, the demands and needs of the audience? That the beneficiaries of this confession (the "worms and the elves') are "whining" (the syntax is ambiguous, rendering "whining" applicable to subject and object alike) is an early indication of the ambivalence about the audience which emerges more explicitly in later poems such as "Talking to Sheep" and "Making a Living."

In the final stanza, the speaker proclaims, and the emphatic use of the past tense confirms, her transcendence of the prohibition against confessional poetry:

> I have ridden in your cart, driver,
> waved my nude arms at villages going by,
> learning the last bright routes, survivor
> where your flames still bite my thigh
> and my ribs crack where your wheels wind.

The punctuation and enjambment of "routes, survivor / where" (addressed either to the witness/survivor who survives her, or, self-referentially declaring herself as the "survivor / where . . .") confirm that she has weathered public ridicule. She lives to tell the tale, hence the shift to the present tense in the last lines. "Ridden" with its aural pun on "written" indicates that it is the writing which invites punishment. That she waves her "nude arms" is, again, a provocative and defiant gesture, invoking the metaphors of nakedness, self-revelation, and shame which are typical of confessional criticism. Jones, for example, argues that "the persona is naked ego" and Phillips suggests that confession "gives the naked emotion direct" (14; 8). Yet as the circular, perpetual, and repetitive nature of these metaphors suggests ("still bite" and "wheels wind" are significantly described in the present tense), the risk of punishment is ever-present. The penalty for writing in a new and distinctive way, for being "twelve-fingered" or excessive, for writing about the life of the mind, and for being "a woman like that" is played out, finally, on the woman's body in images of torture. She is burnt at the stake, stretched on the rack, or broken on the wheel. Barbara Green traces similar public displays of the private female body to the early women's suffrage campaigns, reading it as a "feminist strategy" (2) and a "political act," particularly when it takes place in "inventive and unpredictable ways" (6). We might read Sexton's poem in this way: The female subject, ostensibly denied agency, defiantly claims a form of authority of her own.

The poem bears comparison with Sylvia Plath's "Witch Burning" (from the sequence "Poem for a Birthday"). As Middlebrook explains, "Her Kind" was first drafted in 1957 under the title "Night Voice on a Broomstick." It was revised as "Witch" and completed and given its final title in July 1959 (*Biography* 113). At this time, Sexton was making the final selection of poems for her first book, primarily by testing them in Robert Lowell's Boston University poetry workshop and seeking the advice of her tutor and fellow students, including Plath who was briefly auditing the course. The poem which began life as "Night Voice on a Broomstick" may, then, have been known to Plath. Although she had left Lowell's class by the time it achieved its final form, its early drafts arguably influenced her "Witch Burning" (written at Yaddo between late October and November 1959).[4] There are many points of comparison between Sexton's "Her Kind" and Plath's "Witch Burning." Both offer defiant articulations of female poetic subjectivity and both open with the witch/woman writer literally and figuratively hovering on the margins of society and determining to transcend the quotidian. Both settings are emphatically domestic, and both speakers figure themselves as the cook and provider, or, metaphorically, the person charged with satisfying the emotional needs of their avaricious audience.

In both poems, the first-person speaker reveals a sense of dislocation or self-alienation. Each sees herself as though from the outside (an example of what Laura Mulvey calls the woman's "to-be-looked-at-ness" [17]) and identifies herself as a misfit. Sexton's speaker is a "lonely thing, twelve-fingered, out of mind," she is "not a woman quite." Similarly, Plath's subject "inhabit[s] / The wax image of myself, a doll's body." The next and final section of Plath's "Poem for a Birthday" ("The Stones") develops this synecdoche. It features multiple images of dislocated organs and limbs ("the stomach," the "mouthhole," the "ear," the "pink torso," "any limb"). Here, as in numerous Sexton poems ("Consorting with Angels" or "Live," for example), autotomy (the casting off of parts of the body) is fundamental to the confessional process. In an entirely self-reflexive gesture, the female poet's body is dislocated, splayed, dissected for examination by her audience. In both poems, it is the fingers and the mouth as metonyms of the processes of writing and speaking the poem which are displaced and thus emphasized.

At the heart of "Witch Burning" and of "Her Kind" are images of fire and of the witch woman's sacrifice or immolation. Sexton closes with the subject defiantly approaching the pyre. Plath's poem echoes this in tone, language, and imagery. Sexton's vision of torture (the "wheels wind") reemerges in stanza two of Plath's poem where "the smoke wheels from the beak of this empty jar." Plath's speaker, like Sexton's, sacrifices her body ("hand and ankles" in Plath; "arms" and "ribs" in Sexton) to the flames. There are the same rhymes and half rhymes ("beak"/ "crack," "thigh"/ "bright"/ "bite" / "light") and, crucially, the same latently sexual image of the bright flames encroaching on the woman's thighs. In Plath's poem: "My ankles brighten. Brightness ascends my thighs. / I am lost, I am lost, in the robes of all this light;" while in Sexton's: "Your flames still bite my thigh / and my ribs crack where your wheels wind." In both poems, the persona of the witch is profoundly ambivalent, signifying latent power and the role of marginalized, oppressed victim.

"Her Kind" is an entirely characteristic Sexton poem. It problematizes the process of writing, showing it to be subject to particular and persistent pressures. Although it evokes freedom, liberation, spirit, and independence, it is predicated on images of containment, circumscription, and punishment. Sexton's own comments about the poem replicate this tension:

> I have never given a reading without reading "Her Kind" first off. I always say "I'll read you this poem, and then you'll know just what kind of a poet I am, just what kind of a woman I am. And then if anyone wishes to leave, they may do so." (Crawshaw [5] 1–2)

The Crawshaw lectures, referred to on several occasions above, give an important insight into Sexton's understanding of the confessional mode and of her place in it. The lectures, entitled "Anne on Anne," were delivered at Colgate University where Sexton held the Crawshaw Chair in Literature (1972). Coming towards the end of her career, some thirteen years and five books after her first publication, these lectures provide a retrospective summary of what, to Sexton, was either significant or "misunderstood"—or possibly both—about her work.

It is apparent from the first of the lectures alone that Sexton is keen to dispel the view that her poetry is autobiographical, that it is the spontaneous expression of her own prior lived experience. Thus she implicitly takes issue with many of the founding definitions of confessionalism. From the tone of her "prefatory remarks" at the beginning of the lecture series, it is evident that Sexton is acutely aware of, and determined to confound, her audience's reading of her and her writing: "Today we meet only for a few minutes, and in those few minutes I will give you warnings and intimations. You might wonder what an Anne on Anne class could be about" (Crawshaw [1] 1). Thus, with Sexton, what you see may not be what you get. There is something simultaneously playful, self-dramatizing, and deceitful about such an introduction: a depiction of the self as elusive, enigmatic, uncontainable, requiring concentration and attentiveness but promising no sureties.

Such comments also make apparent Sexton's own vision of her writing self as constructed or artificial. The assignment which she sets for the course involves the students "reading the various critiques of my work as well as my five books." Thereafter, they are required to formulate questions to ask Sexton but, before putting them to her, to anticipate her likely responses: "You will bring questions to class each week and I will answer them. But not until you have already given your answer. In other words, you are to fabricate my reply." So "Anne on Anne" is asking the students to write "Anne," to authorize her in a process which replicates that by which the confessional persona is constructed by her audience. Sexton develops this idea further by suggesting that the "Anne" who is both the subject and the object of these lectures is not only a construction of her present audience, but also a product of her previous and potential audiences. Admitting to her own doubts and uncertainties about how to introduce the lectures, she depicts herself as subject to the ideas and initiatives of others: "Bruce [the lecture organizer] reasoned that . . . ;" "my students at Boston University persuaded me . . . ;" "they reasoned . . . ." Thus the final format of the lectures represents a consensus of views on "Anne" rather than "Anne on Anne." The lecture concludes: "I hope from this class to learn as much about myself that startles as you will learn about me." In so privileging the dramatic, fictive, or fabricated nature of the experience typically identified as biographically accurate, Sexton provides an important insight into confession. She makes a subtle, but repeated and extremely important, distinction between the "I" as subject and the "I" as object of the text (the "I" who is speaking and the "I" who is being spoken about, or the subject of the enunciation and the subject of the enounced). The effect of this distinction is to confound the kinds of readings which might instantly and unthinkingly conflate the two or which would seek in the "I" of the poem "evidence" about the "I" of the writer.

This theme is continued in the first lecture where, significantly, Sexton takes issue with one of the most important of the critical essays which defined "confessionalism," A. R. Jones's "Necessity and Freedom." Literally, the first thing which Anne says about Anne is in refutation of orthodox views of her writing. She cites Jones's view of the "'unmistakably autobiographical impact'" of her work and his contention that "'the "I" of Sexton's poems [which Sexton, incidentally, misquotes as "eye"] is clearly related intimately and painfully to the poet's autobiography,'" and then comments "I would like for a moment to disagree" (Crawshaw [1] 1). She proceeds by emphasizing the fictionality and the artifice of autobiography which, it emerges, is a simulation: "It is true that I am an autobiographical poet most of the time, or at least so I lead my readers to believe" (Crawshaw [1] 6).

In the final Crawshaw lecture, as in the first, Sexton refutes one of her major critics. She questions Robert Boyers's reading of the autobiographical qualities of her work and demonstrates, instead, the importance of constructed personae:

> I would like to make a few comments about Robert Boyers's article in *Salmagundi* entitled "The Achievement of Anne Sexton." . . . In the poem "Two Sons" I am taking on a persona of an old woman whose 2 sons have married. He seems to think I'm speaking in my own confessional voice. Likewise in "The Legend of the One-Eyed Man," although I admit I identify with him. In "Protestant Easter" the persona is an eight-year-old. He thinks it is me. (Crawshaw [10] 1)

Sexton qualifies the reference to "my own . . . voice" by specifying that this is her "confessional voice," as though this were just one of many idioms available to her. The distinction which Sexton makes between "I" and "persona" is an important one. It replicates John Berryman's disclaimer at the beginning of *The Dream Songs*:

> Many opinions and errors in the Songs are to be referred not to the character Henry, still less to the author, but to the title of the work. . . . The poem then, whatever its wide cast of characters, is essentially about an imaginary character (not the poet, not me) named Henry . . . [who] talks about himself sometimes in the first person, sometimes in the third, sometimes even in the second. (vi)

In an interview with Lois Ames, discussing the process and rewards of writing her play, *Mercy Street* (formerly *Tell Me Your Answer True*), produced off Broadway in 1969, Sexton indicates that her use of disparate personae beguiles rather than reveals:

> With the play, I became each person—I love doing this. I think it's something I can do, too. I do it pretty well. I become someone else.

I tell their story. I love to write in the first person, even when it isn't about me, and it's quite confusing to my readers, because they think everything I write—sometimes I am talking about myself and sometimes not. (Ames 2)

The implication of this is that there is no "true" autobiographical "I" beyond a succession of personae or masks. As Candace Lang summarizes conventional readings of autobiographical writing:

Insofar as it has proceeded on the assumption that the literary work is the expression (however inadequate) of an anterior idea originating in the writing subject and for which that subject was the sole authority, to discern what the writer "really meant to say" has been tantamount to approaching the "core" of the author's being to grasp the truth of the writing subject. (10)

Subjectivity, instead of being understood as the source or origin of the text must, in Antony Easthope's words, "be approached not as the point of origin but as the effect of a poetic discourse." By reading confession as discourse, we can "explain the author as a product or effect of the text, whereas conventional criticism accepts the notion of the author as unquestionable and pre-given in order to be able to define how the text should be read" (*Discourse* 31, 7).

Sexton's manipulation of the persona "I" raises crucial questions about the authenticity and credibility typically regarded as characteristic of confessionalism. It becomes impossible to read her poems in order to identify or evaluate the degree of biographical truth implicit in each. Instead we must acknowledge that just as there are many "I's" (none of which is to be identified with the historical author) there are multiple truths. Sexton offers the example of her early poem "Unknown Girl in the Maternity Ward" in order to demonstrate that it is possible for the writing "I" to identify with the experience of another, to adopt a mask or persona, and thereby to be truthful and false. She is truthful in the sense that, as she explains, the mask offers the opportunity to explore personal feelings of loss on the abandonment of her own small child, and false in the sense that the narrative of the poem traces a fictional story of illegitimacy:

It might be noted that after I published "Unknown Girl" people in the town where my husband was brought up said, "Wasn't he a fine boy to marry Anne after she had had that illegitimate baby?" So much for confession. So much for persona. (Crawshaw [1] 12)

The idea that the confessional writer might be the victim of the confession, although treated jokingly here, forms a sinister undertone in poems such as "Talking to Sheep" (see chapter five). Throughout her Crawshaw lectures, Sexton works hard to shift the critical emphasis from an evaluation of the putative authenticity of the confessional voice to an understanding of its potential inauthenticity. Yet, in a supreme double bluff, having established the equal validity of confessional truth and confessional artifice (the autobiographical and persona "I's"), Sexton undercuts the reliability of this distinction, suggesting that, in fact, the whole debate is predicated on uncertainty. Truth and artifice are not so much equally valid as equally equivocal, and her own authority to determine such questions about her own work, her own value as a witness, are thrown into doubt. As Sexton concludes in her second lecture: "All this was merely my fictions made up out of snatches of my life, lyric instances that I developed, other masks that I pulled over my face and voices who spoke for me. Never, never, never. All a lie" (Crawshaw [2] 10). Notwithstanding her attempt to rationalize her work and to foreground the proactive process of exploring new personae, the complexity of the poetry, and its irreducibility to simplistic and schematic evaluations, resists exposition.

A further perception of confessionalism which Sexton attempts to confound both in the Crawshaw lectures and in her poetry is its exploration of taboo subject matter. She recalls: "I remember when I first wrote poems about mental illness, I was told it was not a fit subject for poetry" (Crawshaw [4] 1). To explore the boundaries of what is permissible, she draws on the example of her 1965 poem "Cripples and Other Stories" which, from this perspective, might be read as a provocative parody of the confessional poem.

"Cripples and Other Stories" opens with a mocking appeal to the speaker's doctor: "My doctor, the comedian / I called you every time," thereby confirming skeptical critics' views of the pathological fixation of the confessional poet. In the first stanza alone are found the essential ingredients of confessionalism as conventionally received: doctor, self, and text (here labeled self-deprecatingly, "this silly rhyme"). The "silly rhyme" also refers, specifically, to the refrain which punctuates the poem:

Each time I give lectures
or gather in the grants
you send me off to boarding school
in training pants.
   (Sexton's emphasis)

Here, we see the relationship of control between doctor and patient, confessor and penitent; a relationship which is predicated on the desire to please and on the withholding of pleasure. The confessing subject wishes to swap roles, to gratify or amuse the confessor (doctor/comedian), instead of being the recipient of his favors: "I called you every time / and made you laugh yourself." The subject, in "calling" the doctor "every time," indicates a desire to wrest back control, a desire which is thwarted because it is the doctor/confessor who retains authority and has the ultimate power to call the shots: "You send me off to boarding school in training pants." As Leigh Gilmore argues, here confirming Foucault's point about the authority of the confessor:

> The vow, "So help me God," seals the courtroom and the confessional account in the presence of a witness authorized to return a verdict, to determine veracity or perjury, to judge innocence or guilt, to decide on absolution or damnation. Some higher authority or recourse to its function is a fixture in scenes where truth is at issue, for it is necessary in this construction of truth telling to speak to someone. (*Autobiographics* 121)

Such a requirement is conceded in a rhetorical question which Sexton poses in the last of her Crawshaw lectures: "How did I come to writing about myself? How did I come to be a confessional poet who vomits up her past every ugly detail onto the page?" The answers which she offers are tentative and ambiguous:

> I started to write about myself because it was something I knew well. . . . With every poem it is as if I were on trial, pleading my case before the court of angels and hoping for a pardon. . . . Mind you, I really have no idea why I do what I do. (Crawshaw [10] 1)

By claiming and then denying authority over her experience, Sexton implies that she does not, after all, know herself "well." As the reference to the penitent's arraignment before the "court of angels" intimates, instrumental to the success of this confession is the "court," or confessor, or audience.

In "Cripples and Other Stories," the scatological metaphor of the "training pants" infantilizes the confessional speaker, rendering her powerless and abject. The "ballad-like nursery rhyme-like technique," as Sexton describes it, helps to "underscore the horror" of the action (Crawshaw [4] 1):

> I'm really thirty-six.
> I see dead rats in the toilet.
> I'm one of the lunatics.

The mundane and the extraordinary are thrown into startling and memorable relief, thus drawing attention to one of the ways in which confessionalism achieves its effects. Subsequent rhymes of "shame" with "nickname," "this" and "orifice," "fever" and "leave her," "tell" and "hell," represent a précis of the confession. The final incestuous horror of the poem is rapidly realized, and brought to a clanging conclusion by the end rhymes:

> Father, I'm thirty-six,
> yet I lie here in your crib.
> I'm getting born again, Adam,
> as you prod me with your rib.

Doctor, father and first man (Adam) are here synthesized into one dominant, controlling, and most importantly, surveillant figure. The pun on "lie here in your crib," with its latent allusion to the truths or lies which emerge on the doctor's couch, and the sense that self-scrutiny will lead to rebirth, form a knowing if sardonic commentary on confessional and psychiatric therapy.

The cast of characters in "Cripples and Other Stories," in addition to the doctor and the disappointed and disappointing parents ("Disgusted, Mother," "father was fat on scotch"), features a mutilated self harboring an awful secret ("Would the cripple inside of me / be a cripple that would show?"). The speaker is full of self-loathing; her self-portrait offers a striking metaphor for the confessional poet:

> My cheeks blossomed with maggots.
> I picked at them like pearls.
> I covered them with pancake.
> I wound my hair in curls.

Here we find the suffering, vilified, abject self relentlessly scrutinizing that self and therein finding emotional and material rewards ("pearls" of wisdom and wealth). A persistent complaint about confessional poetry is the way in which it seems to commodify personal trauma. F. D. Reeve's rather equivocal defense of confession posits that a once-fine tradition (the "rich" and "true" confession of the early modern period) has, in the "so-called 'confessional poetry' that arose in the 1950s" (note the use of scare quotes) been corrupted by commercialism (2) while David Yezzi sets the scene for his criticism of Hughes's *Birthday Letters* by saying, "Autobiography has been doing big business lately" (1). We might agree that market forces have had a distorting impact on the production and reception of certain kinds of poetry and certain narratives. However, it would be a mistake to think that the confessional subject is either unaware of, or unconcerned by, such developments. As "Cripples and Other Stories" and many other poems show, such tensions are precisely Sexton's subject. In "Cripples," the subject in scratching away at her psychic wounds leaves the scars perpetually open, constantly the focus of attention. The image of masking the "maggots" with "pancake" invokes the speaker's application of masks, or the persona "I," which may or may not disguise unpalatable truths. The final reference to hair wound in curls suggests a Shirley Temple–like performance, an overly sexualized attempt by a child to appeal to an adult authority figure. It also connotes the awful power of Medusa who threatens the audience with the dreadful consequences of her persistent gaze.

These multiple horrors read, as I have suggested, as a gross parody of confessionalism. In its extreme appropriation of excess, manipulation of disgust and flamboyant disregard of aesthetic convention "Cripples and Other Stories" dramatizes the point which Sexton, in a rather more restrained tone, puts to her students: "Do you think out-houses and enemas are fit subjects for poetry? We all go to the bathroom. Is it an experience that should be written about?" Of course, by entitling her poem "and Other Stories" and mentioning within the text that "those are just two stories / and I have more to tell," Sexton is also acknowledging the fictive nature of confession. As she asks in her lecture: "What would you think the poem would be like from that title? How does "Other Stories" change it?" (Crawshaw [4] 1). However harrowing the subject matter—in this case, "the enemas of childhood / reeking of outhouses and shame"—the confession is at heart a narrative, a construction, one of many made-up "stories."

2

Narcissism

Overviews of post–World War II American poetry typically read the confessional mode as an unsophisticated, undemanding, and rather regrettable moment in a general move towards a more interesting and challenging poetic style. As Alan Williamson suggests in the provocatively titled collection of essays, *After Confession*, "confessional poetry—almost from the moment that unfortunate term was coined—has been the whipping boy of half a dozen newer schools, New Surrealism, New Formalism, Language poetry" ("Stories" 51). Marjorie Perloff confirms the point when she draws a distinction between the exciting "radical poetries" which dominate contemporary American poetry and an earlier tradition of personal lyricism:

> The more radical poetries of the past few decades, whatever their particular differences, have come to reconceive the "opening of the field," not as an entrance into authenticity but, on the contrary, as a turn toward artifice, toward poetry as making or praxis rather than poetry as impassioned speech, as self-expression. ("Changing Face" 93)

Similarly, Michael Davidson characterizes the interests of current Language poetry by reference to its difference from the "expressive" poetry that preceded it: "By foregrounding the abstract features of the speech act rather than the authenticity of the expressive moment, the poet acknowledges the contingency of utterances in social interchange" (74). Gregory Orr sees the situation as rather more complex, distinguishing between confessionalism (which he depicts as a rather embarrassing trial run) and postconfessionalism (a mode which he values because of its "proportionate ego" and its commitment to engaging "the conditional world") (671, 668).

I begin this chapter by arguing that Sexton's poetry demonstrates many of the preoccupations and concerns more typically identified as characteristic of avant-garde, Language, postconfessional, and postmodern writing. Her work, like some of these other modes, shows an acute and self-conscious interest in its own poetic processes, in language and its limitations, in the indeterminacy of the subject, and in the unreliability—perhaps even the undesirability—of reference. Its primary subject is not the life and suffering of the historical Anne Sexton. Its subject is writing. Yet this textual self-consciousness has not, hitherto, been recognized.

The self-reflexivity which I identify in Sexton's work has typically been interpreted as a sign of an unhealthy (because personal) self-obsession and as evidence of the poet's own culpable narcissism. Joyce Carol Oates summarizes such views thus: "Sexton has been criticized for the intensity of her preoccupations: always the self, the victimized, bullying, narcissistic self" ("On The Awful" 144). Alan Williamson complains, of the "later Sexton," that she has become "the uneasy narcissist, self-indulgent and sarcastic at once" ("Confession" 178). And Patricia Meyer Spacks condemns Sexton's "shrill narcissism" and "insistent mirroring" ("On 45" 188). As Alicia Ostriker concludes: "Anne Sexton is the easiest poet in the world to condescend to. Critics get in line for the pleasure of filing her under N for Narcissist" ("That Story" 263). The term, when used pejoratively in this way, is symptomatic of a reading which sees confession as a pathological response rather than a willful and productive act. It exemplifies a normative approach to poetry: one which assumes that language is referential, that the text offers a reflection of the "real" experience of the author, and that the poem presents a clear, transparent, image of the truth.

I wish to propose that the apparent self-absorption of Anne Sexton (poet) might productively be read as the self-absorption of her writing. What appears to be a personal and regrettable self-regard might, instead, be read as a sophisticated and self-reflexive textual narcissism—that is, as a mimesis of process rather than of product, of the kind delineated by Linda Hutcheon in her book *Narcissistic Narrative: The Metafictional Paradox*. Using Hutcheon's argument as a framework, it is possible to reevaluate the adjective "narcissistic," to efface its reductive and pathological connotations, and to see it as a potentially fruitful descriptor of Sexton's work, as indeed of confessional writing more generally.

Within the context of Hutcheon's argument, the adjective "narcissistic" describes a writing which "self-consciously represents its own creative processes" and which is textually, rather than biographically, "self-reflective, self-informing, self-reflexive, auto-referential" (xii, 25, 1). In "narcissistic narrative" or contemporary metafiction or postmodern fiction, to mention the synonyms which Hutcheon uses—as I will argue in Sexton's work—it is poiesis (the act of making) which is mirrored, not the experience or identity of the maker. In this respect, it may further be argued that in its deeply self-reflexive contemplation of its own discursive processes, Sexton's poetry unexpectedly anticipates many of the practices of postmodernism. This is a point to which I will return. Crucially, Hutcheon regards the poiesis which is being mirrored as a "process shared by writer and reader" (41). The narcissistic text draws attention to and even explicitly thematizes the act of reading in order to demonstrate that meaning and truth are the product of a discursive relationship, rather than the property of some prior, originating author. As Hutcheon explains, "Now it is the reader who is being forced to acknowledge his active creative role" (41). To which we might add that in some of Sexton's work, such as "Talking to Sheep" and "The Letting Down of the Hair" (discussed later) it is the writer who is being "forced" to concede her authority.

Hutcheon's predominant interest in *Narcissistic Narrative* is in fiction. Indeed, she makes the point of distinguishing between poetry and the novel, arguing that in this context poetry is ahead. "Of all the literary genres, the novel is the one which has perhaps most resisted being 'rescued' from the myth of the instrumentality of language. Poetry escaped with the aid of the Symbolists, the New Critics, and others" (87). Further, she suggests that "whereas poetic language is now more or less accepted as autonomous and intransitive, fiction and narrative still suggest a transitive and referential use of words" (88). One might argue, however, that confession, unlike much other modern poetry, has not yet been liberated from this "myth of the instrumentality of language." The language of the confessional text continues to be read as "transitive and referential," as a truthful representation of the lived experience of the author. Sexton's brand of confession, like "narcissistic narrative," resists such readings. It is aware, and it flaunts its awareness that its truths are arbitrary, its authority disputable, and that its putative originality has been displaced by a discursive and productive relationship between text and reader. Thus, Sexton's apparent narcissism masks a knowing, and theoretically astute, engagement with the problematic processes of writing and representation.

The early poems discussed here, "An Obsessive Combination of Onto-logical Inscape, Trickery and Love" and "The Double Image" (both written in 1958) and "For John Who Begs Me Not to Enquire Further" (1959), are narcissistic in the sense that they are intrigued by and reflect on how, ex-actly, their meanings are realized and shared. They seek to reach and con-vey a better understanding, not of the experience ostensibly at the source of each, but of the way in which they themselves work as confession. Mirrors and other reflective surfaces such as windows, glass bowls, and portraits are fundamental to this inquiry, either "covertly" (as in the case of "An Obses-sive Combination" where mirroring processes are "structuralized, internal-ized") or "overtly" (as in "For John" where they are "explicitly thematized") (Hutcheon, *Narcissistic* 7). The textual narcissism which we see here forms the foundation of Sexton's exploration of the dynamics of confession in later poems, such as those in the "Letters to Dr. Y." sequence (1960–1970) with their sophisticated analyses of their own linguistic processes, and in "Talking to Sheep" (1974), which displays an acute consciousness and condemnation of its own audience. Throughout, narcissism is presented as both strategy (re-flection as process) and object (the reflection as material subject of inquiry) and, while generous in proliferating meanings, is also always shown to be susceptible to error, to be potentially distorted and distorting.

It is necessary before proceeding any further with this argument to un-derstand the roots of the concept of narcissism and to assess its resonance, not only in Sexton's poetry, but more generally. The cultural origins of the concept of narcissism are to be found in the story of Echo and Narcissus from Ovid's *Metamorphoses*. Narcissus is a beautiful and proud youth, the object of many observers' unrequited desires—including those of the nymph Echo who "cannot stay silent when another person speaks, but yet has not learned to speak first herself" (83). However, Narcissus spurns Echo's advances and in despair she retreats to the woods and caves, wasting away until only her voice remains. As punishment for his pride, Narcissus is condemned to experience the same frustrated desire. Subsequently he falls in love with his own reflected image in a pool. He is admonished: "The thing you are seeing does not ex-ist: only turn aside and you will lose what you love" (85). Realizing that, like Echo, he will never possess the object of his love, he too wastes away and dies, leaving in place of his body a circle of flowers.

The myth of Narcissus is important to Sexton's poetics in several respects. It offers a framework within which to develop themes of self-love and desire, it offers fruitful metaphors such as those of the mirror and the cave, and it lends the structural and linguistic potential of the echo. As James Goodwin has argued, in the context of the origins of autobiography, "The figure of Narcissus represents complexes—or, in other words, structures of great intellectual and affective force—that are indicative of the functions and consequences of self-knowledge at different stages in our cultural history" (69). The story of Narcissus is also of profound significance in Sigmund Freud's account of human psychology and is instrumental to his recognition and definition of the "superego." In "On Narcissism: An Introduction," (1914) Freud identifies a universal "primary and normal narcissism" (*On Metapsychology* 66). This is an early and necessary stage of ego or self-love which must, nevertheless, be transcended such that the "other" replaces the "ego" as love object if the subject is to assume his or her proper place in relation to parents, to subsequent sex objects, and to the wider world.

In the context of Sexton's exploration and defense of narcissism, Freud's argument is influential because, in contradiction to the opinions of his predecessors and peers, he asserts that narcissism is common and "normal" and that there is contiguity between "healthy and neurotic subjects" (73). Such a contiguity is apparent in "For John" where the "I"/"you" dialogue sustained throughout confirms the reciprocity of the subject's and implied reader's experience. Freud's analysis is valuable too because although describing in psychoanalytic terms the narcissist's tendency to turn inward, "away from the external world" (66), it also traces the necessary route outwards by which "our mental life . . . pass[es] beyond the limits of narcissism" and forms an attachment to objects (78). In addition, "On Narcissism" foregrounds the psychological importance of observing and "being observed" (91). It recognizes—and this is crucial to an understanding of confessional writing and its reception—the compelling attraction of someone else's narcissism: "It seems very evident that another person's narcissism has a great attraction for those who have renounced part of their own narcissism and are in search of object-love" (82–83).

In Freud, then, we find the first of several psychoanalytic defenses of narcissism, a defense which Jacques Lacan was later to take up. For Lacan, narcissism—or the gaze in the mirror—initiates the infant child's realization and confirmation of his or her identity. The mirror is vital to the two finally inextricable processes of finding and naming (or textualizing) the self. In Lacanian terms, it is by means of the mirror stage ("le stade du miroir" [*Écrits* 2]) that the aspiring subject leaves the realm of the imaginary and gains access to the symbolic order of language. Such a journey is invoked in Sexton's poem "The Double Image," discussed later.

Richard Sennett and Christopher Lasch, writing about contemporary American culture at the end of the 1970s—the period which had, contentiously, been labeled the "me decade" (Lasch 238)—study the growth and dominance of narcissistic "personality traits" in the "prevailing social conditions" (239). Sennett identifies a problem with the erosion of boundaries between public and private life, between external and internal worlds. Narcissism, he insists, flourishes in historically and culturally specific environments (12, 333). Lasch, too, considers narcissism in the context of changes in American domestic, cultural, and political life. Narcissism, he suggests, represents a reaction to and retreat from a general loss of faith in contemporary society, in the lessons of the past, and in the promise of the future (xv–xvii).

For Sexton, however, narcissism is broader, more complex, and finally more productive. Paradoxically, the self-disclosure in her work is made always with a view to its external reader or audience. While ostensibly focusing inwards, it also looks outwards and turns away from the self. Crucially, Sexton's poetry is predicated on restoring the "connection with the world" which Lasch sees as absent in narcissism and with flamboyantly laying bare the processes by which this connection is established. As Sexton's "An Obsessive Combination," "The Double Image," and "For John" indicate, the "I" can only be comprehended, or the self only known, by placing itself in conjunction with an other. All three poems are predicated on this persistent and sustaining dialogue. In this context, a narcissistic perspective denotes not a solipsistic devotion to the self but recognition that the self can only be perceived as part of a larger social context, as one among many.

The seeds of this interest in the fertile and discursive possibilities of narcissism, understood as a purposive textual strategy rather than as a symptom of debilitating self-absorption, are apparent in one of Sexton's earliest and uncollected poems, "An Obsessive Combination of Ontological Inscape, Trickery and Love." The poem was drafted in 1958 and first published in *Voices: A Journal of Poetry* in 1959. It is striking for the way in which it anticipates and makes explicit concerns which are developed subsequently in her writing. For example, we see here the roots of a sustained interest in the function and fallibility of language, expressed subsequently in poems such as "Is It True?" and "Hurry Up Please It's Time" and throughout the posthumous volume

The Awful Rowing Towards God (1975). "An Obsessive Combination" is paradigmatic of Sexton's poetics in its determined and self-conscious exploration of its own linguistic and representational status.

To look first at the title of the poem, the adjective "obsessive" seems to lay itself open to typical accusations of confessional compulsion and self-absorption. However, it transpires that the obsession is not with the self but with writing. The word "Love" in the title gives the lie to readings of confessional poetry as an expression of personal angst; this is a purposive and fertile, rather than sterile and inadvertent, act. Similarly, "ontological" shifts attention away from direct, lived experience to a more abstract, impersonal consideration of the condition of being. "Combination," too, has considerable resonance in the context of Sexton's poetics, signifying the meeting of minds or the discursive relationship between speaker and reader required for the truth of the confession successfully to be created and disseminated.

"Inscape" is the lodestone of the poem and plays a key role in disclosing Sexton's larger poetics. The noun is defined by *Webster's New International Dictionary* as

> Inward significant character or quality belonging uniquely to objects or events in nature and human experience esp. as perceived by the blended observation and introspection of the poet and in turn embodied in patterns of such specific poetic elements as imagery, rhythm, rhyme, assonance, sound symbolism, and allusion.

"Inscape" encapsulates the complex and seemingly contradictory process, subsequently explored in "For John," by which looking out and in, or "blend[ing] observation and introspection," become synonymous. It connotes the way in which meaning is realized in the dual and seemingly contradictory sense of being made apparent (here "embodied in patterns") and being received. Thus, Sexton's poem describes that moment at the heart of the confessional endeavor which is both hermetic and expressive. In the words of Gerard Manley Hopkins, the most notable proponent of the notion of "inscape": "*Oftening, over-and-overing, aftering* of the inscape must take place in order to detach it to the mind and in this light poetry is speech which afters and oftens its inscape, speech couched in a repeating figure" (xxii [Hopkins's emphasis]).[1] The inner essence is projected outwards by the same kinds of linguistic and syntactical patterning, repetition, and palindromic construction as we see in Sexton's poem.

For Sexton, the term "inscape" is suggestive of a number of disparate and resonant possibilities. It anticipates the exploration in this and a number of other poems of the inner landscape or geography of the mind. It also, in its own punning and rhyming multivalency, connotes the relationship between the inside (suggested by inscape) and the outside (implied in [e]scape). In one of her Crawshaw lectures, Sexton describes this dual perspective: "One writes of oneself . . . in order to invite in" and "to find the way, out through experience" (Crawshaw [9] 1). The word "inscape" reconciles or resolves the polarity of in/out, private/public which was central to poetics in the period. In a 1950 essay that Sexton cites in her Crawshaw lectures, poet Richard Wilbur had argued that poetry should be a window, not a door—meaning that it should show the metaphorical interior, while framing the perspective and limiting the viewer's access. This debate about the ethics and the aesthetics of revelation versus restraint, public versus private display engaged poets of a whole generation.

Sexton's poem achieves its effects by the kind of "generative [word] play" and "linguistic self-consciousness" identified by Hutcheon as characteristic of narcissistic narrative (*Narcissistic* 120, 118). Moreover, in its performative and playful aspects, the poem displays some of the defining features of post-modernist writing. Hutcheon sees as typical of such texts linguistic features, such as acrostics, anagrams, cryptograms, and puns which serve to "call the reader's attention to the fact that the text is made up of words, words which are delightfully febrile in creative suggestiveness" (119; 101). "An Obsessive Combination" employs many of these devices, featuring numerous aural and visual puns, homonyms and anagrams ("tiers," "tries," "rites," "right," "routes"). It also incorporates, and explores the resonance of, the palindrome ("RATS" / "STAR")—a device whose innate symmetry and mirroring potential offers a supreme example of narcissistic word play.

The opening lines of "An Obsessive Combination" ("Busy, with an idea for a code, I write / signals hurrying from left to right") confirm the self-re-flexivity of the title. The prominence in the first sentence of the word "Busy" suggests not only that the speaker is preoccupied or "obsessive" but also that this is important work (busy-ness/business). The fascination is not with personal experience, but with thoughts, ideas, semantic and epistemological sequences—with an "idea for a code" in the first line and with "reasons" in line four. That the poem is "a code," and that writing "signals," confirms the persistent linguistic self-consciousness of Sexton's writing and its sustained interest in the hermeneutic process by which words emerge and are deciphered. The metaphor of the "code" indicates that the confessional text might obscure (as we will see in a moment, I use the verb advisedly) rather than lay bare its secrets. The line break after "write" suggests, as the rest of the poem confirms, that the "signals" are autonomous. The poet writes, yet in what seems to be a distinct movement, it is the "signals" which hurry across the page. Language in this poem, as elsewhere in Sexton's oeuvre, preexists and dominates the subject; it constructs rather than reflects experience.

In "An Obsessive Combination" writing is potentially disordered (and disordering). Hence, these "signals" are "hurrying"

> from left to right,
> or right to left, by obscure routes,
> for my own reasons; taking a word like "writes"
> down tiers of tries until its secret rites
> make sense.

The religious and judicial connotations of "rites" make it a deceptively powerful metaphor for confessional poetry. The text exposes the seemingly magical process by which "write" becomes "right." This notion of writing as magical, as a trick or ritual, and therefore as autonomous and beyond the control of the author recurs in Sexton's work. In "You, Dr. Martin" (1958), Sexton writes, "We are magic talking to itself;" in "Flee on Your Donkey" (1962), she refers to poetry as a "trick;" and in "The Doctor of the Heart" (ca. 1970), she ascribes the poet's abilities to "a gimmick called magic fingers." Suzette Henke records a similar finding in H. D.: "The magical iterations of *The Gift*, H. D. tells us, 'abracadabraize something. . . . Th y are the words of the spell . . . that in a sense . . . keep me alive'" (27). In "An Obsessive Combination," Sexton demonstrates how a spell (itself a hidden pun highlighting the importance of a change of spelling, for example, from "tiers" to "rites") weaves magic in the poem.

The image of the physical and orderly progression of language across the page ("left to right") offers a metaphor for the way the act of confession is assumed to put things "right" in the therapeutic sense. However, as this poem demonstrates, it is not the simple act of release, or the "tapping" of the wellspring of inner compulsion that makes things right, but rather the textualization, the act of "writing." Moreover, as the addendum in the next line of the poem ("or right to left") indicates, the act of confession may compound rather than resolve problems, not putting things right, but making them sinister ("left"). The recourse to the "obscure routes" suggests that understanding or illumination—although in classical Platonic thought dependent on the presence of light (Plato 258ff.)—may emerge from the dark, the private, the unseemly or sinister, which is thereby recuperated as a viable source for poetry. In this respect, the poem anticipates "For John," where the inauspicious "narrow diary of my mind" produces and refracts something of dazzling and broad significance. It also paves the way for a number of later poems, including "With Mercy for the Greedy" and "Hurry Up Please It's Time," in which equally abject or occluded experience is "amazingly" transformed into radiant meaning.

In "An Obsessive Combination" language, perception and meaning are constantly changing and multiplying:

> until, suddenly, RATS
> can amazingly and funnily become STAR
> and right to left that small star
> is mine, for my own liking, to stare
> its five lucky pins inside out.

The poem again exposes the arbitrariness of language. Authorial responsibility is denied, hence the passivity of voice and the appropriation of the perspective of astonished ("amazingly," "funnily") witness to these linguistic and ontological transformations. Certainly, Sexton does not go as far as later Language poets in rupturing the bond between signifier and signified: "Rats" and "Star," while locked in a palindromic relationship with each other, do also connote distinct and opposing referents which are metaphorically suggestive within the context of the poem. However, she does place this bond under critical scrutiny, exposing its arbitrariness (the transposition of a letter or phoneme can drastically alter the signification of a word) and its effect. Nothing, Sexton insists, can be made into something. The enthusiastic explanatory rhetoric of the second half of the poem, with its hyperbolic adverbs ("suddenly," "amazingly," and "funnily")and its incredulous and gleeful aside ("for my own liking") gives way, in the final clause, to a more skeptical and resigned tone:

> right to left that small star
> is mine, for my own liking, to stare

its five lucky pins inside out, to store
forever kindly, as if it were a star
I touched and a miracle I really wrote.

The tentative "as if" concedes that words, and by extension the confessional text, may not deliver what is expected of them; language may fail. The epiphany which the poem seems to promise is a transient thing; hence the sudden change from the present tense and immediacy of action of the body of the poem to the conditional and qualified tone of the final line. "An Obsessive Combination" warns that the word play by which "RATS" becomes "STAR," and by which a miracle is conjured, may remain just that: semantic "trickery" or a "spell." Thus we are returned to the textuality of the confessional poem, to its status as "autonomous and intransitive object" (Hutcheon, *Narcissistic* 88). "An Obsessive Combination," one of Sexton's earliest poems, is paradigmatic of much of her later writing and characteristic of postmodern poetry in that it is unable or unwilling to proffer closure. It refuses the temptations of an easy and satisfying conclusion, finishing instead on an open-ended and provisional note: "as if it were."

Similar concerns inform "The Double Image," a complex and profoundly artful poem which contemplates the relationships between three generations of women: the speaker, her dying mother, and her infant daughter. The defining motifs are the fluctuating mental and physical sickness of the speaker and her mother, the patterns of absence and presence which define the three females' relationships, and the dual portraits (or double images) which the mother commissions of herself and the speaker and hangs "on opposite walls" such that the two images mirror each other. Equally, "The Double Image" may be read in terms of Lacan's understanding of narcissism, as an examination of the way in which we comprehend the self, or achieve subjectivity, by perceiving, recognizing, and identifying ourselves in relation to others. In "The Double Image," the apparently referential surface of the poem—the narrative of loss and recovery which ostensibly inspires, shapes, and validates it—masks an equally compelling and effective examination of its own processes of production and reception.

"The Double Image" is not, then, only or primarily about the relationships and experiences which it describes. It is about its own status as confession. It is a metapoem which draws attention to its own mirroring processes in order to display its constructed, contingent, and finally illusory nature. The

"Double Image" of the poem's title gestures towards this double meaning and, implicitly, to its own duplicity. For what the poem describes and finally exemplifies is a succession of doublings or reflections (the dual portraits of speaker and mother, the image of the speaker simultaneously gazing at her own painted image and drafting this textual self-portrait) which mimics only itself. Speaker and reader alike are locked in an endless mise-en-abyme of the kind which one might identify as characteristic of postmodernism and typical of narcissistic narrative; this is a proliferation of images in infinite regress offering no necessary access to reality.

"The Double Image" uses catoptrics both "covertly" and "overtly" (Hutcheon, *Narcissistic* 23). The text itself assumes the characteristics of a mirror and the arrangement of the poem's seven sections represents a near-perfect symmetry of action. In the first three sections, we see the daughter and then the speaker leaving home, followed by the central (fourth) section which hangs in the balance, denoting a liminal moment of uncertainty or indecision. Symmetry is restored in the closing three sections wherein first the speaker and then the daughter return to the family home. There are numerous antonyms, for example contradictory images for catching and letting go and for progression and regression. In the second section of the poem, the speaker's suicide attempt is symmetrically inverted, or replicated in reverse, and represented by the mother in the form of a talismanic portrait—an attempt to defeat death with an image of life. As Sigmund Freud shows in his essay on "The Uncanny," here citing Otto Rank, the double features first as a way of fixing and confirming life and thereafter as a strategy for warding off death.

The subject ("I"), addressee ("you"), and others ("she" or "they") of the poem stand in a finely balanced and mutually reliant role like that of an object, a mirror, and a reflection. The structure of the poem works subtly to sustain this. The opening and closing sections of dense syllabic verse contain the fullness of the poem, establishing first the terms of the debate, and then its resolution. Like an object and its reflection, they are drawn together by the central hermetic mirror—here the concise, self-contained, central section of the poem. The multiple linguistic repetitions within the poem ("Too late, / too late" in section two, "as if," "as if," "as if" in section three) linger like an echo, mimicking the proliferation of reflections which the poem describes. There is a constant, swaying, forward and backward movement within the poem both in terms of narrative and of perspective such that the reader, like the speaker, is required to look from one mirrored image to another and then back again. In this way, the text brings "to readers' attention their central and enabling role" in the production and reception of meaning (Hutcheon, *Narcissistic* xii).

The symmetry of the double images and their implicit polarity is emphasized. The paintings carry resemblances—both women's smiles are described as being held "in place"—but also subtle and crucial differences: The speaker's portrait is illuminated by the "north light," while the mother's is lit from the "south." As Lacan points out, such inversion or distortion is characteristic of the mirror stage. The infant gazes into the mirror and is given back a reflection which is in "a contrasting size (un relief de stature) that fixes it and in a symmetry that inverts it" (*Écrits* 2). In Sexton's poem, the speaker addresses both the mirror image of the mother and the reflection of the self, thus confirming the paradoxical identity and difference which unite the two: "my mocking mirror, my overthrown / love, my first image." That the mirror is "mocking" indicates that it offers an idealized image of what the speaker should be, thus reinforcing her inadequacy. We are reminded of the plight of the humiliated Echo in Ovid's tale and of Narcissus, too, who perceives a "mocking mirror" and experiences the simultaneous enticement and rejection of his "first image."[2]

The closing stanza of the poem offers a further reading of the "double image" of its title. The speaker finally acknowledges to her daughter that "I needed you." She frankly recognizes the nature of the bond between the "I" and "you" suggested in the opening lines. The daughter has replaced the speaker's mother in that it is she, the daughter, who has bestowed (gender) identity on the speaker. In other words, the speaker's daughter makes good the failure of the speaker's mother:

> I, who was never quite sure
> about being a girl, needed another
> life, another image to remind me.

The "image" is that of the daughter, produced literally and figuratively by the speaker in order to confirm her own identity, just as the speaker's mother created first the speaker and then an image or portrait of her in a vain attempt to cling to life. Hence, the speaker's final admission: "And this was my worst guilt; you could not cure / nor soothe it. I made you to find me." This is a compelling conclusion. However, the real interest lies in the confession, not that the speaker made the daughter biologically but that she has constructed the daughter in the poem textually. These final lines confirm my reading of the poem as textually narcissistic, for the ultimate referent of "the double image" is the poem itself and the strategies which it employs in its construction and aestheticization of relationships, experience, and subjectivity. The "worst guilt" to which the speaker refers pertains to her fabrication and manipulation of the mother/daughter relationship in order to construct this very poem and thereby to create or found—and emphatically not to reflect—her singular identity as poet: "to find me."

Narcissistic narrative, as we have seen, is concerned with the role of the reader. Sexton's early poem "For John Who Begs Me Not to Enquire Further" is noteworthy for the way in which it exemplifies this interest, addressing in particular the discursive relationship between speaker and reader, penitent and confessor. Diane Middlebrook describes "For John" as a "defense . . . of the whole genre of poetry that would soon be labeled 'confessional'" (*Biography* 100), while Caroline King Barnard Hall argues that "For John" should be read as "a credo . . . for Sexton's entire oeuvre" (14). The importance of the poem as an expression of Sexton's poetics is beyond dispute. Its real significance, however, lies in its exemplification of how confession functions, rather than in its defense of what it reveals.

To briefly explain: The images of the "cracked mirror" and glass bowl in "For John," in addition to representing Narcissus's pool, signify primary subjective narcissism ("the cracked mirror / or my own selfish death") and may be read as metaphors for the creative process ("I, the poet, look to myself and show you a reflection of what I see"). Moreover, in this particular poem, the reflective glass symbolizes and instigates the "calling in" of the reader and the transfer or exchange of responsibility between reader and writer in the act of perceiving and interpreting confessional meaning. The poem is predicated on the paradox that, in order truthfully to tell us about telling the truth, the speaker must weave a "complicated lie." The poem's manipulation of successive shifting mirror images confirms the potential multiplicity and unreliability of self-representation. In place of a coherent subject, faithfully mirrored, we see only fleeting, oblique glimpses of a fragmentary reflection.

"For John" achieves its effects in part by anticipating, even parodying, orthodox expectations of its speaker's narcissism. It parades its insistent first-person voice (which, in another context, the poet Denise Levertov suggests is gratuitously narcissistic ["Biography" 11]), its emphatically domestic concerns ("the commonplaces," the "kitchen"), and its protagonist's prolonged self-scrutiny in the mirror. The poem resounds with images for the self; for self-admiration, idealization, and subjective pleasure. Lines end with terms of self-absorption ("beautiful," "mind," "mirror," "me," "myself," "private," "special," "dear," "face") which emphasize the narcissistic impulse at play. Yet the text's flamboyant narcissism is beguiling, masking the absence or dissipation of the self. Marjorie Perloff argues of postmodern poetry that "the Romantic and Modernist cult of personality has given way to what the new poets call 'the dispersal of the speaking subject,' the denial of the unitary, authoritative ego" (*Dance* x). However, I would contend that this fracturing or "dispersal of the speaking subject" is not unique to postmodern poetry and is carefully mapped in this case. The fragmentation of the "unitary authoritarian ego" is represented in multiple and proliferating images of fracture and dissipation, reminiscent of those in "The Double Image" and owing something in turn to the characteristics of narcissism as perceived from a psychoanalytic perspective. Susanna Egan discusses a number of modern writers, from Stein and Woolf through Hemingway to Breyten Breytenbach and Audre Lorde, who similarly manipulate the metaphor of the mirror as they explore the process and limits of self-representation: "By virtue of being multifaceted," she argues, "mirror talk reflects the very indeterminacy of life in crisis" (226).

The pleasurable self-abandonment evidenced in the opening lines of "For John" is countermanded by a contradictory impulse towards clarification and control ("not that," "order," "worth learning," "lesson") and by a recognition of the demands of a community of others ("you," "your," "something outside," "someone," "anyone"). The characteristic confessional "I" does not emerge until line five and is swiftly counterbalanced by the "you"—the explicit ("John") or implicit (unspecified) addressee —whose presence, although always latent in and instrumental to confession, is here unusually rendered visible within the text. The backward and forward movement of both dialogue and action replicates that of a confession, wherein the penitent speaks and the confessor listens. It anticipates the exchanges between speaker, mother, and daughter in "The Double Image" (which is placed immediately after "For John" in *To Bedlam and Part Way Back*, although it was written one year earlier). Further, the speaker and "John"/any reader are depicted in the finely balanced nuances of the poetic language—such as the final couplet "my kitchen, your kitchen, / my face, your face"—to be in a situation of mutually vengeful and predatory fate akin to that of Narcissus and Echo. Neither is able to satisfy his or her desires, both have reached the limits of identification, and neither can penetrate the boundary between self and other. Thus the ever-present risk for confession, that it will not find an auditor and achieve realization, is acknowledged.

Sexton's poem addresses the critical hostility which seems to sustain many readings of confessional poetry. The text's specific origins probably lie in Sexton's response to a letter which she had received from her mentor, the poet and teacher John Holmes, in which he expressed reservations about what he perceived to be the narrow narcissism of her work. Latent in the "I"/"you" exchange in the poem is a dialogue between Sexton (the implied author) and Holmes (an implied addressee). In identifying this letter as a possible source, I do not imply that it explains or limits the poem's potential meanings; as Bonnie Costello argues of the overdetermination of sources in Marianne Moore's work: "This multiplicity of sources is quite different from the multiplicity of references" (6). What I would contend is that Holmes's letter may be taken as a catalyst for the poem's self-conscious examination of larger confessional processes.

Scrutiny of the letter to Sexton, dated 8 February 1959, four days before she began work on the poem, reveals the extent to which "For John" repudiates confessional poetry's detractors. Her privileging of the "selfish death" offers a challenge to Holmes's view that she should efface her "hospital and psychiatric experiences [which seem] to me very selfish." Holmes's letter accuses her of "forcing others to listen" and complains that, in her work, there is "nothing given the listeners, nothing that teaches them or helps them." He abjures her to "do something else, outside yourself" (HRHRC). Sexton's speaker counters that she does teach something, that she offers a "lesson" which is "worth learning." This is "something special" and defiantly "something outside of myself."

"For John" insists that there is "sense" and "order" in even the most private and seemingly abject of experiences:

Not that it was beautiful,
but that, in the end, there was
a certain sense of order there;

something worth learning
in that narrow diary of my mind,
in the commonplaces of the asylum.

By opening the poem with the emphatic "Not," Sexton confronts, from the outset, the criticisms which she anticipates encountering, and proceeds to refute them with her arguments in the subsequent two lines. The syntax of the first line refuses the chief motivation ascribed to Narcissus, that is, love of his own beauty. Sexton suggests that it is "not" the product (the "beautiful" object) which is worthy of attention but the process—the ordering, the reading, the making of "sense."

More generally, the opening lines of the poem foreground the hermeneutic processes of reading and evaluation by which meaning will be received. The opening line postulates a subject "it" ("not that it was beautiful") which is never fully defined, remaining elusive and ambiguous throughout the poem in spite of the speaker's best and repeated efforts to identify and represent it. The reader's commitment and interpretative powers are first solicited and then held at bay by this persistent ontological uncertainty. The reader is made complicit with the speaker; he or she is coerced to share the speaker's uncertainty and frustrated desire for resolution. In this way, the poem self-consciously inscribes within itself an interpretative space for the reader.

Fundamental to Sexton's explanation in "For John" of how meaning is realized and dispersed are the metaphors of mirrors; first, the "cracked mirror" of line seven, and later the inverted glass bowl which shares many of its properties. The mirrors function overtly to portray or mirror the text's own processes of contemplation and reflection. The poem concedes that narcissism is a frustrating and limiting practice as the confessing subject's initial self-scrutiny in the mirror offers no reassurance: "my own selfish death / outstared me." She seeks in the mirror confirmation of her identity, yet is met with a disfigured reflection which is in contrasting or disproportionate size (hence the excessively "selfish death" which dominates, or "outstare[s]") and which is inverted; the living subject looks for signs of life, and finds only evidence of death. Looking in the mirror should be a rewarding and progressive moment—in Lacanian terms, a necessary step towards successful assumption of the "function as subject" (*Écrits* 2). In this poem, there is no such progression. There is no pleasure in this literal and metaphorical introspection (nor, by extension, in the act of confession), and considerable psychic risk.

"For John" inscribes a place for the reader within the body of the text and renders inescapable Sexton's point about the larger, public significance of what had once seemed merely "private." It demonstrates that the narcissistic gesture becomes productive and meaningful only when it is shared. The "selfish" gaze must, if it is to mean anything "outside of myself," be subject to dispersal and dissemination, and it is the fragmentation of the cracked mirror which is instrumental in bringing this shift to multiplicity about. The mirror in and of the text offers no clear image; instead, it proffers fragmented and diffuse but nevertheless suggestive shards. A similar process is encapsulated in the image of the lucky star in "An Obsessive Combination" which shines its "inside out." It is only by refraction that it externalizes its meaning and thus communicates to the reader. Similarly, the language of the poetry is both elusive and multiplicitous. It functions less as a mirror than as a prism which first splits and then projects fractured and elliptical images of its subject. Self-reflection is not, then, what it seems to be and gives back an image which is attenuated, fractured, and dispersed into myriad pieces, like the component colors of white light when viewed through a crystal.

Similar tropes are found in poetry by women from earlier in the century. In Amy Lowell's "Opal," for instance, the closing lines gesture towards the narcissistic process, declaring, "My heart is a frozen pond." But here, as with Sexton, this is not the site of mere introspection; the vision projects outwards, "Gleaming with agitated torches." In H. D., too, we find extensive use of crystalline imagery, promising clarity and precision but often disclosing refraction, opacity, and diffuseness. Throughout *Heliodora*, for example, and "The Flowering of the Rod," reflection and symmetry, doubleness, and "the desire to equilibrate" emerge (169). In "Tribute to the Angels," the qualities of the crystal or prism are exploited to show the richness and multiplicity of white light (metaphorically plain truth or insight) which, it transpires, is "all—color" (163). Edward Comentale, citing Eileen Gregory, points to the liminality of much of H. D.'s work, arguing that it reveals "a constant mediation of 'boundaries between inner and outer, between self and other'" (485). More recently, Sylvia Plath in "Hardcastle Crags" and "Crossing the Water" and Sharon Olds in many of the poems collected in *Strike Sparks* have experimented with similar metaphors of female creativity.

The image in "For John" of the "inverted" or convex glass bowl permits further exploration and development of the metaphor of the mirror:

I tapped my own head;
it was glass, an inverted bowl.
It is a small thing
to rage in your own bowl.

Like its obvious palimpsest, Sylvia Plath's bell jar, the inverted glass bowl discloses whatever lies within it.[3] The inversion of the bowl lends it the same imperfect, unpredictable capacities as the earlier "cracked mirror." Indeed, an inverted glass bowl and a mirror share many qualities. Both have reflective and distorting surfaces which give back fragmented images of the viewing object. Jonathan Miller points out that "in contrast to a plain or flat surface, which faithfully reproduces the proportions of whatever it reflects, a curved surface systematically disfigures it" (43). The image represents, and alerts us to, the confessional text's own distortions and unreliability. It teaches us that confessional poetry is not after all, only transitive and realistic.

The bowl uniquely reveals both its inside and its outside and thus forms a perfect self-referential metaphor for the confessional poem and the larger narcissistic process by which the subject reaches a reconciliation with the object world. Other Sexton poems, as the next chapter explains, manipulate similar metaphors, for example, images of plate glass and picture windows, in order further to explore the relationship between private and public realms. That the speaker "tapped" her "own head" confirms the potential contiguity of self and other and the fluidity of the boundaries between the private and the public. For "Tapped" signifies both the process of siphoning or extracting insights from inside the head, perhaps for personal relief, and the act of striking or hammering or beating out a pattern (a poem?) on the outside for the edification of others. The image insinuates the indivisibility of subject and discourse, product, and process.

The image of the simultaneously luminous and reflective glass bowl which dominates "For John" stands as a metaphor for Sexton's larger poetics. With this in mind, one might argue that Sexton's writing is Janus-faced, that it looks both inside and outside simultaneously and to that extent is always doubled, or split, or fragmented in its perspective. Mimesis is to be treated warily; there is no such thing as direct, unproblematic reflection. Instead, the act of mirroring is fraught with uncertainty and duplicity. The representation of subjectivity or experience which confessional poetry offers is to be understood as a copy of or approximation to the original, but not as identical with it. What confessional writing does is contemplate and expose the complexity of identity, the absence or elusiveness (even in this apparently self-expressive mode) of a unified, homogenous subject. Christina Britzolakis makes a similar point in connection with Plath's use of metaphors of mirrors in her *Journals*: "Ironically, these are almost invariably linked with moments of specular mis- or nonrecognition in which the subject is encountered as abject, resistant otherness" and are seen as "the sign of a self-reflexivity which is alternately paralyzing and enabling" (16, 17).

Sexton's poem explicitly acknowledges and confronts the reader's reluctance to participate in the hermeneutic process which it reveals. Her defiant wielding of the bowl, specifically in line 27, but more generally in the poem as a whole, forces the reader to participate in the narcissistic process and prevents him or her from looking away:

> And if you turn away
> because there is no lesson here
> I will hold my awkward bowl,
> with all its cracked stars shining
> like a complicated lie,
> and fasten a new skin around it
> as if I were dressing an orange
> or a strange sun.

Sexton's bowl radiates meaning. However, this is born not of authenticity, but of artifice. Recognizing that alone it may not compel or retain the audience's attention—indeed that its very transparency or nakedness may repel them—the speaker takes steps to render her "lesson" more acceptable, dressing or disguising the bowl in luminous "orange" so that it shines "like a strange sun." As the poem's argument develops, what we see is emphatically not a pure, unmediated reflection of lived experience as might be expected of confessional poetry. Rather, it is a fabrication, an object masked or disguised, dressed with a "new skin." Truth and artifice, here, are synonymous: The "cracked stars" shine "like a complicated lie." In a genre apparently predicated on revelation, this metaconfession that the essence of confession lies in dressing up rather than undressing, in disguise rather than nakedness, in deceit rather than honesty, is supremely telling.

The concluding section of "For John" is anticipated in, and deflects the reader's attention back to, the beginning:

Not that it was beautiful,
but that I found some order there.
There ought to be something special
for someone.

The structure functions as a strategy of containment, like the frame of a mirror or the rim of a bowl or the banks of Narcissus's pond. The reader, like Narcissus, has become enthralled by the reflection glimpsed in the mirror/text and entranced by the possibilities that it proffers. Just when we think that we have achieved a resolution and may break free, we are taken back to the beginning in an endless, circular mimesis—an inverted bowl whose unbroken circumference traps speaker and reader alike.

In "The Changing Face of Common Intercourse," Marjorie Perloff posits a difference between postmodern and lyric forms of poetry based on a distinction between "artifice" and "authenticity." I would contend that Sexton's simultaneously reflective and luminous bowl refuses to choose just one of these aesthetics and functions as both. The "glass bowl shining" reflects and reveals at one and the same time. What we must note, however, is that both devices are imperfect. The reflective surface is "awkward" and "cracked" and "complicated," offering no clear mimesis. The sun, which should figure illumination and insight, is, in order to seduce its necessary audience, veiled and disguised. Dressed in a "new skin," it cannot penetrate with directness or clarity but must carefully screen its message. In both cases, something apparently transparent or luminous is rendered translucent such that the (confessional) subject ostensibly being reflected or expressed is hidden from view, obscured by a crazed or veiled surface. However, what "For John" does do in self-consciously selected metaphors suggestive of the refraction and diffusion of light is ensure that its meaning is similarly shared. Something reputedly singular, personal, and solipsistic is made multiple, social, and discursive.

The poem presents a fundamentally narcissistic moment, a moment of crisis in the subject's sense of self and her relation to the external world which is laid bare for contemplation by both speaker and reader. It is the potential communality of experience here, the fact that narcissism forms "a place in the regular course of human sexual development" (Freud, *On Metapsychology* 65), which forms the heart of Sexton's argument and aesthetic defense. We all go through this process, and the poem reminds us of this, forcing us to revisit it:

> This is something I would never find
> in a lovelier place, my dear,
> although your fear is anyone's fear,
> like an invisible veil between us all . . .
> and sometimes in private,
> my kitchen, your kitchen,
> my face, your face.

The quiet closing lines of the poem with their symmetry and soft diminuendo mimic the gentle sound of an Echo fading out of hearing. The implicit ("I" / "you") dialogue which has sustained the whole poem is here rendered more generally inclusive; "us all" encapsulates speaker and readers alike. In the simultaneously transparent and reflective bowl, we look for self and find other, we look for other and find self. What we see is both "my kitchen" and "your kitchen," "my face" and "your face." Narcissism is revealed to be a public and discursive rather than a private and hermetic gesture.

John Holmes's concluding message to Sexton in the letter which, arguably, inspired the poem, specifically alludes to Ovid's tale. Holmes's anxiety about Sexton's writing is galvanized by his fear that Sexton's fate may mirror that of Narcissus: "You must liberate your gift, and let it create new life, not gaze always hypnotized on death and the wreck of nerves." "For John" ultimately answers confessionalism's critics by expressly embracing the very process against which they rail. It not only explains, it shows. Mirrors, reflective surfaces and symmetries are, in Hutcheon's terms, "thematized or allegorized" within the text (*Narcissistic* 142) and the voices of Narcissus and Echo are persistently present. Sexton demonstrates that narcissism does not necessarily mean introspective stasis. As in Ovid's tale, where Narcissus's legacy is "a flower with a circle of white petals round a yellow centre" (*Metamorphoses* 87), Sexton's speaker's self-absorption is productive. It is transformed into "something outside of myself," something that at least "ought" to be "special / for someone."

3

Suburbia

Thus far we have seen Sexton exploring the parameters of the confessional mode and identifying her own place in it, and we have noted the profound self-consciousness of her work, that is, its preoccupation with its own discursive processes, its production and reception. It would be wrong, however, to read Sexton's writing as immune from its historical, political, and cultural contexts or as hermetically sealed from the social and ideological imperatives of 1960s America. What may seem intimate, private, and narcissistic may, if we reenvision narcissism in the way I have proposed, be reevaluated as a means of integrating private and public, self, and other or, at the very least, as a way of exploring the contiguity between these apparent poles. From this perspective, confessional poetry is not hermetic, self-contained, and "cut off from greater social, political, moral engagements" as Graham and Sontag put it (7). Rather, it is deeply embedded in, and has much to say about, the larger culture into which it emerged and has continued to be read. Sylvia Plath famously delineated the duties of her generation of poets (a generation which included Sexton and Rich) thus: "Personal experience is very important, but certainly it shouldn't be shut-box and mirror-looking, narcissistic experience. I believe it should be relevant and relevant to the larger things, the bigger things such as Hiroshima and Dachau and so on" (Orr, *Poet* 169–70). I will argue below that Sexton concurs with Plath in refusing this dichotomy.

The chapter which follows does two main things. First, it traces the emergence of Sexton's poetry within a specific place, time, and set of cultural and ideological expectations (that is, within the domestic spaces of postwar suburban America).[1] Second, it examines Sexton's poetry in terms of its broader sense of its political and historical responsibilities. It is unusual to read Sexton, or the work of most other confessional poets, in these terms. Adrienne Rich has widely been perceived as the one poet of Sexton's cohorts to have risen to the challenge of addressing contemporary ideologies, although recent work by Tracy Brain, Robin Peel, and Deborah Nelson has succeeded in recuperating Plath's voice in such debates. Sexton's writing has less visibly—although not, as I will argue, less attentively—concerned itself with political issues.

Her poetry, like confession more generally, explores what Deborah Nelson has identified as "the changing boundaries of public and private domains" in postwar American culture (xii). It shows us that it is often in personal experience or in the private domestic sphere (for example, in the 1961 poem "The House") that broader ideological crises are most painfully played out.

Marilyn Chin has commented of a trend towards the private and domestic in recent American poetry: "Poetry has moved to the suburbs. . . . I suppose this was first inspired by the confessional poets. . . . Their poems are self-centered, shortsighted; they don't extend to larger concerns" (qtd. in Graham and Sontag 6). My point is that the private and domestic sphere usually identified as the locus of Sexton's oeuvre is inescapably political. It is deeply implicated in "larger concerns," not only in the sense that it is the place where femininity is constructed and played out (although this is an important part of the story), but in the sense that it is here that the subject takes her place in history. The perception that confessional poetry has little or no interest in anything beyond the limits of the self is a long-lived one. Throughout the 1950s, as Edward Brunner shows, American poetry was riven by debates about the relative values of a politically engaged poetry on the one hand, and a poetry of intimacy, quietude, and introspection on the other. Even then, though, there were voices which recognized the possible dovetailing of the two. Philip Blair Rice of the *Kenyon Review*, writing in 1954, noted that "poetry which could resemble an apparent retreat may also be in dialogue, albeit obliquely, with large and disturbing issues" (qtd. in Brunner 238). Of late, the shift towards suburban concerns has come to seem demographically inevitable, yet, as Robert von Hallberg explains, contemporary poetry of the suburbs (for example, the work of Robert Pinsky) remains committed to the examination of major concerns, for example, about nation and identity, about history and progress, and about writing and American social life (228–44).

In a 1962 letter, Sexton confides, "I am actually a 'suburban housewife' only I write poems and am sometimes a little crazy" (*Letters* 143). This characteristically nuanced and deceptive declaration shows Sexton first positing, then complicating, and finally demurring from a particular personal identity.

She acknowledges, albeit tacitly, the complexity of the contradictory parts which she is required to play and the difficulty which she has in reconciling them. As she goes on to explain: "I fear I am not myself here in my suburban housewife role." Christina Britzolakis makes a similar point of the influence of Sylvia Plath's social context on her self-representations: "The different and often contradictory versions of 'Sylvia Plath' constructed by the letters, journals, short stories, and *The Bell Jar*, are entangled with myths of selfhood, femininity, and nation attendant upon a particular place and time" (12).

Where confessional poetry has typically been read as focusing on the subject's inner life, or the landscape of the mind, I suggest that Sexton's writing deviates from this model, valorizing instead a distinct, unexpected, and poetically fertile locale. Hers is a peculiar suburban world of open-plan lounges and modern kitchen appliances, of picture windows, backyards, and barbecues, of intense neighborliness, high-pressure childrearing, and carefully demarcated gender roles; and of difficult but necessary marriages. Significantly, her 1973 sequence, "The Divorce Papers," is dominated by metaphors of suburban domesticity under crisis. The accouterments of the average suburban life—of wedding rings and children, vacations and kitchens, of televisions, aprons, washers, and dryers—are juxtaposed in surreal and disturbing ways. Marsha Bryant has noted the same strategy in Plath's writing. In both cases, the effect is to illuminate the "unstable boundaries of postwar domesticity" (Bryant 287). In Sexton's work, the American suburbs represent both a literal place and a figurative space, one whose meanings and parameters have to be constantly negotiated and repeatedly tested in order fully to accommodate the multiple identities (housewife, poet, and madwoman) which she proposes to install there.

In the first part of the chapter, I examine the rhetorical and metaphorical uses to which Sexton puts the suburbs, for example, in poems which depict the self in the modern suburban home as dislocated and fragmented or in poems which devise a complex rhetoric of voyeurism and display entirely appropriate to contemporary suburban experience. I proceed to consider Sexton's suburban poems in their particular historical moment. Deborah Nelson has shown that the ascendance of the confessional mode of poetry coincides with two key factors: the emergence of the suburbs as the apotheosis of American living, and the pervasiveness in Cold War America of a culture of anxiety, hostility, and surveillance. Sexton's work is produced and read within an environment which, while it permits a "loosening of the social/cultural prohibitions against self-disclosure" (Nelson 19), is also characterized by suspicion. Thus, it bestows contradictory messages about privacy and community: "The suburban home was supposed to offer the opportunity to live out the democratic dream of privacy in postwar America. And yet . . . suburban homes . . . were associated with a profound deprivation of privacy as well" (85). These contradictory messages are reproduced, affirmed, and recirculated in the new architecture of the period with its open-plan layouts and picture windows. Both of these seem to invite association and deny privacy (or to assert the "visibility principle" as contemporary commentator William M. Dobriner puts it) while functioning to enforce strict geographical, gender, and familial boundaries (9).

Sexton is, of course, not the first or only poet to enter this field. Phyllis McGinley, writing from the 1930s through to the 1950s, made the suburbs her literal and figurative home and was popularly known as the "housewife poet." However, in her poetry, like in Sexton's (and like in the work of a more recent "suburban" poet from a different context, the Irish writer Eavan Boland), the private sphere, while representing a retreat from a larger public context of anxiety, surveillance, and threat, also invokes a range of new conflicts and pressures. In McGinley's "June in the Suburbs" or "Spring Comes to the Suburbs," for example, we find an undertow of tension, violence, and latent aggression (the sound of whimpers, roars, and explosions in the former) and of competitive consumption and display (metaphors of begging, mending, earning, giving, and conspicuously spending in the latter). Her "Sonnets from the Suburbs" present a catalogue of grotesques to surpass those of Sherwood Anderson's *Winesburg, Ohio*.[2] A number of prose writers of the period (John Updike, John Cheever, and Joyce Carol Oates, for example) have written about suburban values and crises. What is interesting and unique in Sexton's case is the way in which her own experience is melded with an acute and informed reading of contemporary ideology and a sophisticated and self-conscious aesthetic.

Implicit throughout this chapter will be my sense of the productive relationship between the profound self-reflexivity of Sexton's work and its suburban roots. My point is that the self-consciousness of her writing (its awareness, in particular, of its relationship with its audience, its concerns about truth and deception, its anxiety about personal revelation) replicates a wider self-consciousness about privacy and surveillance, about seeing and being seen, about social and gender conformity which characterize suburban domestic life at this time.

To summarize Sexton's suburban origins: She was raised in the outskirts of Boston and spent the summers at her grandparents' affluent home on the Massachusetts coast, a place which is immortalized in "Funnel," discussed below. She moved to the new suburbs of Boston as a young housewife and mother and took sporadic jobs outside the home (selling cosmetics door to door, for instance). However, with her husband away for long periods of time as a salesman, she remained in the suburbs as the main homemaker. These suburban roots have been noted by other commentators, often as an accusation or as a way of showing what the suburbs did to her and other women of what has been called the *Feminine Mystique* generation (after Betty Friedan's 1963 book). Such readings situate Sexton in a passive relationship with these discourses, whereas I wish to suggest that Sexton actively, persistently, and consciously—albeit often with considerable ambivalence—evokes the suburbs as the site of her poetry, as the source of her poetic voice, as a badge of difference with which to counter dominant metropolitan and masculine literary models, and as a profoundly political space.

Sexton's suburban poems may be said to "write back" to those of her contemporary and one-time instructor, Robert Lowell. Lowell's emphatic and long-lived association with the metropolis and with Boston Brahmin culture is countered by Sexton's marked recognition and articulation of the different spaces which she inhabits, as for example in her poem "Man and Wife," a response to his "To Speak of Woe that Was in Marriage," discussed below.[3] Sexton's flamboyant championing of the suburbs in poems, letters, and paratextual comments, marks a defiant assertion of poetic identity and a self-conscious annexing of this implicitly gendered place and of the complex perspectives, relationships, and experiences which it represents. Moreover, the modern home provides a rich source of metaphor which, in particular, gives Sexton the means to explore and critique some of the tensions and contradictions of contemporary women's experience. *The Feminine Mystique* had recently shown that beneath the public face of the "suburban housewife" lay a private narrative of violence, breakdown, failure, and resentment—a secret life which Sexton's poetry exposes. In the poems discussed below, the female subject in the modern suburban home is dislocated, fragmented, and split ("Self in 1958") or inauthentic ("Housewife") or she is figured as food—as offering herself up in and to a culture which overvalues consumption ("The Death Baby").

Sexton manipulates or exploits readerly expectations of the role of suburban housewife and mother, provisionally identifying with that label and then utterly traducing its efficacy. She does this not only by the sardonic or despairing tones of the poems discussed below but also visually in her use of photographic portraits. Here she exploits to great effect the transgressive value of the apparently passive suburban housewife turning and assertively speaking. Arthur Furst concedes as much in his introduction to *Anne Sexton: The Last Summer*, the book of still photographs which he took at Sexton's home in the summer of 1974 and published in 2000. Furst, like others before him, notes the discursive impact of the incongruity between Sexton's suburban setting and demeanor and the anger, sexuality and explicitness of the poems:

> Anne was sitting at her kitchen table, amid the gingerbread men and women of her wallpaper and matching curtains, her back to the refrigerator, the message board and phone. . . . Virginia Slims, lighter and ashtray were positioned in front of her. Her hair was carefully coiffed, and she was wearing a silk blouse and slacks. It was the dark side of the 1960s image of a homemaker, if you could imagine Betty Crocker composing "The Fury of Cocks" and "When Man Enters Woman." (viii)

This is an incongruity which, as we will see in chapter five, has also been noted of Sexton's physical performances on the stage.

Sexton's move to the suburbs in 1953 is characteristic of her generation of young American newlyweds. As the authors of a 1961 book, *The Split-Level Trap*, note: "Between 1950 and 1959, nearly two-thirds of [America's] increase appeared in the suburbs; the central cities . . . increased in population by about 1½ % during those years; the suburbs increased 44%" (Gordon et al. 27). The movement which *The Split-Level Trap* records and which Sexton's experience exemplifies was, however, almost exclusively a white phenomenon. Elaine Tyler May shows that although the suburban population more than doubled between 1950 and 1970, "blacks were excluded from the suburbs by *de facto* segregation and the FHA's [Federal Housing Authority's] redlining policies" (152). Many of the poems in Sexton's first collection, rather like those in Lowell's first avowedly "confessional" work *Life Studies*, take as their ostensible subject a particular kind of privileged white American upbringing or, more specifically, the threats to its stability and status as turn-of-the century standards gave way to the Great Depression years, to the economic growth stimulated by American's role as supplier to the World War II effort, and to the retrenchment and countercultural movements of the Cold War era.

Elizabeth Bishop famously applauded Lowell for the ability she saw in early drafts of *Life Studies* to associate his own personal past with national history. This was an ability which derived, as she acknowledged, from the historic association of the Lowell family name with the history of Boston and, by extension, of the nation: "All you have to do is put down the names! And the fact that it seems significant, illustrative, American, etc., gives you, I think, the confidence you display" (351). Of Sexton's early poetry, she was less complimentary. In a 1960 letter to Lowell she wrote: "Sexton I think still has a bit too much romanticism and what I think of as the 'our beautiful old silver' school of female writing, which is really boasting about how 'nice' *we* were" (386–87). Bishop's comments arguably underplay the ambivalence in these poems. In both cases, the speakers are struggling to negotiate their positions in relation to these families and to this history. They are unsure of what to make of the past, they demonstrate a lack of confidence in what it can give them in the present. This is not a perspective peculiar to Sexton alone. Christopher Lasch sees such a loss of faith in the lessons of the past as characteristic of contemporary, demoralized, alienated American life (xvi, xviii). This is a society, he suggests, which lives in and for the present, which seeks and is satisfied with immediate gratification. This tension is played out in a number of Sexton poems. In "You, Doctor Martin," for example, the opening poem of *To Bedlam and Part Way Back*, the past is lost to the speaker ("once I was beautiful") in ways which are simultaneously regretted and welcomed. Authenticity and identity belong in the present: "now I am myself." Similarly in "The Bells," the here and now is all: "the children have forgotten / if they knew at all." The denial or erasure of the past is represented, albeit equivocally, as a form of escape.

Sexton's circa 1958 poem "Funnel" registers the disappointment attendant on the move from the city to the suburbs, from the extended to the nuclear family, from the traditions of the past to the uncertainties of the present. "Funnel" records the containment and mediocrity of modern suburban life, particularly when contrasted with the freedom and abundance of the past. It

opens with an account—biblical in its idiom and heroic in its proportions—
of the scale and importance of the past:

> The family story tells, and it was told true,
> of my great-grandfather who begat eight
> genius children and bought twelve almost new
> grand pianos.

But from this expansive opening (the mouth of the "funnel"), the poem begins to retract and diminish. The hyperbolic adjectives of these opening lines
are replaced with weaker, lesser ones: "hushed," "marginal," "musted." The
grandeur of the past (the family of "eight children," the extensive grounds
planted with "thirty-six pines," the confidence with which the patriarch or
"bearded man" surveys his domain) gives way to the mediocrity of present-
day life in the suburbs:

> Back from that great-grandfather I have come
> to puzzle a bending gravestone for his sake,
> to question this diminishing and feed a minimum
> of children their careful slice of suburban cake.

Sexton referred to poetry as a lifeline, as a means of escape from the debilitating conditions of suburbia—or "disturbia" as Gordon and Gunther
label it (34). To the poet Oscar Williams she wrote on 3 April 1963 of her
receipt of a generous travel award: "I am off this August (out of the suburbs
as you always told me, as you always told me I must go out of the suburbs)"
(HRHRC). In a similar context, she wrote of her need to be "unchained" from
her everyday life (*Letters* 114). To Fred Morgan, editor of *The Hudson Review*
who had accepted some of her early poems, she wrote: "I would be here in
the suburbs and going nowhere if it weren't for such as you" (31 March 1966
HRHRC). And to poet Carolyn Kizer she confided, "I would be no one at all
without my new tight little world of poet friends. I am kind of a secret beat-
nik hiding in the suburbs in my square house on a dull street" (*Letters* 70). As
Lewis Mumford explains, "Beginning as a mechanism of escape, the suburb
has turned into its very opposite" (492).

Nevertheless, the suburbs are elsewhere—and this is a crucial contradiction both in Sexton's representation of the suburbs and in their very nature—
depicted as a sanctuary, as a welcome relief from the frightening conditions

of urban life. Sandy Robartes, one of Sexton's neighbors who was dragooned into accompanying her into Boston for her Robert Lowell poetry classes, explained that at first Sexton was too frightened to leave her own house. Sexton's biographer comments that "Anne, who still panicked when she had to walk alone on a city sidewalk, liked being able to run across the lawns" to see her suburban neighbors (Middlebrook, *Biography* 49, 229). The suburbs then are simultaneously a prison and a haven.

Sexton's 1963 poem "Man and Wife" exemplifies her self-positioning or perhaps self-invention as suburban housewife and poet. The title "Man and Wife" alludes to the Christian marriage service and already signals the loss of identity for the woman who is here defined by her relationship with the man. Both title and epigraph, "To speke of wo that is in marriage," look back to Chaucer's "Wife of Bath's Prologue" and to Robert Lowell's poems "Man and Wife" and "To Speak of the Woe that is in Marriage" (both from *Life Studies*).

"Man and Wife" diagnoses the condition of married life in the suburbs as one of alienation, dislocation, and despair. Idealistic expectations of marriage as a union of love or companionship or, failing that, of bare familiarity, are emphatically exposed. We should note the disclaimers, negations and denials ("not lovers," "not even," "nothing") in these opening lines:

> We are not lovers.
> We do not even know each other.
> We look alike
> but we have nothing to say
> We are like pigeons ...

Sexton's speaker likens the couple not to the doves or love-birds of lyric convention but to a pair of lost pigeons. Pigeons are reputed to mate for life. One might read this as a sign of commitment or, as in this poem, of claustrophobic restriction. The simile conveys the couple's dislocation and disorientation as they land, seemingly inadvertently, in the suburbs. The only thing that binds the two is their shared misery—a misery which they experience "in unison," hence the use of the first-person plural "we."

Just as idealized expectations of married life are undermined, so too are preconceptions of suburbia. In stanza two, the city ("Boston") from which the couple have fled signifies squalor, deprivation, and danger with "blind walls" against which the subjects collide, "traffic that kept stamping /

stamping," and "worn out" fruit stalls onto which the couple's own exhaustion is displaced. Yet the suburbs prove little better. Indeed, the speaker describes herself and the husband as "that pair who came to the suburbs / by mistake." Lewis Mumford describes the move from city to suburbs as a quest for "liberation from the sometimes dreary conventions and compulsions of an urban society" and, ironically in Sexton's case given her personal history of mental illness and hospitalization, as a search for "asylum" (485, 486). "Man and Wife" shows us the abject failure of such aspirations.

Sexton drafted this poem in 1958 (and sent a copy of the draft to Robert Lowell as part of her application to join his poetry class), she then returned to and revised it in May 1963. This was almost certainly while she was reading, with great enthusiasm, the newly published *The Feminine Mystique*. On 6 June 1963, Sexton wrote to a friend, Irene Orgel: "Have you read *The Feminine Mistique* (spelling?) [*sic*]. If not, hurry and do so. Motherhood is beautiful but it sure ain't everything" (HRHRC).[4] Friedan's book famously analyzes the "problem that has no name," or the profound dissatisfaction experienced by a generation of women in mid-century and, specifically, suburban America. As its opening lines explain, "The problem lay buried, unspoken, for many years in the minds of American women. It was a strange stirring, a sense of dissatisfaction, a yearning that women suffered in the middle of the twentieth century in the United States. Each suburban wife struggled with it alone" (13). Friedan's study found that women's lives in "the suburbs, those ugly and endless sprawls which are becoming a national problem," were characterized by frustration, ennui, and ultimately an amorphous pathological condition diagnosed as "housewife's fatigue" (219). Sexton's poem dramatizes such a context, and such a condition—this "problem" that resists articulation and reveals itself only somatically in physical and emotional collapse:

> They are two asthmatics
> whose breath sobs in and out
> through a small fuzzy pipe.

Elaine Tyler May opens her study of American Cold War culture, *Homeward Bound: American Families in the Cold War Era*, with a vignette about *Life* magazine's 1959 feature on a newlywed couple who elected to spend their honeymoon in a fallout shelter. In a letter of 15 September 1961 to Tony Hecht, Sexton notes, "Everyone in the suburbs is building fallout shelters" (HRHRC). "Man and Wife," written only months after the Cuban missile

crisis of October 1962, imagines such a scene in its true horror. Her couple
are forced into a squalid and finally antagonistic intimacy "like strangers in
a two-seater outhouse, / eating and squatting together." The military metaphors are significant given this Cold War nuclear context:

> They have teeth and knees
> but they do not speak.
> A soldier is forced to stay with a soldier
> because they share the same dirt
> and the same blows.

We have here the squalid intimacy of suburban marriage: silence, alienation,
violence, tension (Gordon and others identify an "increased tension" and
"tremendous emotional stresses" as characteristic of suburban life in this period [29,7]). In her lecture notes on this poem, Sexton comments on its evocation of "forced intimacy, dumb instincts" (Crawshaw [6] 5). The paradoxical situation of being "together / like strangers" refers both to the couple and
to the wider suburban community of which they are a metonym. Trapped in
a suburban prison of their own choosing, the couple seem paralyzed by their
situation. Silent "exiles," they cannot fully participate in the life of which they
dream. They can only "gasp in unison beside our window pane, / drunk on
the drunkard's dream." The window here, as in a number of other poems, is
a metaphor for isolation and belonging, for privacy and communication, for
seeing and being seen. It is redolent of contemporary suburban architecture
and of an ideology which, as Deborah Nelson has shown, both invites and
repels intimacy.

Plate glass, picture windows, and glazed patio doors are a notable feature
of postwar suburban architecture. To a generation who moved to the suburbs from overcrowded and ill-lit urban housing, one of the most attractive
features of new suburban housing developments was the space, light, and
perspective which such windows promised. However, these windows bear
an ideological as well as a practical significance. Lynn Spigel notes that the
introduction of plate- and sliding-glass doors "mediated the twin goals of
separation from and integration into the outside world" (32). Sexton's work
frequently uses images of plate-glass and picture windows to represent the
contradictory processes of observing and being observed fundamental both
to life in the suburbs and to confessional poetry.

Although as I have suggested glass windows were celebrated as a technological and aesthetic advance in modern suburban America, Sexton and other writers and commentators of the period do voice misgivings about the exposure which they invited. John Keats's tellingly entitled book *The Crack in the Picture Window* featured a caricature of a suburban couple, John and Mary Drone. Welcomed into their newly built tract home, one of countless built as a consequence of the postwar G. I. Bill, John and Mary Drone find "a nine-by-twelve rug spread across the largest room wall to wall, and there was a sheet of plate-glass in the living-room wall. That, the builder said, was the picture window. The picture it framed was of the box across the treeless street." The Drones learn that having the means to look out inevitably gives someone else the power to look in: "Through their picture window, a vast and empty eye with bits of paper stuck in its corners, they could see their view—a house like theirs across a muddy street, its vacant picture eye staring at theirs" (xv, 21). There is a reciprocity here which betokens either communality or a stultifying anxiety about constantly being on view.

The suburban home represents both a place of privacy and safety and one of vulnerability and public scrutiny. To quote Lynn Spigel, the modern home with its large picture windows, and open-plan living areas was "designed as a space for looking. . . . The new tract homes of the mass-produced suburbs featured sliding glass doors, bay windows, and open plans that were designed to maximize the visual field" (2). This leads to a specific kind of exposure, and a particular threat to privacy and autonomy—one felt acutely by women who were typically at home much more than husbands who were employed out-side the suburbs. As Friedan explains, the design of typical open-plan homes "give[s] the illusion of more space for less money. . . . There are no true walls or doors; the woman in the beautiful electronic kitchen is never separated from her children. . . . A man, of course, leaves the house for most of the day. But the feminine mystique forbids the woman this" (216). In a letter to Hollis Summers on her return from a writers' conference, Sexton complains:

> My suds, I'm back in the suburbs, the children are having an acorn fight on the front lawn, it is 95 in the shade . . . a ham is cooking itself and me in the oven (my desk is situated in the dining room, but at the door leading into the kitchen . . .) (*Letters* 83)

Another poem, "What's That," written in March 1959, confirms that the window, like the parameters of the suburban home and the boundaries of the self, is permeable and thus potentially vulnerable. There is a collapse in

"What's That" of the barriers between private and public, internal and external, self and other (hence the equivalence of "calling me, calling you" in the final line). In this curious poem, it is never clear whether the unnamed presence which lurks outside the "kitchen window" is to be feared or welcomed:

> Before it came inside
> I had watched it from my kitchen window,
> watched it swell like a new balloon,
> watched it slump and then divide,
> like something I know I know—
> a broken pear or two halves of the moon.

The object ("it") might signify some alien threat or a fear of recurrent depression. Yet the images also signify some kind of inspiration, even a visitation from the muse (hence the metaphors of the pear and the moon, both of which connote female fertility). The situation which the poem contemplates is all the more astonishing for taking place in such an unlikely environment, observed from the "kitchen window" while "outside cars whisk by on the suburban street / and are there and are true." The poem anticipates Plath's "Balloons," written some four years later, in which a similarly uncanny or *unheimlich* presence intrudes into domestic sanctity. In "Balloons" and many of the other *Ariel* poems, Plath constructs what Marsha Bryant refers to as the "domestic surreal." Here we find "an intensity charged by strange combinations of housewifery with the supernatural and mechanical" (279).

The speaker in such poems—her vantage point on the outside world notwithstanding—is engaged primarily in a process of inner surveillance or self-policing characteristic both of suburban life in Cold War America and of confession. In "Three Green Windows," for example, the speaker simultaneously sees and is seen, she is subject and object of observation. Trapped in a Foucauldian panopticon, behind "three green windows" looking west, south, and east, the speaker both occupies an excellent vantage point and feels herself to be open to everyone else's gaze. Most importantly, though, she is scrutinizing, judging and correcting her own behavior. Although the poem proceeds in a mood of free-floating reverie, that reverie is guarded. It is interrupted repeatedly by negated and therefore, according to Freud's "On Negation," very real anxieties about family and friends and about personal and social responsibilities ("the sewers and the drainage / the urban renewal and the suburban centers"). It is her own perceptions and observations which the subject must keep under closest watch, must correct and deny:

> I have misplaced the Van Allen belt,
>   the sewers and the drainage,
> the urban renewal and the suburban centers.
> I have forgotten the names of the literary critics.

There are some things which she cannot permit herself to have seen and known, although the presence of these issues and objects is ineradicably confirmed by the succession of denials and negations through which they are detailed: "I do not think of the rusty wagon on the walk. / I pay no attention to the red squirrels."

These poems are explicit about the spectacular and gendered nature of contemporary suburban existence. "The Touch" and "Housewife," for example, figure the female body as an extension of and indivisible from the modern home. Le Corbusier's "machine for living in" becomes, in Sexton's eyes, a mechanism of domination and despair. In "The Touch," the father "comes with the house and even at night / he lives in a machine made by my mother." And "Housewife" (1961) declares:

> Some women marry houses.
> It's another kind of skin; it has a heart,
> a mouth, a liver and bowel movements.
> The walls are permanent and pink.
> See how she sits on her knees all day
> faithfully washing herself down.

Women and the home are linked in a perpetual cycle of consumption and waste (in a later poem, "The Sickness Unto Death" [1973], the speaker likens herself to "a house full of bowel movement"). Such metaphors replicate the anxiety, shared by poet and critics alike, about the potentially noxious impropriety of confessional poetry. In "Housewife," the modern home demands abjection, sacrifice and obeisance from the woman who is implicated in an endless ritual of cleansing. As Lynn Spigel explains of contemporary suburban architecture, the "antiseptic model of space was the reigning aesthetic at the heart of the postwar suburbs" (34).

In "The Death Baby" from the 1974 volume *The Death Notebooks*, the modern kitchen is the altar for the immolation of the female subject. In this curious and disturbing poem, the speaker plays out her own sister's murderous dream whereby, in the reported words of the sister:

> "The baby turned to ice.
> Someone put her in the refrigerator
> and she turned as hard as a Popsicle."

Modern domestic appliances, which had seemed to promise liberation to housewives of the period, here signal their imprisonment and annihilation. Ruth Schwartz Cowan has shown that middle-class women setting up home on either side of the Second World War typically had a smaller home than their own mothers, fewer—if any—servants and more domestic appliances accompanied by the tacit expectation that she would operate them (172). Plath's 1962 poem "Lesbos," which opens "viciousness in the kitchen!," similarly stages the trauma of suburban domesticity. According to Bryant, "in the topography of the domestic surreal, the housewife inhabits a colorful, electrified and animated household full of strange happenings—especially in the kitchen" (284). The "strange happenings" here, though, are profoundly unsettling; the speaker is engaged in a perpetual battle against forces (the husband, the in-laws, the children, pets, appliances, food and finally the abject self) which threaten to overwhelm her (Plath, *Collected* 227–30).

Sexton's "Self in 1958," originally "The Lady Lives in a Doll House," was drafted in 1958 but then put to one side and not completed until 1965. The time span is important, stretching as it does over the early years of the nascent second wave of feminism. In her unpublished lecture notes Sexton comments: "in the next poem we have me stopped as the perfect housewife, as the advertised woman in the perfect little ticky tacky suburb. . . . It is a picture of me before madness became my friend." Her comment suggests both a critical distance on, and some kind of accommodation with, the conditions it describes. "Stopped" is an interesting choice of word; it connotes a state of frozen inanimation, of arrested development. Sexton proceeds to interrogate the situation the poem describes: "Why do I call myself a plaster doll? Why do I live in a doll's house? (because I feel unreal, because the furniture, the scenery is perfect but I am unreal)" (Crawshaw [6] 6). The poem opens with a huge question: "What is reality?" This introduces the sequence of images of impermanence and superficiality which follows ("plaster," "shellac," "nylon," "advertised clothes"). Femininity here is a form of masquerade or performance

("I am a plaster doll; I pose"). "Self in 1958" describes a profound inauthenticity (hence the strange syntax of "am I approximately an 'I'?") which is tied up with rituals of consumption and display: "am I approximately an I. Magnin transplant?" (I. Magnin was an upscale department store chain). Femininity is medicalized or pathologized ("plaster," "cut," "transplant," "cut open"). Rather like in "Housewife," it is remorseless, continuing "without landfall or nightfall" and requiring endless reiteration. "Housewife" and "Self in 1958" bear comparison with Plath's 1961 poems "Face Lift," "Tulips" and "In Plaster." In both poets' work, we see the female confessional subject relentlessly cutting herself open, displaying her inner demons for the edification of some anonymous audience. Susan Bordo suggests that the textual representation of the female body, particularly of the hysteric, anorexic, or agoraphobic body, is historically specific and ideologically constructed, offering, as in Sexton and Plath, "exaggerated, extremely literal, at times virtually caricatured presentations of the ruling feminine mystique" (16).

Femininity is played out in front of the mirror (implicitly in stanza one, the speaker is looking at her own reflection although I do not think we can read this as a Lacanian moment of pleasurable self-realization; there is blankness here, dislocation, and disorientation) or it is played out in front of a camera ("life enlarges," "flash") which is also a gun ("life takes aim"). Crucially, femininity is played out in the "all-electric kitchen":

> Someone plays with me,
> plants me in the all-electric kitchen,
> Is this what Mrs. Rombauer said?
> Someone pretends with me—

Sexton gestures here towards the infamous "kitchen debates" between Soviet leader Khrushchev and U.S. Vice President Nixon. These took place at the 1959 Moscow trade fair at the height of the Cold War when Russia and America were in deadly competition for military and ideological dominance. For Nixon, superior domestic appliances stood for all that was best about modern America and, by extension, for an idealized femininity. Friedan confirms the point: "The American housewife—she was the dream image of the young American woman and the envy, it was said, of women all over the world" (15). Sexton's speaker/doll demurs from this position and questions the ideal. She is placed in the kitchen against her own volition and uncertain how to perform once she is there; hence, the repeated questions, exclamations, and parenthetical dashes. Where for Nixon, the "all-electric kitchen" liberates ("what we want is to make easier the life of our housewives"),[5] for Sexton's speaker, it is a kind of prison. She is unable to "spring open the doors" and remains "rooted" to the wall.

Domestic spaces, then, are where larger ideological crises are crystallized. It is here that the subject must learn to take her place in history. As Elaine Tyler May explains, the post–World War II period was one of ever-increasing anxiety for Americans (16). There was concern from many that the apparent prosperity of the wartime economy (a prosperity that Sexton's father, and thus Sexton as a child, had enjoyed through the success of his wool company in providing the material to make military blankets and uniforms) would give way, as it did in the aftermath of World War I, to economic depression. There was also a persistent awareness during this period of the fragility of world peace with conflict in China, the onset of the Korean War, Vietnam, and increasing threats to the environment from industrial, nuclear, and other sources. This was also the time of the Cuban Missile crisis, the escalation of Cold War hostilities with communist regimes, and McCarthyism, heralding a culture of deep suspicion of, and anxiety about, knowledge, power, and betrayal.

A careful reading of selected poems, from the early collections *To Bedlam and Part Way Back* and *All My Pretty Ones* to the later *The Awful Rowing Toward God* and the posthumous *Words for Dr. Y.* demonstrates the importance of these contexts for Sexton. Even where her poems seem to be most intimate, most personal, most "confessional," they must be understood to be speaking also about larger public concerns. "The Truth the Dead Know," a double elegy for the speaker's mother and father, is emphatic about this. The poem exemplifies a key problem for confessionalism; how to reconcile the personal and immediate, the solipsistic even, with an awareness of larger, shared, universal, and inescapable realities. Although written in explicit memory of the parents whose dates of birth and death are detailed in the epigraph, the poem is not only about their deaths or the speaker's own loss. These, the poem insists, are not the only people to be mourned: "In another country people die." This is an ambivalent note, serving both to defamiliarize and depersonalize death (this happens all the time) and to register its inescapable omnipresence.

"All My Pretty Ones," the title poem of Sexton's second collection, sets its elegy for the lost father against the background of historical change. As the speaker sifts through the residue of her father's estate, she marks the passing of a whole way of life, not necessarily with regret, but rather with a rueful recognition that it was precarious and self-deluding. The poem records the slow dismantling of the father's identity, an identity constituted by material signs of wealth: "a gold key, your half of a woolen mill, / twenty suits from Dunne's, an English Ford." By extension it offers a critique of a certain class of American bourgeois society—a group which was wealthy in the early years of the century, threatened by the Wall Street Crash of 1929, resurgent in some cases during World War II, and always desperately shoring itself up with material markers of prosperity, such as photographs of speedboat races at Nassau and of prize-winning horses. All, though, is now as fragile and obsolete as old newspapers, "as crackling now and wrinkly / as tobacco leaves." The earlier substance, it transpires, masks a sordid life of personal and, by implication, cultural failure. The poem reads as a Gatsbyesque allegory of the excesses and the excessive confidence of the period. The final stanza confides the father's "alcoholic tendency" and the mother's complicity in concealing it. The text is explicit about the connection between the power of the father in the home, and patriarchal power on a larger scale.

The first poem in *Live or Die*, "And One for My Dame," is set in the context of World War II and similarly asserts the relationship between micro- and macroauthority. It exposes the ways in which patriarchy and the violence with which it is concomitant are perpetuated. Central to the narrative are relationships of exploitation and strategies of expansion; the salesman, like the military, is engaged in appropriating and colonizing the land and its people (hence stanza five's likening of the father figure to a "merchant and an Indian chief"). The poem opens with a recognition of the importance of propaganda in consolidating these relationships; "A born salesman / my father" seduces both the customers for his products and the beneficiaries of his wealth, the daughter and family:

> At home each sentence he would utter
> had first pleased the buyer who'd paid him off in butter.
>
> Each word
> had been tried over and over, at any rate,
> on the man who was sold by the man who filled my plate.

The nursery rhyme title and repetitions seem to underplay the seriousness of the poem's concerns, subtly reflecting the power of such propaganda in inculcating an acceptance of the status quo. Home is the heart of an ever-expanding nexus of male power and violence:

Each night at home
my father was in love with maps
while the radio fought its battles with Nazis and Japs.

America here is anthropomorphized; the body politic is simply one more territory to be won: "its cemeteries, its arbitrary time zones, / through routes like small veins, capitals like small stones."

The March 1961 poem "The House" offers a long and nuanced contemplation of similar issues. It revisits, as though in a nightmare, the house (notably not "the home") of the subject's childhood experience and draws on World War II and Cold War national and racial stereotypes in order to convey the hostility and menace which the child associates with it. The house is figured as a noisome melting pot. Like "some gigantic German toy," set on a "kelly-green lawn," it has been infiltrated by the enemy—the Germans and the Irish (hence "kelly-green"). Women are represented paradoxically both as the vulnerable subjects who need to be protected and as the potential weak point in the domestic defense. The threat is sexualized, for example in stanza two where the "Irish boy / who dated her" pushes his way into the family home. The purity of the dominant W.A.S.P. household is thus contaminated. Such stereotypes have a long history in American culture. Kerry Soper suggests of turn-of-the-century caricatures of the Irish, that "sexual promiscuity" was a key accusation (263 n.12). Rachel Blau DuPlessis discusses Eliot's Sweeney poems in similar terms, seeing in them a pernicious stereotype of the "savage or simian Irishman" (151). Interestingly, Sexton's own "Sweeney" poem (1969) refuses such a caricature, opening defiantly: "My Sweeney, Mr. Eliot, / is that Australian who came."

In "The House," the "Japanese" too have gained a toehold: "A quick-eyed Filipino, / slinks by like a Japanese spy." The allusion reflects the fear and panic which followed the Japanese invasion of Pearl Harbor in 1941 and led to President Roosevelt's decision to intern Japanese Americans living in West Coast and other areas of the United States. It reflects the ignorance and confusion in the speaker's, and by extension, privileged white America's mind; unable to distinguish between the Filipinos and the Japanese, both become objects of suspicion. In the long penultimate section of the poem, the speaker imaginatively enters the house. She feels herself to be under threatening surveillance by all of these alien interlopers (the Irish, the Japanese, the Germans) and by the father. Again, it is the young woman who is perceived by the family and by patriarchy to be the greatest potential threat—or the enemy within. Trying to avoid attention, she slips "past the flashing back of the Japanese spy." The erroneous simile of the first stanza which sought to compare Filipino with Japanese spy has here been turned into a metaphor, thus the likeness is concretized. The final stanza of the poem pulls back from this dream/nightmare of the past but retains that sense of deep paranoia. This is represented in the present by "Russia," America's postwar enemy:

> All day long the house sits
> larger than Russia
> gleaming like a cured hide in the sun.

The poem captures and traces the historical precedents for the fear of invasion or nuclear annihilation that dominated American life in this period:

> All day long the machine waits: rooms,
> stairs, carpets, furniture, people—
> those people who stand at the open windows like objects
> waiting to topple.

The closing line of the poem which foresees the family members exposed by, and finally "toppl[ing]" from, the windows belongs with a number of similar poems which, as we have already seen, depict the suburban picture window as the contradictory place of insight and exposure, of safety and vulnerability.

Sexton returns to similar themes in her late poem "Daddy Warbucks" (1974). Like "Funnel" or "The House," it makes explicit the connection between material wealth and forms of power, particularly patriarchal or sexual power. "Daddy Warbucks" looks back to World War II America and to the ostentatious wealth of a certain elite and it asks about the kinds of collusion which rendered such profligacy acceptable, even desirable. The price of male power, the poem suggests, is female subordination, silence, and denial. As in "Three Green Windows," the poem is notable for its strategies of repression and negation:

> I never bled?
> I never saw a man expose himself.
> No. No.

The poem closes in the present tense with a rejection of the pretenses of yesterday and an admission of latent violence, self-loathing, and fear. Again, like in "The House," the enemy is Nazi or Japanese or a conflation of the two: "'Daddy,' I died, / swallowing the Nazi-Jap-animal." The subject is swallowing or incorporating or absorbing the enemy—that is, either annihilating it or making it part of herself. She learns to perceive herself as the enemy, as a threat to the security of the self, the family, the home and thereby the nation. Images of eyes signifying remorseless scrutiny and surveillance dominate, and the poem closes with a scene of violence within and thereby against the self:

> It keeps knocking at my eyes,
> my big orphan eyes,
> kicking! Until eyeballs pop out.

The subject becomes her own tormentor, beating the truth out of herself in a masochistic and also, finally, a self-reflexive way. Physical self-flagellation and the self-flagellation of Sexton's particular brand of poetry are one and the same thing. Political brutality and the brutality of confessional self-revelation are, it is implied, fundamentally equivalent.

Other poems which were written in the shadow of the Cuban Missile Crisis and at the height of the Cold War say something about the ideological tensions and anxieties of their time. They depict a culture which is secretive, suspicious, alert to all kinds of threat. "Venus and the Ark," an early and rather atypical Sexton poem, conveys in its opening lines its contemporaneous Cold War and space race contexts and the atmosphere of surveillance and suspicion which underpinned both; "the missile to launch a missile / was almost a secret." The poem was written after the first spacecraft (the Russian Sputniks I and II) had gone into orbit (1957) but at least four years before the first pictures of the surface of the moon were seen and seven years before the first pictures of the planet Venus. An apparently whimsical fantasy—and a poem which has been largely overlooked by most commentators—"Venus and the Ark" becomes first a biting indictment of the patriarchal military-industrial machine and finally a curious form of creation myth. A palimpsest in this poem about military secrets and their revelation is the story of Ethel and Julius Rosenberg (the subject, of course, of the famous opening line of Plath's *The Bell Jar*). The Rosenbergs were arrested in 1950 on suspicion of selling U.S. atomic secrets to the USSR and were executed in June 1953 after all appeals were exhausted.

The initial tone is mocking but the poem opens out into a far more profound and moral fable than the dismissive early lines suggest. Sexton's villains or, as it transpires, her victims, are "two male PhDs," "picked" presumably by some anonymous superpower to turn the missile into a modern-day ark which is to be "stuffed" with a disparate range of creatures and objects; snakes, black rats and white rats, the "necessary files." The combined might of the male PhDs, the missiles, and the military behind them are overwhelmed in Sexton's poem by the "oozing," fecund, and female power of Venus. As it approaches the planet, the missile/ark is transformed into a soft, malleable balloon shape. Like a tired child turning to its mother it

> sank like a sweet fat grape,
> oozing past gravity to snuggle
> down

Maternal forces overwhelm patriarchal and phallic ones (the missile-charged missile) and the Earth is left to its own murderous and poisonous devices.[6]

Another early poem, "Noon Walk on the Asylum Lawn" (1960), traces both a personal and indeed pathological condition and a more general, shared, and historically determined set of circumstances. The speaker's "noon walk" is through a threatening, poisoned landscape. The "asylum lawn" is figured as Psalm 23's "valley of the shadow of death"; the air is first drained away —"it sucks the air / and looks around for me"— and then suffocating —"The sky breaks. / It sags and breathes upon my face." This is a nightmare scene where the air itself—permeated, perhaps, with invisible nuclear fallout—threatens to poison the speaker. Edward Brunner notes the impact of the development and testing of the hydrogen bomb in the 1950s: "The H-bomb offered no advance on security; if anything, it only underscored the threat of silent and invisible radioactivity, an enemy against which there could be little defense" (230).

The atmosphere is secretive: "The summer sun ray / shifts through a suspicious tree." Some unknown assailant keeps constant watch, tracing the subject's every movement: it "looks around for me," threatening her in silent and vicious ways; "the blades extend / and reach my way." Even in this place of ostensible "asylum," "the world is full of enemies. / There is no safe place." Of course, it is possible to read this as the expression of individual, clinical paranoia, but its specific historical context gives it a far broader resonance. The poem's closing lament exemplifies what Deborah Nelson identifies as a primary concern and contradiction of postwar American life or what she calls the Cold War's "governing paradox: In the interests of preserving the space of privacy, privacy would have to be penetrated" (xiii).

Wars in Korea and Vietnam form the explicit subject matter of a number of Sexton's poems. "For Johnny Pole on the Forgotten Beach" takes militarism as its subject. Set, we might gather, during World War II or the Korean War or any modern conflict, the poem uses metaphors of successive summers (an infant's summer, a ten-year-old's summer, a twenty-year-old's summer) to connote a golden age and a passing of time which must, we feel, inevitably end. In tandem with this are metaphors of shells and beaches connotative in contradictory ways of seaside and battlefield scenes. The poem uses both of these metaphorical strands to establish a split perspective. This pits the idealized child's beach with its "nursery crafts" and harmless "sparklers" glinting from the waves against the stinking, menacing "first beach of assault" with its "junkyard / of landing craft" and "fire" from the sea. Johnny Pole, the speaker's brother, is balanced—poised as though surfing the crest of a wave—between the two, seized halfway between child and adult, between life and death. The structure of the poem with its two stanzas of twenty-two lines each, balanced on either side of a two-line cusp ("Johnny, your dream moves summers / inside my mind") emphasizes the precarious symmetry of the narrative and the fragility of the two poles. And indeed, such a position proves untenable. As the second line of the second long stanza puts it, "There was no balance to help." Only memory remains and retains the capacity to (re)construct and (re)vitalize the past.

I qualify my use of these terms because "For Johnny" is famously an invented confession—a construction rather than a reconstruction. It is an example of what Sexton herself termed a "fiction": "I'll often confess to things that never happened." She cites it as an example of the possible confusion in her work between truth and lies, confession and invention, real and representative experience. As she explained in an interview:

> I remember Ralph Mills talking about my dead brother whom I've written about. And I met Ralph and I said, "Ralph, . . . I had no brother, but then didn't we all have brothers who died in that war?" (Heyen 136)

"Johnny Pole" closes with a sense of the power both of death (the end of history) and resurrection (its return). The motion of the poem mimics the fall and rise of the tide, the perpetual motion of the sea and affirms the importance of imagination ("I think") in recognizing either:

> I think you die again
> and live again,
> Johnny, each summer that moves inside
> my mind.

The long sequence, "Eighteen Days without You," written in 1966 and published in the 1969 collection *Love Poems*, while ostensibly an epistolary love poem in which the subject apostrophizes the absent other, hides rather more complex and nuanced depths. It is a poem which is embedded very much in a specific historical context, a context which it reveals cumulatively but nevertheless emphatically. Rather tellingly, Sexton draws on historically resonant images of loss, violence, and betrayal to represent the lovers' relationship. The poem begins with natural images suggestive of decay, decline, danger, and death: "The cornstalks are broken / in the field, broken and brown" while "a cat-green ice spreads / out over the front lawn." The poisonous "hemlocks" are "the only / young thing left." These unpromising natural images soon give way to human and, therefore, political anxieties, starting at the micro level ("mother slamming a door") and then weaving in and out of the public and private spheres: "a criminal in solitary," "you dragged me off by your Nazi hook." The backyard which the speaker is gazing out on as she summons these images comes to seem more and more sinister and threatening. The separation between self and lover which the poem laments mimics other more permanent, devastating, and publicly symbolic ones: "the day Jack Kennedy was dying" and "Oswald's November." Suspicion, fear, and disappointment in the national news foreshadow the same on the personal level.

By day seven (the "December 7th" section), the poem cannot transcend its broader context, cannot free itself from its wartime roots. Written on the anniversary of the Japanese attack on the U.S. naval site at Pearl Harbor, Hawaii, the name "Pearl Harbor" tolls like a bell at the beginning of each of the first two stanzas. The events of that day—the catastrophic and unexpected bombing of the site, the huge loss of life leading to U.S. entry into World War II and, ultimately, one might argue, to Nagasaki and Hiroshima—all form a palimpsest here. They give a particular and threatening nuance to images of the ice storm (signifying perhaps broken glass or bullets or an atomic blast) and of airborne predators pitted against vulnerable prey: "Owls force mice into the open. Owls thrive / The ice will do the birds in."

The late and posthumously published sequence, "Letters to Dr. Y.," produces one of Sexton's most explicitly political poems. Simply dated "December 17, 1969," the poem describes one of the most horrific events of the Vietnam War, the My Lai Massacre. "I'm dreaming the My Lai soldier again," the poem starkly begins. Throughout, it is vivid in its clipped, precise detail, conveying the shock of the massacre which had, only a few weeks previously, become known to the U.S. public. The speaker's dream foregrounds the chilling horror of the events—the invasion of the privacy of the home and of the safety of the village by the American soldier who is pictured "ring[ing] the doorbell like the Fuller Brush man." How is it, the poem seems to be asking, that ordinary domestic routine can be so brutally interrupted?[7]

The vividness of the color (the "green . . . intestines" and "yellow gasses") is a particular characteristic of the poem and registers the fact that the atrocity had been publicly exposed with color images in *Time*, *Newsweek*, and elsewhere. The detail and authenticity of the photos provided incontrovertible evidence of the nature of the massacre. The specifically gendered and sexualized nature of the attack is reflected in the poem's repeated allusions to babies and mothers and to the vision of the soldier "pointing his red penis." We should note, too, the soldier's attempt at self-exculpation: "saying / Don't take this personally." Most importantly, Sexton's speaker depicts herself as part of the scene; she identifies with the victims of male violence sufficiently to place herself—"me"—in the line of fire.

The soldier's admonition not to "take this personally" seems particularly to engage Sexton and to speak to the larger concern of all of the poems I have been discussing here. What is the relationship between the personal and the political? What is the place of the confessional subject in history? Again and again these poems register the significance of historical events by very visibly negating them. "To Lose the Earth," for instance (written in Europe in 1963), opens by cataloguing key contemporary issues:

> The wreckage of Europe or the birth of Africa,
> the old palaces, the wallets of the tourists,
> the Common Market or the smart cafes,
> the boulevards in the graceful evening,
> the cliff-hangers, the scientists,

and the little shops raising their prices
mean nothing to me.

Thus, these poems expose a dreadful inability or refusal to witness; it is sins of omission which Sexton seems to be confessing.

The question of what history means "to me," or of how I can continue to live in the shadow of history, is a central question of our time and one that Sexton's poetry repeatedly—albeit often tacitly—addresses. "Loving the Killer," for example, the 1966 poem based on her and her husband's safari trip to Africa, uses violent Holocaust imagery as it conflates domestic violence and genocide:

> Oh my Nazi,
> with your S.S. sky-blue eye—
> I am no different from Emily Goering.
> Emily Goering recently said she
> thought the concentration camps
> were for the re-education of Jews
> and Communists. She thought!

Most importantly, the text closes off any opportunity for self-exculpation. The exclamation mark after "she thought" registers incredulity at Emily Goering's stance and also implies the importance of taking personal responsibility for public affairs. In "After Auschwitz," the speaker parodies her own susceptibility to anti-Nazi propaganda. The pat rhythm emphasizes her point:

> Each day,
> each Nazi
> took, at 8:00 A.M., a baby
> and sautéed him for breakfast
> in his frying pan.

In the best traditions of satire though (we are reminded in particular of Swift's "A Modest Proposal"), the brutal point remains: The Nazi regime—and individuals within it—were responsible, directly or indirectly, for the deaths of millions.

In poems such as these, it is precisely in the silences, in the refusal to give testimony, that the true horror becomes most clear. These are, as Dori Laub and Shoshana Felman describe Holocaust testimonies, forms of "impossible,

unspeakable confession" (xix). Sexton's 1973 poem "Courage" confirms the
point: "It is in the small things we see it," as the poem begins. Inspired, perhaps, by the peace movements of the 1960s and early 1970s, "Courage" seems
to advocate a policy of passive resistance. Silence, not shouting, is the most
powerful weapon:

> Later,
> if you faced the death of bombs and bullets
> you did not do it with a banner,
> you did it with only a hat to
> cover your heart.

This is a powerful rhetorical point, but one that risks conceding the futility
or impossibility of poetry. As Theodor Adorno famously put it: "To write
poetry after Auschwitz is barbaric" (34). However, if we situate Adorno's
comment in the broader trajectory of his argument, we can see that what he
is seeking, against what he perceives to be the odds, is a way of making literature matter, a connection between culture and the world, between poetry
and history, and a way of describing that connection. Sexton, we might say, is
engaged in a similar search.

PART 2

Self-representation

4

Autobiography

Sexton writes in a mode that seems to promise autobiographical revelation. Yet the relationship between subject, personal experience, and its representation is less straightforward and less reliable than might be assumed, particularly for the female subject. As Rita Felski argues, autobiography or confession

> cannot uncover a miraculously intact female subject. . . . There exists no innocent place outside the symbolic order. The "self" which women find will continue to be marked by contradictions, schisms, and tensions, some relating to the more general problems of subjectivity, others to the specific conditions of marginalization and powerlessness that have shaped much of female experience. ("On Confession" 91)

In the light of this and other recent readings of the complexity of autobiographical representation, it is apposite to rethink Sexton's relationship with the genre. I have already proposed reading the confessional mode as a form of discourse whose subject and truth are discursive, even performative, effects produced in and by particular circumstances and exchanges. Here I propose to read the larger genre of autobiography in the same light.

Sexton manipulates the rhetorical possibilities of the genre and exploits the reader's expectations of it. As we have seen, her declared intention is to "lead my readers to believe" in the autobiographical basis of her work (Crawshaw [1] 6). With autobiography, as with confession, Sexton is interested in the possibilities of the form. She is as exercised by the problems and issues arising from the attempt to write the self (that is, by the process) as she is by the problems and issues experienced in the life in question (the object of the narrative). In her experimentation with autobiography, she uses it to playful, imaginative, and inquisitive effect, and she grapples with its failure to deliver the coherent, self-identical, singular sense of self which it so erroneously seems to promise.

The poems discussed in this chapter are drawn from throughout Sexton's oeuvre, thus indicating the persistence of her interest in this area. Early poems such as "Some Foreign Letters" (1960) explore the status and vulnerability of memory, demonstrating that an autobiographical—that is, written—memory is always already inflected by other texts. Others, such as "Just Once" (1968), reflect the temporality and thus fragility of self-understanding. A late poem, "End, Middle, Beginning" (1974), parodies orthodox expectations of the unity, chronology, and teleology of autobiography; it summarizes, pointedly in reverse order, a lifetime's achievements. A number of poems from this late period develop elaborate conceits in order to experiment with and problematize the conventions of the genre. The "Horoscope Poems" narrate, in anticipation, the story of the subject's own future, while "Love Letter Written from a Burning Building" records, as though from beyond the grave or beyond the limits of self-life-writing, the narrative of the subject's own death. Sexton's strategy in these cases replicates the technique which Gilmore has elsewhere identified as characteristic of Gertrude Stein's writing; it is a way of "mobiliz[ing] the recognizable constituents of autobiography . . . against autobiography itself" (*Autobiographics* 200).

Sexton, perhaps surprisingly given the apparent self-referentiality of her poetry, seems to find it difficult to present a coherent prose narrative of the self, for example when asked by publishers or fans to provide an autobiographical sketch. Part of the barrier preventing Sexton from relating her "life story" in prose seems to be the impossibility of identifying and thereafter representing any fixed, unitary, coherent, and consistent identity which will transcend the specific discursive context in which it is constructed and to which it belongs. In a long letter to Jon Stallworthy, her publisher at Oxford University Press (dated 24 September 1965), Sexton gives valuable insight into her reluctance and inability to deliver the autobiographical sketch which her publisher has asked of her. The letter begins: "No. I just can't face that woman . . . with an accounting of my '"life story."' I did write that other rather sweet and old woman a letter . . . but life story. DEAR GOD!" (HRHRC)

Having confessed her inability to provide a "life story," Sexton proceeds to attempt one, although only on the tacit understanding that the "story" will be edited or made coherent by Stallworthy. Within the first lines of this draft autobiography, Sexton is at pains to emphasize the disjunction between the many different, albeit simultaneous, lives she leads, and the discrepancy between her own sense of self and her publicly perceived identities as poet, housewife, and mother: "I do not live a poet's life. I look and act like a housewife. My daughter says to her friends 'a mother is someone who types all day.'" The difficulties of defining and appropriating a coherent and recognizable identity are emphasized. Sexton is all of these things and none of them: "I am a lousy cook, a lousy wife, a lousy mother, because I am too busy wrestling with the poem to remember that I am a normal (?) American housewife." Such contradictory demands, or "discursive injunctions" as Judith Butler terms them, generate disruption. It is, as Sidonie Smith says, "as if the autobiographical subject finds him / herself on multiple stages simultaneously" ("Performativity" 110).

Sexton's conscious autobiographical sketches struggle with the demands of articulating a coherent picture of a self which cannot be said to exist outside the text itself, or which cannot be made to cohere with the image of the self given in earlier poems. In correspondence with Rise and Steven Axelrod, she confirms the point: "The poems stand for the moment in which they are written and make no promises to the future events and consciousness" (*Letters* 421). The self, when understood as a discursive effect, must be re-created anew in each and every text and reading. As Antony Easthope argues (here referencing Derrida): "Discourse is 'a sort of machine,' and subjectivity in poetry—'the Poet'—can never be more than an effect of discourse, a god or ghost produced (by the reading) from the machine" (*Poetry as Discourse* 30).

Given these difficulties with autobiographical representation, what is it that might "lead" the readers to "believe" that Sexton is an "autobiographical poet"? The most instantly identifiable of "autobiographical" poems are those in which the subject attempts to represent her own identity by reference to the familial roots from whence she came, to situate her experience within a genealogy and tangentially, as we have seen, a broader historical and political context. In a group of poems written over a period of at least four years (1959–1963) and published in two different volumes (poems which I collectively nominate "Memoir" poems), Sexton repeatedly contemplates questions of origins and ancestry, of personal history as it determines life lived in the present day. In "Some Foreign Letters," "Crossing the Atlantic," and "Walking in Paris" she appropriates and problematizes the practices and tropes of the memoir. She uses, but only in order to undermine or disallow, complacent and nostalgic readings of the past, exposing the selectivity and fabrication inherent in any representation of one's personal history, and, by implication, in autobiography in general. She interrogates the relationship between introspection and retrospection and specifically foregrounds the textuality of the past as represented in these poems by written documents handed down through the family. Perhaps dissatisfied with the limits of the genre, Sexton—like Woolf and Stein before her—offers a portrait of the self in the guise of a biography of another.

"Some Foreign Letters," addressed to Nana (Sexton's great-aunt, Eliza Dingley), offers a meditation on Nana's autobiographical letters home from a turn-of-the-century European tour. The poem contemplates change and identity, memory and loss, the past and the present, and the potential and limitations of language in representing any of these. Indeed, the poem is as much about reading autobiography as it is about writing it. As Candace Lang suggests, reading one's own past "as one would a book" is a characteristic of the genre (11). The process of reading and ascribing meaning to the great-aunt's letters functions as a metaphor for the way in which we, as readers, ascribe meaning to the contemporary autobiographical text.

The title of the poem reflects both the geographical foreignness of these letters from abroad and the historical strangeness of the Victorian aunt's experience. One of the ways in which the poem achieves its effects is in its juxtaposition, not only of past and present, but of America and Europe. We are shown the letters' disorientating "foreign postmarks," and we hear the strangeness of the language (trapped in "the towers of Schloss Schwöbber, . . . the tedious / language grew in your jaw"). We see the "yankee girl" exposed on a foreign mountain and, later, struggling with her "New England conscience" against a backdrop of the Roman Forum. If we read the "letters" of the title as signifying writing in general, we can see that Sexton's poem self-reflexively contemplates its own "foreign" impenetrability and indeterminacy, the difficulty of translating memory into language.

The poem opens with a dialogue symptomatic of its larger attempt to communicate with the past, to forge a bond between the "I" of the present and the "you" of history: "I knew you forever and you were always old, / soft white lady of my heart." The form of the letter is instrumental in confirming this split between "I" and "you." The prosopopoeia plays with notions of absence and presence, addressing an "other" who is both here in the sense that they are being addressed and not here precisely in the sense that they can only thus be addressed. Janet Altman characterizes letter writing as a "communication with specters, not only with the specter of the addressee but also with one's own phantom, which evolves underneath one's own hand in the very letter one is writing" (2). The act of reading the aunt's letters permits the speaker to cross the divide between self and other, to enter into this life (bios) and claim it in writing (graphia) as her own (auto):

> I knew you forever and you were always old,
> soft white lady of my heart. Surely you would scold
> me for sitting up late, reading your letters,
> as if these foreign postmarks were meant for me.
> You posted them first in London, wearing furs
> and a new dress in the winter of eighteen-ninety.
> I read how London is dull on Lord Mayor's Day.

These opening lines also establish a sense of the passing of time, although the poem's true interest may be described as an exploration of the ways in which autobiography misleadingly refuses this passing. Sexton commented of the poem that it has a "dual outlook toward the past and the present. It combines them in much the same way that our lives do—" ("Comment" 16). The poem unsettles our sense of chronology and narrative coherence. It mixes tenses throughout; in the first stanza alone, we see the past ("I knew"), imperfect ("were always"), conditional ("you would scold / me"), simple present ("London is dull"), continuous present ("reading your letters") and future ("you will / go"). The effect of this, again, is to problematize this present act of reflection on the past.

Implicit in Sexton's seemingly self-explanatory, even slight and sentimental, memoir of a beloved aunt is a sense of voyeurism, intrusion, and risk. We are engaged in an illicit reading of illicit experience. The original letter-writer (Nana) entices her reader with accounts of the thrilling and macabre events of her journey, and the recipient of the letters (the speaker of the poem) conveys these to her contemporary audience to similar effect. The poem exemplifies the vicarious desire and pleasure which sustain, and are produced in, any reading of the autobiographical text. The use of the verb "guided" ("You guided past groups of robbers, the sad holes / of Whitechapel") may be read as a metaphor for autobiography. This is a genre which offers access and apparent insight, but only ever at the behest, and under the control, of the autobiographer or "guide."

Throughout "Some Foreign Letters," as I have suggested, metaphors of reading and writing dominate. Yet, as Lang notes,

> the description of the autobiographer as "reader" of his past is not as simply "metaphorical" as it may first appear: autobiography is "literally" the analysis of one's past discourses, of one's acts and utterances, insofar as they signify within a social and linguistic context. (11)

Sexton's speaker does not, then, "read" the past but "past discourses"—that is, her aunt's earlier readings and interpretations of the past. Nana is only knowable, only reachable as a text and cannot be made "real." As the stanza concludes, the speaker tries "to reach into your page and breathe it back . . . / but life is a trick, life is a kitten in a sack." The ellipsis after "breathe it back . . ." adds to the suspense of this moment. We are witnesses to a perverse Victorian music-hall spectacle. Magic is about to be performed when, by sleight of hand, the promised object (Nana), instead of being materialized, is whisked out of sight, condemned to the dead past from which she came. Notwithstanding the urgency of the speaker's desire, the depth of which is emphasized by the plaintive "I try" placed at the end of a line, she is unequal to the task of transforming writing into life.

Here, the poem gives the lie to one of the orthodoxies of autobiography, particularly autobiography by women. This is the expectation that by rewriting one's past, by textualizing one's foremothers, one can reforge an actual or meaningful bond with them. Such an expectation is encapsulated in Virginia Woolf's assertion that "We think back through our mothers if we are women" (*Room* 76). "Some Foreign Letters" indicates that the attempt to reclaim the past and to rebuild a nurturing and reciprocal relationship with one's foremothers (or what Gilmore describes as "the feminist nostalgia for an identity discourse") is destined to fail (*Autobiographics* 237). The grotesque image of the suffocated kitten implies an angry rejection of any attempt to learn about oneself or others in this way. This includes the attempt represented by psychotherapy, an analogy which Sexton herself draws. In 1963, taking the aunt's letters with her as her "guide," Sexton undertook what she called in a 15 May 1963 letter, her own "grand tour" (HRHRC). In Belgium, the letters along with

Sexton's car and other possessions were stolen. In a letter home, Sexton comments on the theft:

> The shock of losing it all just doesn't sink in. I lost all the books! Even
> Nana's letters from Europe and grandfather's too. I did value and love
> those two books... but they are in the thief's wastebasket I guess... and
> life must go on not backward (just this fact makes me feel better, the
> trouble with therapy is that it makes life go backwards . . .). (Sexton's
> ellipses; *Letters* 191)

The metaphor of "reach[ing] into the page" in "Some Foreign Letters" is
used elsewhere in Sexton's poetry to interrogate the validity and usefulness of
searching the past for the key to present identity. In "45 Mercy Street," Sexton
refers to her life "And its hauled up / Notebooks"; in "Flee on Your Donkey," which also explores the backwards/forwards, regression-as-progression,
paradox, she describes the process of "dredg[ing]" or trawling her dreams for
insight; and in "The Hoarder," she proposes a relationship between digging
a hole and excavating the truth about the past. In her *Paris Review* interview,
Sexton comments on the "buried self" and "creative depths" which were part
of her identity before the writing of poems, or the process of "dredging" and
"digging" brought them to the surface (Kevles 309).

One of the characteristics of autobiography, if understood as a discursive
process, is that the subject's authority is moderated, if not nullified, by the
voices and interpretations of the reader or other. In her Crawshaw lecture
on "Some Foreign Letters," Sexton highlights the importance of the reader's
hermeneutic role:

> There is some persona going on in "Some Foreign Letters" because it is
> not all true. It is not all the confessional Anne Sexton speaking for her
> great-aunt. Some of it isn't true and some of it is. I'd like you to guess
> which. But is it important which? That's a job to be left to potential
> biographers, but then aren't you all biographers in a sense? (Crawshaw
> [3] 3)

In the poem, the death of the great-aunt serves to dramatize this situation,
paradoxically opening up a space ("This is the sack of time your death va-
cates") in which she may be reconstructed, or remembered, by others—first
by the descendent/writer and thereafter by the reader of the poem. Autobi-

ography represents an opportunity to fill or complete this gap, or "void" as Rousseau's *Confessions* terms it (17). Autobiography is neither a release nor a revelation (there is nothing to release from an "empty sack," there is no pre-textual subject to unveil), but a process of fabrication and plenishment.

"Some Foreign Letters" lays bare these processes of supplementation, interpretation, and speculation: "Tonight your letters reduce / history to a guess. The Count had a wife." Here, as at other key points in the poem, it is impossible to distinguish between autobiography ("letters"), truth ("history"), and fiction ("a guess"). Each, it transpires, offers a subjective representation of experience, and each is subject to processes of condensation, displacement, denial, and omission. Of these, guesswork, or interpretation, dominates. This is exemplified in stanza three, which depicts the aunt's deeply symbolic climb up "Mount San Salvatore." We are told that this is her "first climb" and, clearly, a sexual encounter is being intimated. The confident, explanatory reportage of the earlier two stanzas here dissipates and we find a more urgent, snatched snapshot of the scene. There are few verbs, and, instead, a rapid description of the young Nana, the object of the count's gaze:

> This is the rocky path, the hole in your shoes,
> the yankee girl, the iron interior
> of her sweet body.

"History" is, indeed, reduced to a "guess" and the metaphorical references to "hole," "girl," "interior," and "sweet body" invite us to "guess" that sex is the subject. The poem foregrounds the uncertain truth-status, first of the letters from Nana, and second of their representation in this poem. Is this what Nana reported of her experience? Or is this the speaker's "guess"? What is the status of the reader's interpretation of the meeting on the mountain? Which of these versions, if any, may be regarded as true?

Stanza five further explores, and then complicates, these questions by admitting a new set of memories to supplement those relayed in the aunt's original letters. The warm, detailed, and apparently clear memories of the earlier stanzas are not, it transpires, the strongest. Like Virginia Woolf's "Sketch of the Past," where the "first memory" is not in fact the most significant, Sexton's key memory emerges later. Part way through this stanza, the perspective shifts, and the "I" who has hitherto been responsible for reporting or mediating Nana's experience inserts more insistent memories of her own:

When you were mine they wrapped you out of here
with your best hat over your face. I cried
because I was seventeen. I am older now.

The final stanza of "Some Foreign Letters" insists on the primacy and immediacy of the first-person autobiographical voice. The insistent "Tonight"
and "Tonight" at the beginning of lines one and three acts both as a rejection of the past which no longer matters and as a defiant carpe diem defense
against the future which cannot be known. In her 1966 television documentary, Sexton reads the poem and comments on the apparent intimacy and immediacy of address in this stanza: "I break up a little bit because I'm speaking
to her then; if you understand the difference in time." There is an oracular
sense of urgency here which invokes the larger historical context in which
this journey was played out and again undercuts the apparent sentimentality
of the narrative:

Tonight I will speak up and interrupt
your letters, warning you that wars are coming,
that the Count will die, that you will accept
your America back to live like a prim thing . . .

In her "Comment on 'Some Foreign Letters,'" Sexton emphasizes the strange
alienating qualities of both the original letters home and her own autobiographical meditation on and mediation of them. She refers to the surprise
and dislocation which she experiences on rereading the poem, or revisiting
her own autobiographical representation: "It is, for me, like a strange photograph that I come upon each time with a seizure of despair and astonish-
ment" (16). The textual representation of a life—and this includes Sexton's
self-representation in this poem—remains just that: some foreign letters.

Two subsequent poems, "Crossing the Atlantic" and "Walking in Paris,"
develop these themes. They are placed consecutively in the volume *Live or
Die,* in which Sexton, unusually, dated all of the poems, noting in her preface
that she thought "the order of their creation might be of interest to some
readers." The poems complement each other and create a sense of autobiographical narrative. In the first of these, Sexton reflects on her sea voyage
from America to Europe, which she undertook as the first recipient of the
American Academy of Arts and Letters traveling fellowship. In a move which

mimics John Berryman's journeys in the *Dream Songs*—281 ("I rush back to the haunts of Yeats / & others") and 282 (which inquires about "our meaning to the Old World, theirs to us")—Sexton contemplates the strangeness of her journey and of the reversal by which she sails east in search of her past in contradistinction to her ancestors' voyage west in search of their future.[1]

In "Crossing the Atlantic," like in "Some Foreign Letters," the distance between past and present is elided by the act of writing about it. The writer from the past sailing into the future and the writer from the present sailing back in time are destined to meet on this hostile sea:

> We sail out of season into an oyster-gray wind,
> over a terrible hardness.
> Where Dickens crossed with mal de mer
> in twenty weeks or twenty days
> I cross toward him in five.

"Crossing the Atlantic" is a poem of multiple reversals, metaphorically confirming the complexity and acausality of autobiographical representation: The ship sails the "wrong" way (it sails east) at the wrong time of year ("out of season"). It leaves behind a "wake," signifying both the ship's tracks and a funeral commemoration, which is also a "ragged bridal veil." The journey across the Atlantic, like the images of digging and dredging discussed earlier, symbolizes a regression into a dark, labyrinthine underworld:

> The ship is 27 hours out.
> I have entered her.
> She might be a whale,
> sleeping 2000 and ship's company,
> the last 40¢ martini
> and steel staterooms where night goes on forever.
> Being inside them is, I think,
> the way one would dig into a planet
> and forget the word *light*.
> I have walked cities,
> miles of mole alleys with carpets.

The text dramatizes the autobiographical process, depicting it as an act of looking back and down, of searching the labyrinths of memory for meaning and identity. In a Crawshaw lecture on the poem, Sexton explains: "There was no ocean there, there was no sky. It was a tunnel, there was a cave" ([10] 9). In the underworld, the subject loses contact with her sense of self (here, symbolically represented by a loss of voice); she loses sight of the light (traditionally the source of human understanding); and she experiences her identity as split, alien and incomprehensible: "Inside I have been ten girls who speak French. / They languish everywhere like bedsheets." The metaphor of ship as underworld reminds us of Orpheus's predicament and of the punishment he suffers as a consequence of his inability to resist looking back.

The journey across the sea, into the past, or into the self is a painful, violent, even rapacious one:

> She will run East, knot by knot, over an old bloodstream,
> stripping it clear,
> each hour ripping it, pounding, pounding,
> forcing through as through a virgin.

Sexton amplifies the point: "I am like the ship, ripping through the ocean of my mother's and grandmother's lives, stripping it away, cutting through life. . . . (The ocean never stops, neither does the street of the bloodline")" (Crawshaw [10] 9). Such metaphors of stripping, ripping, pounding, and forcing anticipate what Peter Brooks identifies as an insight to be learned from the autobiographical quest: "Truth is not of easy access; it often is represented as veiled, latent or covered, so that the discovery of truth becomes a process of unveiling, laying bare, or denuding" (96). In "Crossing the Atlantic," this "unveiling" is both a revelation and an act of exposure, a clarification and an exploitation.

"Walking in Paris" takes these ideas a stage further, rendering yet more personal and immediate the attempt to revisit the past initiated in the earlier "Memoir" poems. Here, the speaker is not simply reading about, but physically retracing the ancestor's footsteps in a figurative and literal journey which, like autobiography, is fraught with difficulties and disappointments. The poem overstates the speaker's rights of possession over the Victorian aunt or, alternatively, the autobiographer's desire for interpretative control over the past. The poem's opening line announces: "I have come back to your youth, my Nana"—a reference both to the speaker's actual return to the place of Nana's "grand tour" and to this poem's metaphorical return to the concerns of the earlier poems. Again, we find an intense dialogue between the "I" and the "you"; although in "Walking in Paris," even more than in the earlier poems, we are conscious that the "you" is always mediated or reported by the "I," hence the possessive "my":

> I come back to your youth, my Nana,
> as if I might clean off
> the mad woman you became.

The reliability and referentiality of the aunt's letters and, by extension, of any writing is cast into doubt. Stanza two opens:

> I read your Paris letters of 1890.
> Each night I take them to my thin bed
> and learn them as an actress learns her lines.

The apparently sincere and intimate "letters home" are presented as a dramatization or a masque—a theatrical rendering (in the sense of a surface representation) of the truth to be performed or reenacted by an other. Many commentators have noted that Sylvia Plath's *Letters Home* function in a similar way; they present a dramatic or performed identity, one which is further mediated by the recipient (Plath's mother) who is also the editor, even the impresario. In her own letters home from Europe, Sexton appropriated Nana's affectionate and cheery greeting: a demonstration that she has, indeed, "learn[ed] her lines." Such a performance chillingly masks Sexton's misery and loneliness on the actual journey, which culminated in a breakdown and a swift return home, recorded in a terse telegram which seems worlds apart from this spectacle: "ARRIVING BOSTON SUNDAY OCT 27" (HRHRC).

The deep anxiety about the ethics and the referential accuracy of autobiography surfaces throughout "Walking in Paris." In seeking to establish parallels between Nana's experience and the speaker's own, the poem has been forced, for the sake of rhetorical and autobiographical symmetry and narrative coherence, to erase whole epochs of history: "1940 never happened." By juxtaposing her own private acts of erasure—her attempt to sanitize the great-aunt, to evoke a past stripped of any complexity—with the large-scale obliteration of Paris's wartime past, the speaker concedes her own complicity and guilt:

> In Paris 1890 was yesterday
> and 1940 never happened—

the soiled uniform of the Nazi
has been unravelled and reknit and resold.[2]

This reference to the erasure of Paris's past serves as an implicit reminder of the dangers of such forgetting. Sexton's speaker, by eliding or manipulating historical experience, is a collaborator in its betrayal. These images may be read as a self-reflexive and, indeed, self-critical commentary on the autobiographical poem's own processes. The "soiled uniform of the Nazi," like the dirty, mad old woman, has been "unraveled" (cleaned off, peeled back) and rewoven so as to be suitable for public consumption, this time in the guise of a poem. Paris, like the speaker's Nana, has been remodeled for public display and "resold" for financial gain. "Walking in Paris" exposes its own bad faith, its dissatisfaction with the masquerade of autobiography, and indicates Sexton's own guilt and ambivalence about the genre. Yet the concerns of this stanza are ostensibly belied by its closing declaration: "To be occupied or conquered is nothing—/ to remain is all!" This is a defiant credo which again foregrounds—although not without some anxiety—the subject's power to appropriate and attenuate a particular version of the truth.

In the subsequent stanza, the speaker concedes the extent of her transgression, but nevertheless continues to strip back the layers, to push back the boundaries of recall and representation:

Having come this far
I will go farther.
You are my history (that stealer of children)
and I have entered you.
I have deserted my husband and my children,
the Negro issue, the late news and the hot baths.

The speaker exposes the extent to which she has "unravelled" her own past: cleaned off ("deserted") her husband and children, the American present ("the Negro issue, the late news"), and domestic responsibilities ("the hot baths"), in order to rejoin Nana. That she is able to disregard current political issues is a further reminder of the speaker's dangerous complicity in the erasure or misrepresentation of the past.

The final stanza, like the penultimate stanza of "Some Foreign Letters," synthesizes the rigorously demarcated "I" and "you" of earlier stanzas to form the pronoun "we." The complexities of the past are eclipsed by the two women's newfound communion:

> Come, my sister,
> we are two virgins,
> our lives once more perfected
> and unused.

Middlebrook comments of "Walking in Paris" that "the imagery of being a virgin suggests that one of Sexton's coping strategies [during her European tour] was the fantasy of starting life over" (*Biography* 205). Although I concur with this reading, I would add that the key motivation for Sexton, as evidenced in this and the other "Memoir" poems, is the chance not to live a new life, but to rewrite one, to generate a new textual identity by appropriating the aunt's letters. All three "Memoir" poems demonstrate that the acts of reading and writing allow the subject to modify or erase earlier "selves" and to construct new ones: self as sister, virgin, and intrepid traveler free of "all that is American and forgotten." As Leigh Gilmore suggests "the autobiographical subject is produced not by experience, but by autobiography" (*Autobiographics* 25).

Gilmore's comment implies that autobiography produces presence out of absence, unity out of fragmentation, coherence out of chaos. It confirms the point which Sexton makes in a letter of 1963: "My poems only come when I have almost lost the ability to utter a word. To speak, in a way, of the unspeakable. To make an object out of the chaos" (*Letters* 171). She develops the point in her interview with the *Hudson Review*:

> There is a big change after you write a poem. It's a marvelous feeling, and there's a big change in the psyche, but I think you really go into great chaos just before you write a poem, and during it, and then to have come out of that whole, somehow is a small miracle, which lasts for a couple of days. Then on to the next. (Marx 82)

Such apparent coherence is beguiling, though. Any unity is sporadic and temporary.

The aural pun on "whole"/hole (to "come out of that whole") is particularly worthy of note given that we have seen Sexton, in the "Memoir" poems, constructing an identity by plumbing the depths or by descending into the underworld. In "The Hoarder," she depicts the poetic process in terms of a sustained metaphor of digging a hole in the ground:

> There is something there
> I've got to get and I dig
> down.

Thus, one emerges "whole" as a consequence of excavating a "hole" (surely a metaphor for the promise of psychotherapy). Deryn Rees-Jones notes a similar trope in Sexton's angel poems where the image "denotes a sense both of emptiness and completeness" (292). This brings to mind the writing process which Virginia Woolf depicts in "A Sketch of the Past." Describing the effect of sudden shocks in her life, Woolf notes:

> A shock is at once in my case followed by the desire to explain it. . . . I make it real by putting it into words. It is only by putting it into words that I make it whole; this wholeness means that it has lost its power to hurt me; it gives me, perhaps because by doing so I take away the pain, a great delight to put the severed parts together. ("Sketch" 83–84)

Sexton uses similar rhetoric to describe her own writing:

> When writing you make a new reality and become whole. It is as if I were operating on myself and suturing on the arms and legs, placing the heart, settling the intestines. Much of my poetry is the poetry of a cripple, and yet the act of creation cures for a time. (Crawshaw [9] 4)

However, this marks a reversal of the tropes used elsewhere in her work whereby autotomy (the casting off of parts of the body) and corporeal synecdoche are used to signify subjectivity in crisis. Indeed, the evidence of many of the poems belies any claim to the achievement of wholeness, subjective unity and coherence through the act of writing. "Just Once," for example, offers the tantalizing promise of self-presence in momentarily displaying a vivid, unified, coherent self. The poem opens with a moment of insight: "Just once I knew what life was for. / In Boston quite suddenly, I understood." The speaker's epiphany is played out against the holistic background of the elements (earth, air, fire, and water: that is, her nighttime walk along the banks of the river, lit by stars). She implicitly figures herself as the center of this particular universe. Her presence centers all points of the compass:

> I walked my love
> on the night green side of it and cried
> my heart to the eastbound cars and cried
> my heart to the westbound cars.

The "neoned and strobe-hearted" lights shine for her, announcing her presence by "opening / their mouths as wide as opera singers." The choice of theatrical metaphors, however, implies that her apparently solitary, soul-searching walk is, at bottom, a performance.

"Just Once" is, in many respects, an extremely egotistical poem. It asks not how "I" fit into the world, but how the world shapes itself around me. Yet such autobiographical confidence is temporary. The transience of the moment, indicated already in the title and opening line, and subliminally confirmed in the impermanence of the images throughout: flickering strobe lights, flowing river, twinkling stars, is reiterated in the poem's final lines when the speaker hurries home "and hoarded these constants into morning / only to find them gone." The diminution in this last line, with its few and monosyllabic words and final sonorous "gone" provides a stark and telling contrast to the excited, rapid, syntactically varied preceding lines. The sense of identity here—of self as a whole, taking one's place in a larger whole—is fleeting and ephemeral; it occurs "just once" and gratuitously. There are no "constants"; hence, the dream or fairy tale metaphor in the penultimate line: Such nighttime gifts never last. And it follows that any sense of self is, to borrow Virginia Woolf's words, simply a "moment of being"; an impression, a simulation, an effect which quickly fades "and then on to the next."

Sexton's work raises important questions about the possibilities or, more accurately, limitations of autobiography for the subject who experiences herself in this way: as impermanent or fragmented. Although autobiography demands that one scrutinizes one's self, the self—particularly the female self—who is both subject and object of the search is always split, and never fully present to herself. One of Sexton's responses to this problem is the abandonment of any attempt to write the self "whole" and the use, instead, of synecdochic representation of the lives of a disparate collection of parts of the body. In "Killing the Spring" (1971), for example, Sexton depicts the piece-by-piece closing down of the body and its senses, or the grotesque body in crisis. This attempt at writing the self is characterized by self-effacement (the head, eyes, and ears are buried or drowned) and by an extreme form of self-negation, with the speaker explicitly comparing herself to a "young person" who "died for no reason."

Most often in Sexton's work, it is the hands or fingers or arm (all metonyms of writing) which are the objects of attention. Diana Hume George notes that "hands remained synecdoches for self throughout Sexton's canon." They "represent . . . and then become the whole" (*Oedipus* 64, 66). However, I would suggest that Sexton's synecdochic objectification of parts of the body is less amenable to coalescence and closure than this suggests. The parts do not always form a "whole"; and the significance of the hand is not necessarily as a synecdoche for "self," but as a synecdoche for writing. In a number of places, in "Cripples and Other Stories," for example, the subject who writes is specifically figured as impaired and partial or as incapable of constituting a "whole."

In "The Touch" (1966), the metaphor of an amputated hand indicates that the writing or autobiographical self is dissociated from the life which it is thought to represent: "For months my hand had been sealed off / in a tin box. Nothing was there but subway railings." It is significant that the hand is "sealed off" such that it is unable to gain access to the underground or unconscious. This reading is confirmed later in the poem's opening stanza where the hand with its "thin underground veins" simply "lay there like an unconscious woman / fed by tubes she knew not of." The dormant hand is "like an unconscious woman" because it lies unresponsive, gathering energy, awaiting its moment of action and revelation.

One important feature of this and Sexton's other poems about dissociated, objectified, or amputated hands and arms is that it is only one hand which is so treated.[3] In "The Touch," it is clear that an active hand remains and is able to display ("turn over," write about) the "sealed off" one:

> I turned it over and the palm was old,
> its lines traced like fine needlepoint
> and stitched up into the fingers.

This represents the way in which the autobiographical subject may be both present in, and detached from, the life which is its focus. The third stanza of "The Touch" opens resignedly: "And all this is metaphor." The poem is noteworthy for its conscious interrogation of the importance and limitations of metaphor as a means of comparing like with like, as a way of translating experience into text, and as a way of bringing into figurative proximity two disconnected objects—life and writing, hand and subject. In her Crawshaw lectures, Sexton explains: "In metaphor two things that are not quite alike are likened. Therefore they take on a new color and a new brightness. They take on a new character" (Crawshaw [7] 4). The figure of metaphor works in two seemingly contradictory ways: it permits the speaker to compare her experience with something completely separate and different, and it permits her to emphasize latent contiguities. In "The Touch," metaphor is depicted as a mere rhetorical or textual figure, as an artificial way of constructing likeness where none exists:

> And all this is metaphor.
> An ordinary hand—just lonely
> for something to touch
> that touches back.[4]

Yet, as is indicated by the subsequent and immediate appropriation of another metaphor in line seven of this stanza ("I'm no better than a case of dog food"), metaphor remains an insistent and inescapable figure.

Sexton here articulates one of the obstacles to autobiography. She demonstrates the impossibility of ever presenting a "true" picture of oneself: all that can be achieved is a "likeness"—a representation in terms of similarity, or contiguity—which is never, finally, self-identical. There is no clear depiction, there are only metaphors, metonyms and tropes which embody varying and indeterminate proximities to the subject of representation and to each other. It is impossible to write the self without displacing or deferring the representation down a metaphorical line ("I" am an amputated hand, "I" am a case of dog food, etc.). As Sexton suggests in an unpublished introductory talk, prepared in 1962 for students at Boston College: "I am the one who creates, not the one who thinks . . . and if by mistake I should think—it is in symbols and metaphors . . . and I must remind you that I am not responsible for what they mean" (HRHRC).

Subject and reader alike can only ever circle, or circumvent, the truth—itself a metaphor used by Sexton to discuss the writing process. In a 21 February 1964 letter, she describes her poems "With Mercy for the Greedy" and "For God While Sleeping" as "circl[ing] obsessively" around the same theme, while in a 12 August 1965 letter to the editor of the *Hudson Review* about an interview which she had recently given for the journal, she complains, "I feel the interview with Patricia Marx is simply awful. I really do. And who am *I* to be saying anything. What I say in it spirals around the truth and the lie as a snail shell held close for inspection" (HRHRC). These circumventory images suggest a wariness born of experience. They confirm that the route to memory, and to identity, may not be straightforward and obvious but may instead be indirect and meandering. Peter Brooks relates such circumvention to the kinds of metonymy and synecdoche which I have identified in Sexton's work. He characterizes the gaze which can never see the object whole, but only ever as a collection of parts, as a "frustrated attempt to fix the body in the field of vision [which] sets off the restless movement of narrative, telling the story of approach to, and swerve away from, that final object of sight that cannot be contemplated" (102–3). Thus, it may be argued that autobiography can only ever skate around the edges of the truth. It offers snatches of insight and brief moments of contiguity or wholeness, yet perpetually denies closure. Autobiographical truth, like all others, is endlessly deferred, displaced, indeterminate.

The profound ambivalence about the efficacy of the figures by which one may write the self persists even to the superficially redeeming end of "The Touch." Here, the damaged, dissociated, and dying hand is brought back to life and into productive creativity by the loving touch of another:

Your hand found mine.
Life rushed to my fingers like a blood clot.
Oh, my carpenter,
the fingers are rebuilt.
They dance with yours.

These lines appear at first to suggest that if the sealed-off hand can be restored, it may, through the act of writing/remembering, bring the dismembered self back to wholeness. It may reconstitute itself as a successful writing self ("My hand is alive all over America"). In a comment which she made about the poem in a 1974 interview, Sexton seems to confirm that writing generates a sense of wholeness, plenitude, satisfaction: "'The Touch' shows something about my feeling that there's God everywhere, although I didn't know it when I was writing it [Sexton quotes the final stanza] I just wrote that. I didn't look into it" (Fitzgerald 195). However, we find that the act of regeneration in the poem is implicitly and unavoidably life threatening. The oxymoronic line "Life rushed to my fingers like a blood clot" links life with death. The simile reveals an anxiety about the possible risks of permitting life (blood) to flow back into the writing hand—a fear, perhaps, of what writing might reveal.

"Love Letter Written in a Burning Building" similarly promises and then denies a satisfying resolution. Here, as in "Just Once" and the earlier "Memoir" poems, we are provided with a wealth of apparently autobiographical detail sufficient to persuade the reader that he or she is party to lived experience. The "Love Letter" opens "Dearest Foxxy," and we are permitted insight into the speaker and addressee's shared past:

> I am in a crate,
> the crate that was ours,
> full of white shirts and salad greens,
> the icebox knocking at our delectable knocks.

Here, however, the speaker is in the process of self-destruction. The setting of the poem, a burning building, is apposite given the prominence in Sexton's ostensibly autobiographical poems of metaphors of female subject as house or room (see, for example, "Housewife" and "There You Were") and of writing as fire ("Her Kind," "The Fire Thief" and "Talking to Sheep"). Plath uses metaphors of conflagration in similar ways, for example in "Witch Burning" and "Lady Lazarus." Fire represents both self-transformation and self-destruction, and, most importantly, a form of self-expression akin to the Pentecostal gift of tongues. In "Witch Burning," for instance, "the red tongues will teach the truth."

In "Love Letter Written in a Burning Building," the speaker is unable to complete the "whole story" of the self:

> If my toes weren't yielding to pitch
> I'd tell the whole story—
> not just the sheet story
> but the belly-button story,
> the pried-eyelid story,
> the whiskey-sour-of-the-nipple story.

Yet it is always possible that the "whole story" is, after all, what is being told. Paradoxically, the "whole" story is a dreadful narrative of fragmentation, destruction, and disintegration. We find a similar trope in "The Fierceness of Female" (ca. 1974) which achieves closure through disintegration, juxtaposing metaphors of spinning with metaphors of unknitting or unraveling to show the self constructed and the self deconstructed as two sides of the same coin of female identity.

The "whole" story in "Love Letter Written in a Burning Building" is that the subject is not whole, but is at this very moment engaged in, and reporting on, an act of self-immolation:

> Despite my asbestos gloves,
> the cough is filling me with black,
> and a red powder seeps through my veins.

However, in spite of the speaker's claim not to be telling the "whole" story, we find an inalienable sense of resolution. "Love Letter Written in a Burning Building" was one of the last poems which Sexton wrote (dated just one week before her death), and in its final lines, it looks back to, and confirms the premonitions of the much earlier poem, "Her Kind":

> we seem to be going down
> right in the middle of a Russian street,
> the flames making the sound of
> the horse being beaten and beaten.

As this anticipation and then confirmation of a death not yet experienced (autothanography, instead of autobiography) would indicate, one of the major conceits which Sexton develops in order to subvert the conventions and promise of autobiography is the reversal of the genre's conventional chronology and narrative causality. "End, Middle, Beginning" and the "Horoscope Poems" in the "Scorpio, Bad Spider, Die" sequence, for instance, may be regarded as parodic in the way in which they present the autobiography of the future, or reverse a sequence of events, so as to make a nonsense of conventional notions of cause and effect. The "Horoscope Poems" do not scrutinize past life events for significant information about present character (a characteristic of autobiography, according to Philippe Lejeune: "A retrospective account in prose that a real person makes of his own existence stressing his individual life and especially the history of his personality"); instead, they look to the future for such signs (qtd. in Olney 18).

"End, Middle, Beginning" parodies the archetypal life-story. Although written in the third person, its blatant appropriation or perhaps misappropriation of the idioms, structure, and concerns of the "life story" induce me to read it as a poem about autobiography, and indeed, as autobiographical. Sexton's subject is objectified, dramatized, and coldly scrutinized from the outside. The use of the third person pronoun helps to sustain this judgmental distance. Like T. S. Eliot's "East Coker," the poem begins with the end. However, unlike Eliot, whose use of this achronology may be regarded as a framing device, Sexton completely and persistently reverses the time sequence to considerable rhetorical effect. Eliot states his premise: "In my beginning is my end," and Sexton exemplifies it: "There was an unwanted child. / Aborted by three modern methods." The paradox that my beginning is my end is my beginning is found in a number of Sexton's other poems (for example, in "O Ye Tongues," which begins, "Let there be a God as large as a sunlamp to laugh his heat / at you" and ends "For God was as large as a sunlamp and laughed his heat at us / and therefore we did not cringe at the death hole"). The effect of these rhetorical, even chiasmic, figures is to suggest that ends, middles, and beginnings are equal and indeterminate, and may be read in any order. This marks a rejection or at the very least a questioning of the teleology which would see all experience as leading, systematically, to the construction of the subject which we see before us.

"End, Middle, Beginning," like some of the fairy tale poems in *Transformations*, appropriates and then distends the conventional structures, idioms, and themes of the fairy tale. From the archetypal "Once upon a time there was a beautiful baby," we are faced, suddenly, with a grotesque image of rejection, violation, and hate (the "unwanted child," aborted not once but the magical "three times"):

> There was an unwanted child.
> Aborted by three modern methods
> she hung on to the womb,
> hooked onto it
> building her house into it
> and it was to no avail,
> to black her out.

There is a succession of complex paradoxes at play here. First, the "unwanted child" is, in fact, the "wanting" child, the child who desires so much to live that she escapes "three modern methods" of abortion. Second, the child seeks to live in order to achieve death. There is a strong "instinct towards death or destruction" (to quote Freud) which manifests itself in this poem in the unwanted child's silent acceptance of pain and punishment:

At her birth
she did not cry,
spanked indeed,
but did not yell
instead snow fell out of her mouth.

The silence reproduces the condition of Freud's death instinct ("which works in silence") and is found again in stanza three where the growing child is buried under rocks "to keep / the growing silent" (Freud, "Autobiographical" 105). The reference to snow signifies the death instinct's tendency to reduce living matter to a cold, lifeless, "inorganic state" (Freud, *Civilization* 310). Throughout, the unwanted child, having clawed ("hooked") her way into the world, seeks stillness and nothingness. She is passive, immobile, death-like:

They locked her in a football
but she merely curled up
and pretended it was a warm doll's house.

As the poem moves into its final (or, to mimic the reversed trajectory indicated by the title, its "beginning") stages, we learn that the speaker did "once" escape this stultifying drive towards death:

Then once,
by terrible chance,
love took her in his big boat
and she shoveled the ocean
in a scalding joy.

The dramatic "then once" echoes the fairy tale tone of the earlier stanzas, and has the effect of enhancing the fictionality of the experiences being evoked. It is significant that the death instinct is thwarted by an encounter with its opposite element: with "scalding" Eros. The hot passion, however, bears the seeds of its own destruction: "Scalding" suggests burning danger and possible death while its aural pun "scolding" implies disapproval and punishment.

The slow, emphatic final stanza, with its single-word opening lines ("Then, / slowly") and long, attenuated assonance ("love seeped away") emphasizes, as it dramatizes, the final victory of the death instinct and the turn to stultification, lifelessness, silence:

> The boat turned into paper
> and she knew her fate,
> at last.
> Turn where you belong,
> into a deaf mute
> that metal house,
> let him drill you into no one.

The image of the paper boat may be read as a metaphor for the transience and inevitable failure of self-life-writing. That the subject knows "her fate, / at last" merely confirms what the rest of "End, Middle, Beginning" has demonstrated: that the beginning (birth) inevitably brings us to the end (death); indeed, that the "beginning" is the end in the sense that it closes the poem. The final admonition subtly takes us back to the beginning of the poem (the "end" of the title). For this concluding line reads like a perverse metaphor for conception. The speaker anticipates, and indeed seeks to avoid, the moment of impregnation which must have preceded the need for abortion. The final invocation is a plea against being "drilled" (planted and fertilized like a seed) and thereby brought to birth. It is a plea for death pure and simple and thus for a preemption of the otherwise inescapable battle with Eros. So "End, Middle, Beginning," like "Love Letter Written in a Burning Building," functions as a perverse anti-autobiography, as a record of life which is a narrative of death. Such a conceit exposes and undermines many of the conventions and techniques of autobiography, and, most perniciously, its underlying premise: that there is a life worth living and worth writing.

Performance

Early accounts of confessional poetry postulate a mutually beneficial relationship between poet and reader. The suffering and overburdened subject is said to experience relief as a consequence of releasing her emotions, and the audience identifies with the subject and is thereby vicariously relieved of its own anxieties about modern experience. Even a poststructuralist theorist such as Foucault—notwithstanding his recognition of the power differential which underpins the confessional process—sees it, finally, as a purposive and beneficial act, as

> a ritual in which the expression alone, independently of its external consequences, produces intrinsic modifications in the person who articulates it: it exonerates, redeems, and purifies him; it unburdens him of his wrongs, liberates him, and promises him salvation. (*History* 61–62)

One might argue, however, that in confessional poetry the relationship between speaker and reader is neither as positive nor as productive as this suggests. Indeed, as the striking and little-known texts discussed in this chapter indicate, there is a fine line between collaboration and exploitation, symbiosis and parasitism.

It is in staged readings or performances of Sexton's work that the pressure on both parties (speaker and observer) is most acute, and that the problematics of the confessional process are thrown into sharpest relief. Paradoxes and contradictions are here foregrounded, even exaggerated. The paralyzing double bind, in which the audience is both necessary and despised, in which the penitent's own punishment must be first enticed and then laid bare, is in public performances dramatically writ large. New questions arise: Is the Anne

Sexton on the stage the "real" Anne Sexton? Is the "I" performed on the stage a scripted, that is, constructed, prescribed "I"? Does the speaker's physical presence and her vocalization of experience offer a guarantee of truth? Who benefits from the dramatic reenactment of the scene? Sexton's mentor, John Holmes, complained in a letter dated 8 February 1959 that Sexton's writing was "all a release for you" and asked "what is it for anyone else except a spectacle of someone else experiencing release"? (HRHRC) What difference does the staged recapitulation of the confessional moment make to readings of confession as compulsive, necessary, and therapeutic?

Something about the repetitiousness of these displays and images seems most to disturb. It is not that Sexton tells or shows us these narratives once; it is that by offering them up in successive readings or performances, or in endlessly reiterative texts, the authenticity of the narrative is defused. As the confession becomes readable (and thus repeatable), it risks becoming incredible. Problems such as this unsettle the audience. Mary Russo makes a similar point of Charcot's infamous photographs of female hysterics:

> The photographs of Salpêtrière especially strike us as uncanny because of the repetitiveness of the hysterical performance. It is not only the content of the hysterical behavior that strikes us as grotesque, but its representation: if hysteria is a display, these photographs display the display. (68)

Sexton's 1974 poem "Talking to Sheep," first published in *The Death Notebooks*, foregrounds the spectacular and deceptive nature of confession, or, more properly, of confessional performance. "Performance" is an accurate term in that it signifies the fundamental artificiality of the mode, it confirms that the "I" of the poem may be a persona or dramatic mask, and it invokes the crucial relationship between poet/penitent/performer and reader/confessor/spectator. "Talking to Sheep" is one of the few poems in which Sexton explicitly refers to "confession," and is interesting not least because it offers a sustained critique of the audience's expectations of the mode and an account of the speaker's attempt to escape its demands. It manipulates the conventions of confessional poetry in order to challenge them. For example, it concedes but then problematizes the compulsiveness assumed to be at the heart of confessional discourse: "Yes. It was a compulsion / but I denied it, called it fiction." The first line of the poem, "my life," dramatically, even melodramatically, announces itself as a personal confession of the subject's life story.

However, as it proceeds to make clear, "my life" cannot be represented in the magnificent isolation promised by the syntax of this opening line. Rather, "my life" can only be revealed within a fraught framework of power and punishment. It cannot be "confessed" without the involvement and finally the assent, by whatever strategies these might be obtained, of the hostile auditor.

Ted Hughes's final collection, *Birthday Letters*, is equally exercised by the difficulties and complexities of confession. It includes a poem, "Chaucer," which we might almost want to subtitle "Talking to Cows." In it, the speaker depicts its subject (perhaps Plath) declaiming lines from Chaucer to an audience of cows. Just as in "Talking to Sheep," the subject must hold her audience's attention; she is simultaneously in command and at their mercy, she must make sure that they keep listening and they must make sure that she keeps talking. The speaker must first gain the attention of her audience by posturing and gesticulating; she raises her arms, partly for balance, but partly "to hold the reins of the straining attention / Of your imagined audience." Speaker and audience then move to an equilibrium: "You were rapt. And the cows were enthralled" but soon the attentions of the audience become overwhelming, excessive. What would happen, the speaker asks, "If you were to stop? Would they attack you, / Scared by the shock of silence, or wanting more—?" This curious, dangerous and deeply symbolic relationship is entirely characteristic of that at the heart of the confession.

"Talking to Sheep," like Hughes's poem, dispels any residual notions of the satisfaction which the confessional speaker achieves in the act of confession. She is subject to the same sense of shame and revulsion as critics of the mode have noted and she achieves neither sympathy nor absolution. The naked self-revelation thought by some to be a narcissistic indulgence on the part of the speaker is shown, by Sexton's use of the passive mode, to be a regrettable source of violence and humiliation. This is a relentless rape (hence the repetitions in line three and four) rather than an exhibitionist gesture:

> My life
> has appeared unclothed in court,
> detail by detail,
> death-bone witness by death-bone witness,
> and I was shamed at the verdict.

The power of shame should not be underestimated. There is, first, the shame of the original act (the inspiration for and object of the confession) and there is the additional shame of confessing it, of laying bare these intimate secrets for public judgment. Added to this, there is the terrible shame of enjoying or gaining some kind of satisfaction from the confessional process—an enjoyment which, I would argue, both subject and confessor, writer and reader, share. As I have already suggested, it is the propensity for repetition which makes this so dangerous, and exponentially so shameful. J. M. Coetzee detects behind the desire to confess a desire to deceive and behind this a desire to be "admired for one's candor":

> We are at the beginning of a potentially infinite regression of self-recognition and self-abasement in which the self-satisfied candor of each level of confession of impure motive becomes a new source of shame and each twinge of shame a new source of self-congratulation. (282)

"Talking to Sheep" generates cause for shame in its very shamelessness. To quote Jacqueline Rose, "Shame only arises when someone knows, or fears, they have been seen. Shame relies on the art of exposure, even if exposure is what it hates most, and most militantly struggles against" (*On Not* 1). Despite her naked vulnerability and her humiliation in the courtroom, "I went on / . . . confessing, confessing." "I went on" yields a pun, both on the speaker continuing to speak notwithstanding the imperative to stop, and on her taking the stage ("she goes on" and "the show must go on"). It transpires that this is no simple victimization of vulnerable subject by predatory others. Rather, it is a product of the symbiotic—verging on the parasitic—needs of poet and audience alike:

> Then I accosted winos,
> the derelicts of the region,
> winning them over into the latrine of my details.

The confessional poet's desperate thirst for an audience is presented as an addiction. Like an alcoholic, hence the image of "the winos," she is forced to take aggressive and debased steps ("the latrine") to fuel her habit. In an interview, Sexton explains that poets "dig right into the heart and let it spurt out and I think this kind of life makes alcoholics of them" (Balliro 13). Yet the metaphor also signifies the contempt in which the confessional speaker holds her audience. The image of "winos" connotes their addiction to her trauma as much as her addiction to its public display. And regardless of her contempt, it is these debased creatures who retain power and who must thus be "accosted" and "w[on] over."

In stanzas three and four, the speaker steps back in order to contemplate the aesthetic process of, and historical precedents for, this painful and problematic confession. Sexton's speaker concedes that the confessional text may be a sublimation or the product of unconscious processes hence the metaphors of sleep and dreaming: "I keep making statues / of my acts, carving them with my sleep." She also indicates the noncoincidence of the "I" of the confession with the historical author; the "I" of the poem may wear a costume or disguise. The phrase "not my life" here belies the ostentatious "my life" of the opening line:

> or if it is not my life I depict
> then someone's close enough to wear my nose —
> My nose, my patrician nose,
> sniffing at me or following theirs down the street.

The poem recognizes the instinctive distaste or revulsion which seems often to have characterized critical responses to the mode. Alicia Ostriker points out that confessional poetry is regarded as producing a "a nasty odor" ("Nerves" 75). "Talking to Sheep" confirms the point: "Even five centuries ago this smelled queer." The final line expresses an anxiety about the audience seeing "too much" and being harmed or corrupted by the object of the gaze. Witnessing a confession is thought to taint the auditors, burdening them with traumas which they then need to confess or discharge. The "only cure" is "to sit in a cold bath for six days, / a bath full of leeches, drawing out your blood." The metaphor of "leeches" sucking the confessors' blood significantly echoes the image Sexton uses elsewhere to describe the penitent's role as "a kind of blood letting"—a crucial metaphor, and one to which I will return.

In "Talking to Sheep," the only way of avoiding the condemnation which "five centuries" of historical precedence indicates will greet the act of confession is by escape into disguise, silence or incomprehensibility:

> It was wise, the wise medical men said,
> wise to cry *Baa* and be smiling into your mongoloid hood,
> while you simply tended the sheep.
> Or else to sew your lips shut
> and not let a word or a deadstone sneak out.

Silence, or the refusal to speak sense, becomes a form of power—indeed, the only power remaining to the speaker. Meanwhile, the text (the cry *"Baa"*) and its performance ("smiling into your mongoloid hood") function as a screen with which to appease and deflect the audience. We are reminded of Plath's "The Bee Meeting" with its hooded central character, silenced, vulnerable, and disguised. As Karen Jackson Ford comments of Plath's poem, the subject/speaker "makes passivity a performance and tinctures the funereal atmosphere with the carnival" (144). This is crucial to our understanding of both poets' work; the spectacular and the macabre coexist. For Sexton, the power to perform and, importantly, the power to refuse to perform or to remain silent are fundamental to the delineation of female subjectivity. Mary Russo in her study of the female grotesque proposes that "There is a way in which radical negation, silence, withdrawal, and invisibility, and the bold affirmations of feminine performance, imposture and masquerade ... have suggested a cultural politics for women" (54).

The conceit of the "cry *Baa*" functioning as a masquerade is borrowed by Sexton from a medieval French farce—a copy of which in French and English remains among the manuscript drafts of *45 Mercy Street* (HRHRC). The farce confirms that the seemingly nonsensical *"Baa"* represents a technique for evading scrutiny, a means of tricking the gullible but nevertheless dangerous audience, and a supreme double bluff. It consciously addresses the audience with a contempt which they cannot credit, and are only able to interpret as a sign of the subject's insanity. Central to the farce, and Sexton's revision of it, is the speaker's knowing disdain for her interrogators; she does indeed "mock the Court" as the medieval manuscript suggests. This reads also as a metaphor for the larger relationship between confessional speaker and auditor. The speaker mocks her needy and predatory audience. She speaks nonsense (metaphorically, the poem which may not be "true," but "fiction") and the audience accepts her word as evidence of her condition, rather than as a conscious and sardonic indictment of theirs.

This strategy becomes the only option open to the speaker in her attempt to escape the attentions of the demanding "populace." The onlookers are described now in more pressing detail ("the multi-colored, / crowded voices"), which emphasizes the distinction between the speaker's singular and vulnerable nakedness ("unclothed in court" and "death-bone witness") and the listeners' dense, protected elusiveness:

I feel I must learn to speak the *Baa*
of the simple-minded, while my mind
dives into the multi-colored,
crowded voices.

In "Talking to Sheep," giving voice offers no escape from traumatic experience. Although the audience is described in terms which implicitly invoke Pentecostal tongues of fire, for the speaker, liberation only comes through an inversion of this motif; through inhibition and silence: "I am the flame swallower" she declares.

Contempt for the audience becomes, finally, contempt for the self. The contempt is born of the speaker's complicity in the dialectic of display, punishment, deceit and retribution. The woman exposed in the witness-box in the first stanza is, in the final section of the poem, still vulnerable and now spotlighted on the stage. The emphatically repeated verb "plays" confirms that the confessional role is a mere masquerade:

Yes! While my mind plays simple-minded,
plays dead-woman in neon,
I must recall to say
Baa
to the black sheep I am.
Baa. Baa. Baa.

The nursery-rhyme allusion indicates that the poem carries no more inherent meaning than the child's song, thus the confessional poem is belittled and the poet disaggrandized. Further, the speaker—like the sheep in the children's rhyme—is destined to give of herself to everyone who demands it (the master and the dame). The depiction of the self as the "black sheep" or disgraced and shameful member of the family demonstrates the speaker's own self-loathing and her assimilation of other people's condemnation. The final "*Baa. Baa. Baa.*," spat out as though in disgust, is arguably addressed both to the audience and to the self. It has been argued that this poem forms a "confessional manifesto" (Hall 155). More than that, it offers a condemnation of the dynamics and latent artificiality of the mode and articulates a strategy for confusing, repelling or escaping the overly intrusive audience.

Sexton's short story, "The Letting Down of the Hair," although described by her as "an allegory for my devotion to poetry," may more usefully be read as an indictment of her imprisonment by poetry. The religious connotations of the word "devotion" ("the fact or quality of being devoted to religious observances" [Shorter Oxford English Dictionary]) encapsulate both the rigorous demands made of the subject and the sense that the object of attention (here the poet/poetry) requires close scrutiny or observation. The simile of self as "novice" or nun in the opening section works in a similar way; the confessing subject (secular or religious) must learn the regulatory framework which will, in time, define her identity. The figure of Mary Magdalene who is reputed to have cleaned Jesus's feet with her hair (Luke 8:36–51) is a possible referent here as, of course, is the fairy-tale figure of Rapunzel and, arguably, the mythical figure of Medusa whose snakelike hair enthralls her audience. Steven Gould Axelrod and Christina Britzolakis, among others, have pointed to the use of Medusan imagery in Plath's poetry where it is used as a figure which both represents and threatens the female self. We should be alert in the context of my argument to the figure of the female confessional poet as a modern day femme fatale. She is seductive, enthralling, and enigmatic while simultaneously embodying danger and risk. Her superficial beauty masks dangerous inner demons. Readings of Sexton's poetry and of her public persona as potentially corrupting, infectious, and dangerous, are symptomatic of such an association. Linda Gray Sexton assimilates some of these associations in her account of one of her mother's readings: "How captivating she was, how slender, burning with excitement, her voice a drowsy rasp, her sexuality palpable in the way she draped herself against the podium, her arms bewitched sirens calling to us all" (*Searching* 161).

"The Letting Down of the Hair" was drafted and revised during the early to mid-1960s, and published first in the *Atlantic Monthly* in 1972 and subsequently in *The Book of Folly*.[1] The story, or "prose poem" as Sexton called it (Middlebrook, *Biography* 359) is spoken in the first person, and tells the story of a reclusive woman's retreat to a "stone room" at the top of the house where her only activity is the care, and daily display, of her long hair. The narrative is divided into eight sections, the first of which opens with the heading: "Attracting Thousands," itself a barely disguised metaphor for Sexton's role as popular poet. The speaker begins by describing her paradoxical isolation: "I live in a stone room. Far from the luxury of draperies and transistors, far from the movie theaters and coffee houses, far from the men in their business suits." Yet such negative invocation of her own asceticism serves only as a disavowal of the latent importance of such objects in her life. It is significant that what are missing are the signs of communication (radio, film, and theater, coffee house conversation, business/publishing transactions). The specifically literary context is confirmed by the reference to the newspapers and letters which are her only sustenance ("I have only the daily newspapers and letters from Ruth") and by the allusion at the end of this short opening section to Emily Dickinson: "To tell the truth, I'm a recluse. I'm as hesitant as Emily Dickinson. Like a novice I'm all dressed in white. A recluse, yes. Yet each day I attract thousands."[2]

This seemingly self-evident comparison begs its own questions, however. How "hesitant" is Dickinson and by implication the speaker? Does the label "recluse" define Dickinson's entire identity (a doubt implied by Sexton's qualifying "yes. Yet . . . ")? Alicia Ostriker suggests that the position of "recluse" was, for Dickinson, a mask or disguise (*Stealing* 38). To what extent should we identify Emily Dickinson with the voice of her poems and, by implication, Sexton with the voice of hers? As Dickinson averred in a letter of 1862: "When I state myself, as the Representative of the Verse—it does not mean me—but a supposed version" (qtd. in Paglia 638). The comparison between self and Dickinson is found elsewhere in Sexton's writing, notably in a letter of June 1965, in which she draws a distinction between her own need of an audience and Dickinson's apparent disinclination to be published: "Emily Dickinson never bothered with the whole thing. She was content to write them. I would not be only content to write and never to publish or share" (*Letters* 263).

The second section of the story expands the description of this particular "room of one's own"; Woolf's essay, the "mad woman's attic," and the Lady of Shalott's tower are all subtexts of this sardonic account of the female artist's life.[3] The stone room is likened simultaneously to a barrier ("the craggy rocks of Gloucester, that desperate sea coast") and to a sacred and aesthetic space ("the steps of Rome," "Michelangelo and his stone creatures"). Moreover, the room is a "cupola" which permits the speaker a privileged view, and tacitly replicates a series of images in other poems of belligerent surveillance (for example, in the exposed spaces of "Three Green Windows" and "What's That?"). In terms of Sexton's poetics, it is significant that the room is spherical ("the shape of a merry-go-round, and eleven feet in circumference. A chalice, a cave, a perch"). Like the "inverted glass bowl" in "For John Who Begs Me Not to Enquire Further," the dome simultaneously contains and offers for display the female object. Moreover, this circular stone room represents an archetypal creative space; it is described as "a hidden place like the inside of a seedpod." It is a womblike site of gestation where the speaker can nurture the seeds of her inspiration.

However, this "cupola" is also experienced as a prison. The speaker explains that "like a lion in a zoo I adjust to my environment." The simile of the "lion" is doubly telling. First, it confirms the speaker's experience of being inhumanly treated, and of being put on display for the entertainment and education of the public—an image which is returned to in Sexton's article, "The Freak Show," discussed later. Second, it subtly revises one of Sexton's habitual metaphors for poetic form in order to make a larger point about the role of the poet. Speaking about her own early writing, Sexton explains that the presence of a secure and restraining poetic structure paradoxically permits her the freedom to release the "wild animals" of her unconscious (Marx 80). Adrienne Rich makes a similar point of her own initial aesthetic control; such formalism, she writes, was "like asbestos gloves, it allowed me to handle material I couldn't pick up bare-handed" (*On Lies* 40–41)

If "The Letting Down of the Hair" is to be read as "an allegory for my devotion to poetry," then the speaker's retreat to the "stone room" should be read as a metaphor for the confessional writer's characteristic introspection. Sexton's speaker describes her room or the locus of her writing as: "A room to crawl into and hide . . . as a child I would enter through a closet, standing tiptoe on a chair, up through the trapdoor into the forbidden—." This is a resolutely private world, inaccessible to others and thus, of course, intriguing. Indeed, in a Foucauldian sense, the desire to see is constructed by the barriers to/prohibitions against seeing: The stone wall provokes our yearning to look beyond it, the external image of the suffering poet stimulates our desire to peer into her mind. In a later section ("The Death of Everyone Except Myself"), we learn that the speaker's literal and metaphorical reclusiveness corresponds with the acquisition of painful knowledge and experience. It is after a period of hostility and rejection by the speaker's parents and brother, and the parents' sudden death that the speaker "came up to my stone room for good." The pun on "good," signifying both "for ever" and "for some beneficial purpose," is noteworthy. It is this introspective act which heralds the audience's voyeuristic fascination; it is her reclusiveness and apparent self-containment which, paradoxically, attracts a crowd: "Each day I attract thousands." The traumatized victim becomes the object of other people's obsessive interest, recipient of multiple "envelopes addressed to the Lady of the Hair. And so forth. Letters from the people." In this respect, the story is uncannily pre-monitory. The subject's plight anticipates Sexton's experience as the recipient of hundreds of fan letters: "The fan-mail collection [at the HRHRC] consists of thirteen folders of letters. . . . The volume averages about eighty letters per year, culminating in a deluge of one hundred sixty-nine items in 1974, the year that Sexton committed suicide" (Luedtke 166).

In section three, subtitled "The Window That Watches the Pru," we dis-cover a possible key to the speaker's incarceration, and to the public's fascina-tion with her: "I have never cut my hair. That's something you ought to know right off. It fills the room the way ten giraffes would, twisting and twisting their long, innocent necks." The hair which has never been cut, and which is the object of the speaker's own scrutiny and care—the story is punctuated by the refrain "Brush. Brush."—stands as a metaphor for personal experience. Acquired over time, carefully cultivated and, as we see later, put on public display, it signifies the confessional poem.

The allegorical relationship between poetry and hair is sustained in the lengthy central part of the story. Caring for the hair, like contemplating the self, has its own routines and rituals, it requires structure and organization, and it demands profound and sustained attention or "devotion":

> Here in my room I have my hair to care for. In the soapstone sink I wash from nine to eleven forty-five in the morning. . . . There is so much hair, so much sucked-up honey, that I must wash it in sections. The room becomes clammy like a sea cave, never dry. I am standing in my bare feet, dipping up and down over the sink probing the mystery.

Here, as in Sexton's "Memoir" poems, caring for the self/hair is figured as a process of dredging, or searching, or gleaning ("dipping up and down," "prob-ing"). Like autobiography, or confessional writing, "It is cumbersome and arduous and yet it is my work in life." Once washed, cared for, picked over, and untangled, like knotted memories, the hair is released from the window of the cupola to dry: "I let it out to dry. I let it out to give it a life of its own." The image stands, too, for the moment of release or publication of a poem when, having been exhaustively worked over, it is free to make its own way in the world.

In "The Letting Down of the Hair," the act of private self-scrutiny becomes public and ritualized:

> Over the years the people have gathered to watch it fall down and dry out. They call out, just as the clock strikes twelve: LADY! LADY! LET DOWN YOUR HAIR! I am becoming a tourist attraction and there is nothing I can do about it.

Paradoxically, in revealing herself, the speaker loses control of her self. However, the hair is only tangentially connected with the subject of self-revelation. It is a synecdoche but never the thing itself. Access to the sight of the hair is not access to the subject's experience and we are misled if we believe otherwise. The erroneous conflation of subject and text, speaker and poem, is exposed in the speaker's admission: "They often write to me. I don't answer them, of course, for my hair cannot speak and it is the hair they write to." In a 1972 letter, Sexton explains of the story: "It's really about the life of a poet and what it's like to have people like your poetry but not know you really" (*Letters* 377).

The "Lady of the Hair" has become pure spectacle: "The Gray Line bus arrives daily with a taped recording of facts—usually false—about what I do and who I am." She is the object of other people's misinterpretations: "And then there is the college crowd who seem to have adopted me." More dangerously, she is the object of other people's misplaced and unwanted devotions. Like the onlookers in Plath's "Lady Lazarus," they seek relics: "There is . . . one obese woman who comes each day and beats out with a stick at the people who reach for the hair and want to tug it. The people have become very devoted or very disgusted." Sexton, here, displaces her own alleged "devotion to poetry" onto the audience, confirming the potential interchangeability of the roles of speaker and reader, penitent and confessor.

As "The Letting Down of the Hair" nears its conclusion, we learn more about the letters from Ruth which are alluded to in the story's opening section. It is apparent that this is the Ruth of the earlier poem, "With Mercy for the Greedy." Ruth, unlike the unfamiliar correspondents who conflate text (hair) with poet ("Lady of the Hair"), understands the distinction between the two, and the special identity of each. She possesses a privileged insight into the nature and significance of the speaker's life: "Today's mail brought a letter from Ruth . . . P.S., she added, I've even discovered what your hair means. It is a parable for the life of a poet." In the final section of the story ("The Sickness Unto Death"), the speaker receives the sudden and devastat-

ing news of Ruth's death by suicide. The knowledge leaves her bereft and terminally uncertain about her own identity and status:

> The clock strikes twelve and I just stand there. It's too late now. I wanted
> to ask Ruth what my life meant. Ask her about my tent. Ask her about
> the parable. Now there is no one to ask. There are the people down
> below calling up LADY! LADY! LET DOWN YOUR HAIR! but I
> could hardly ask them.

The speaker is unable to ask her demanding and vociferous audience because
they are already possessed of a defining, consuming, and above all erroneous, perception of her identity. Thus, rather like in "Talking to Sheep" she
is reduced to silence and paralysis. "The Letting Down of the Hair" is, then,
about the impossibility of "letting down" or disappointing the audience. The
spectators expect, and benefit from, a spectacular and regular display. There
is no therapeutic gain for the speaker who is reduced merely to performing
to their order. The story depicts the terrible imperative—a public pressure,
rather than a private compulsion—to go on.

"The Letting Down of the Hair" marks a bruising realization that the
confessional audience is interested in the spectacle of the speaker's presence,
rather than what she has to say. It is the body rather than the text which is being read. This is true too of photographic images of the poet on book jackets,
as exemplified by Thomas McDonnell's comment: "Not so incidentally, by
the way, Anne Sexton is a strikingly beautiful woman, as anyone can see from
the photo on the back dust jacket of her latest volume" (43). But it is most
apparent in responses to Sexton's physical appearance on the stage. In his per-
tinently titled article, "The Anne Sexton Show," William Pritchard reports:
"She read with spellbinding intensity, to the extent that one wasn't quite sure
just what one was responding to—the poems? Or something else—the life
that was all tied up with them" (390). Muriel Rukeyser notes the dramatic
difference between the image on the stage and the voice of the text—a difference which Sexton, it may be argued, consciously exploits. Rukeyser recalls
seeing her reading at the Guggenheim Museum: "It was a beautiful woman
standing there, in a beautiful dress. The expectation and the gossip around
was one of confessional poetry." Sexton concludes her reading, however, by
admitting: "'It is not true.'" As Rukeyser comments:

When Anne Sexton said, "But it is not true," a waver went through the audience. No, I cannot say that, I can speak only for myself. I thought, "It may very well be true." She had cut through the entire nonsense about confessional writing, and returned me to the poem. (155)

The female body, then, is used as a sign. Laura Severin argues that Stevie Smith uses her own body in performance as a way of "interrogat[ing] and deconstruct[ing] cultural definitions of womanhood" (118) and although the same might be said of Sexton, it is also the case that the body as sign might be read in multiple and entirely unpredictable ways—as captivating or risible, real or fake.

In respect of the confession in particular, as the place where the private and the public most visibly collide, the body and its exposure assume a profound significance to subject and viewer alike. Peter Brooks recognizes the importance of the semiotics of the body in his study of Rousseau's *Confessions*: "Rousseau radically invades privacy—most notably his own—and gives the body an importance in the generation and inscription of meaning" (38). In particular, this is a gendered body which is received and judged in accordance with ideological notions of the ideal. John Mood's report of a performance exemplifies such a perspective: "She is flat-chested by America's inflated standards for such things. And she has that suggestion of a stomach appropriate to all Aphrodites . . . she looked like a fruitful sixteen year old virgin" (110, 116).

It is useful at this point to consider the differences between visual and textual representations, between photographic images of the subject, staged performances of her work and written confessions. As Timothy Dow Adams shows, photography has been posited as the medium by which the uncertainty of life writing, its alleged unreliability and nonreferentiality, can be disputed or disproved. Where the referent of life writing might be understood as a fabrication or chimera, the photograph as concrete image seems to represent certainty, fixity, documentary evidence upon which the structure of the autobiography may safely be assembled. Adams summarizes such views thus: "Because photographs are in a sense physical traces of actual objects, they somehow seem more referential than words" (xv). Persuasive though this is, and interesting in the way in which it interpolates into debates about the relationship between representation and referent, autobiography and experience, a number of problems remain, problems that the use of photographs and, in Sexton's case television film images, exemplify. First, does the subject of autobiography or confession stand in the same relation to the photograph as the "objects" of Adams's example? Second, what difference does the context, reading perspective, and interpretation make to the meaning of the photograph and its perceived relationship to truth? Adams highlights a distinction between the apparent referentiality of the photographic images and the nonreferentiality of language. Is it not possible that the (visual) language of the photograph is equally slippery, intransitive, and illegible? As he goes on to say "reference is not secure in either . . . interrelations between photography and autobiography demonstrate the inherent tendency in both to conceal as much as reveal" (xxi).

Sexton uses visual signs in a similar way to textual or linguistic ones, that is, as a way of exemplifying the uncertainty of truth, identity, and representation. Showing something (the self) visually is no more reliable than reporting it verbally. Both, we find, are shaped, mediated, and questionable in their relationship with subjectivity and truth. It is also the case that images are produced and read in specific cultural contexts; the parts we inscribe and play change in different circumstances, depending on our audience. This is obvious both in Sexton's writing and, for example, in the photographs of her taken in the spring and summer of 1974, first as a commission for a poetry anthology, and thereafter for Sexton's own use. As Arthur Furst, the photographer, explains, Sexton was posing with a view to her own posterity (viii–ix). In *Camera Lucida*, Roland Barthes talks about the ineluctable artificiality of photography—its apparent documentary value notwithstanding. He describes the moment in which the image is captured: "I pose, I know I am posing, I want you to know that I am posing. . . . I constitute myself in the process of 'posing,' I instantaneously make another body for myself" (10). Furst similarly comments on the self-conscious sexuality of Sexton's poses: "Anne was provocative and sexy, using all of her posing skills from her days as a model" (ix). He recollects that his first encounter with Sexton was through the well-known Gwendolyn Stewart photograph of Sexton in a long black and white dress: "smiling, sitting, her legs crossed, her hands gesturing upward with a cigarette in her fingers. She was sexual, tanned, beautiful" (vii). This particular photograph, commissioned for the cover of *The Death Notebooks* but not used because its editor thought it looked "too revealing" (Stewart), has been read in a similar way by Elizabeth Wurtzel who calls it "glorious and alive," although she proceeds to draw attention to the strained posture and motifs it displays: "The poet is shown twisted into place, her legs tightly crossed, her feet in white shoes with a crisscross buckle" (178–79). The photographer herself points to a dichotomy in the image whereby in the top half of the picture, Sexton looks radiant and alive, and in the bottom half with her "legs torturously twisted together" she seems fraught and pained (Stewart).

This paradox whereby the woman poet is both liberated and restrained, free and under control surfaces again in the television film of Sexton, made in 1966 for National Educational Television and shot in her suburban home. Here she constitutes herself in different roles in successive scenes: poet, madwoman, mom. Each time, there is a tension and uncertainty which suggests that this is a terrible pretense which must be sustained. The original film is lost, but what remains is an extensive sequence of outtakes which give some idea of the shape and tone of the original. Sexton's performance here is artful and mannered, and the production is carefully staged and framed. The film opens with a lingering shot of Sexton's mantelpiece. Framed photographs of Sexton and her two daughters stand, like bookends, at either end of the mantelshelf, implicitly referencing the central dual metaphors of Sexton's long poems "The Double Image" and "A Little Uncomplicated Hymn." There is neither voice nor human presence in the long opening shots, we merely share the camera's eye view of the scene—of the room, the photographs, the desk with typewriter, the artfully displayed copies of books, journals, and a folder of worksheets, seen in closeup, and strategically opened to show the typescript of "Wanting to Die." We are thus placed in the role of intruders or voyeurs, stealthily creeping around someone else's private space in an unsettling way which metaphorically replicates our role as voyeurs of and intruders into the private mind of the poet. A part of us feels unsettled by our own presence; we are not sure whether we should be here at all.

Sexton displays a mannered informality which is part professional and part chaotic, responding to questions, pausing for a beer, dropping an earring, riffling through her papers. She reads from and comments on a number of poems, first feigning not being able to find the worksheets of "Live" and then being persuaded to read "Some Foreign Letters," a poem which as we have seen, she claims is too painful to read aloud. Between reading and replying to questions from the interviewer, we see her taking a break with her children. Donning winter coats they move out into the garden, perching precariously—and in Sexton's case, unconvincingly—on a pile of boulders on the lawn (Sexton mutters to her daughter "first time I've been on the rock"). Again, the viewer's sense of voyeuristic intrusiveness is emphasized by the staging; our attention is both solicited and repelled. The camera concentrates resolutely on Sexton, struggling sometimes to stay in focus, and the sound, particularly in the distant shots of Sexton on the boulders, is muffled and barely audible but intrusive enough to demand our careful attention. At times, Sexton manipulates these circumstances, dramatically whispering to her daughter in such a way as both to show us that there is something important that we must want to hear, and ensuring precisely that we cannot. There is a parallel here with the way in which confession works—particularly if we think of it as a form of screen discourse—a mode which seems to reveal all, but in fact shows only a superficial or misleading surface image.

Finally in the film in a supreme, and rather troubling double-bluff, Sexton returns into the house with her daughters. She seems delighted at having reached the end of the performance (as she jumps down from the rock, she declares to camera "here endeth the little scene") and relieved to have carried it off. Perhaps she protests too much; entering the house she nestles up to her daughter and exclaims: "Are we fake? Are we fake? Tell them we're fake.... It's so easy to be natural, when you've got this. I mean that's for real!" Manifestly, the scene has been artfully constructed. The daughters' discomfort, whether with being filmed or with their mother's displays of affection, or both, is almost palpable. Sexton's participation in the film, as in Arthur Furst's photography session, is profoundly self-conscious. Her role bears comparison with Cindy Sherman's artful and staged self-portraits. Paul Jay's point about Sherman's work stands also, surely, for Sexton's: "Like an autobiographical metanarrative about the course of the artist's investigation of subjectivity [they scrutinize] the very concepts of identity and subjectivity in a way that turns that act into a memoir of itself" (199).

Sexton's performances or readings of her work are equally self-reflexive. In a letter of 7 February 1973 in which Sexton cancels a speaking engagement, she explains her increasing reluctance to perform her work on the stage: "I have given up readings. They are a kind of blood letting for me. They make me feel as though I were dancing in the combat zone (if you know what that is) naked in Boston" (HRHRC). The combination of physical, sexual, and religious metaphors here strikes at the heart of the dynamics of confession. Confessional performance is both an entertainment and an act of violence, self-willed and forced, a celebratory gesture of defiance ("dancing") and a sign of vulnerability and victimization ("the combat zone" or red-light district).

Sexton's assimilation of the rhetoric of nakedness and sexual display acknowledges while it rejects, or at the very least problematizes, orthodox criticism of the exploitative and self-revelatory nature of confessional poetry. Jane McCabe laments, "Sexton's flirtatious parading, her glamorous posing, her sexual exhibitionism" (216–17) and Donald Davie, in his response to Al Alvarez's "Beyond All This Fiddle," alleges that confessional poets are "self-hating stripteasers" (472). Donald Hall regrets that "what began as a series of excruciating self-discoveries . . . dissipates in an orgy of exhibitionism" (33). However, it must be said—and this, surely, is the point of Sexton's metaphor of "dancing naked in the combat zone"—that such "exhibitionism" presupposes an observer. Without an audience there is no display, without a witness, there is no spectacle, and, by extension, without a punter there is no stripper. Peter Brooks suggests that privacy and the gaze are inextricably connected: "We know privacy by way of its invasion" (37–38). It may also be argued, of course, that where the gaze is invited, there can be no "invasion" or perhaps, only a masochistic act of self-invasion.

As much of this rhetoric will indicate, confession and particularly the performance of the poems, and more particularly still performance by a woman writer, becomes a form of sexual commerce or commodification, or a "one night stand" (*Letters* 304). The body is offered, read, and finally sold. Sexton herself uses such metaphors repeatedly. In an unpublished autobiographical sketch dated June 1965 she explains: "To begin with, I think it is a kind of prostitution . . . for the poet to try to tell how or why he might be distinctive" (HRHRC).[4] In a 21 October 1965 letter to Elizabeth Bishop, she complains about a forthcoming ten-day reading tour, describing herself as "rather like a whore, I think." Ironically, the justification which Sexton offers for this self-prostitution is that she needs the money: "And yet money drives me—and in the end the 'reading' is a gastly [*sic*] sort of show—an act such as a comedian has. So next Monday I go on the road with my act" (HRHRC). The speaker needs satisfaction from her audience to the same degree as they seek fulfillment from her. In her *Paris Review* interview, Sexton describes, here in contradiction to the antipathy she expresses elsewhere, some of the personal satisfaction—indeed the physical rewards—of public performance: "Then there is the love. . . When there is a coupling of the audience and myself, when they are really with me, and the Muse is with me, I'm not coming alone" (Kevles 334–35). Thus the performance is neither a narcissistic (masturbatory) indulgence nor a one-sided exploitation, but rather a relationship of mutual pleasure.

The metaphor of "blood letting" in the February 1973 letter quoted above encapsulates the visceral nature of confession and, as such, has much in common with the scatological metaphors seen in previous chapters. The image figures repeatedly in Sexton's work. In the "Big Heart" she writes: "The artery of my soul has been severed / and soul is spurting out upon them," and in "The Author of the Jesus Papers Speaks" which recalls a dream about milking a cow: "Blood spurted from it / and covered me with shame." In seminars and interviews, Sexton explains that the poet "spurts images" (Sexton and Kumin seminar) and "dig[s] right into the heart and let[s] it spurt out" (Balliro 13). Gregory Orr notes the use of a similar image in Walt Whitman's "Trickle Drop," a poem which he suggests is at the root of modern confessional writing (651). The metaphor is resonant in a number of ways. It implies, as Brooks argues of Rousseau, that it is the body rather than the mind which signifies or speaks. It draws on an important image from Dante's *Inferno* (an influential text for Sexton) wherein the suicides, or "the violent against themselves," can speak only through the body: "Only through their own blood do they find voice" (112). And it plays on common (mis)perceptions of confessional poetry as some kind of "release," as a way of tapping or leeching a febrile source.

Most importantly, Sexton's comparison of poetry readings with "a kind of blood letting" signifies religious martyrdom. Hers is a gesture simultaneously of self-aggrandizement (I'm like Christ) and self-abnegation (This is only "a kind of blood-letting"). In both cases there is an implied audience which is asked to witness the act of suffering that is performed for its ultimate benefit. In her *Paris Review* interview, Sexton makes explicit the comparison between Christ's "performance" and her own. She explains: "That ragged Christ, that sufferer, performed the greatest act of confession, and I mean with his body. And I try to do that with words" (Kevles 334–35). Here, identity is created in the very act of being offered up. In contradiction to Christ's joyous martyrdom, however, Sexton complains in her "Journal of a Living Experiment" that "When you write you wait three years and then they crucify you" (HRHRC).

"The Passion of the Mad Rabbit," written in April 1974, makes a similar point. The poem opens with a dramatic pastiche of confessional self-exposure: "I underwent a removal, tearing my skin off me." Liberated by this self-efface-ment, the speaker is free to assume a new persona—the nonsensical guise of

"Mr. Rabbit": "A fool walked straight into me. / He was named Mr. Rabbit." Thereafter the poem parodies the martyrdom of this fool. Hers is a negation, in every respect, of Christ's glorious Passion. In the second stanza, we find that the "Good Friday" of the Gospels has been transformed into "Bad Friday." The dignity demanded by the occasion is travestied in a sequence of bathetic images and bizarre juxtapositions:

> Next it was bad Friday and they nailed me up
> like a scarecrow and many gathered eating popcorn, carrying
> hymnals or balloons.

The audience's complicity is rendered explicit in the performance of this spectacle. When the speaker declares that she is crazy, we find that "Some giggled and some knelt." Thus Sexton dramatizes, and indeed makes part of the act, the simultaneous fascination and mockery which typify responses to confessional writing.

In the poem's final, nonsensical scene, the religious and the secular are brought together as the confessional speaker, playing the role of the spiritual martyr, is handed Easter eggs—the pagan symbols of a religious festival. Thereafter she is committed to the flames, singing as she goes:

> My blood came to a boil as I looked down the throat of madness,
> but singing yellow egg, blue egg, pink egg, red egg, green egg,
> *Hallelujah*, to each hard-boiled-colored egg.

Finally, in "The Passion," comes the humiliating realization, marked by the sudden, quiet change to a whisper, that the whole spectacle has been just that: a "little vaudeville act" (*Letters* 304) or a "shamfull [*sic*] display" as Sexton puts it in a 24 September 1965 letter:

> In place of the Lord,
> I whispered,
> a fool has risen.
>   (HRHRC)

From glorification and adoration to mockery and punishment, the trajectory of the confessional poet is encapsulated here. The metaphor of the "fool" anticipates comments which Sexton made in the last poetry workshop which she taught at Boston University just two days before her death:

I have to play the fool. . . . I mean I have to let myself be a fool, and say any damn thing that, you know, appears and blurt it out. . . . That's the hardest thing: to be a fool. You can be anything; you can be stinking, no good, a rotten poet—but to be a fool—nobody wants to be a fool. (Qtd. in Williams, "Sexton" 101)

Sexton's ambivalence about public performance which is realized in self-deprecating references to self as "a little bit of a ham" and to readings as "some sort of racket" (*Letters* 163, 72) finally emerges in her bitter condemnation of what she terms "The Freak Show." Her essay of this title was first published in the *American Poetry Review* in 1973 and was written, according to the editors of Sexton's *Letters*, as a direct response to a "traumatic" reading which Sexton had given earlier that year (397). However, the essay should be read as the culmination of a longstanding anxiety about the spectacular, theatrical, and finally exploitative nature of confession, and as an expression of Sexton's unease with the lascivious and predatory tendencies of the audience. As early as 1962, she can be seen disparaging the nature and purpose of poetry readings: "Readings are a show. Read all around now . . . big show . . . rather depressing. . . . I now make (if you can stand this) 250 bucks a reading plus expenses. Kee rist !!!" (*Letters* 150). In a 1968 interview, Sexton replies to a question about poetry readings: "It takes three weeks out of your life. A week before it happens, the nervousness begins and it builds up the night of the reading, when the poet in you changes into a performer" (Kevles 109). In this interview, and in the opening paragraph of "The Freak Show" ("I asked such preposterous sums that I gave fewer readings than most poets do"), it is the commercial nature of the operation which is foregrounded. The spectators pay money to see her, and she gives them a little part of herself in return. The confessional poet is thus a commodity or object of exchange. This is an exploitative situation (hence her use of metaphors of prostitution) and, as is the case with prostitution, it is sometimes arguable who is exploiting whom. Further, notwithstanding Sexton's declared reluctance, she continued to give readings. Thus we must ask whether the posture of angry, wronged, misunderstood poet is not merely another persona—another dramatic role used to entice sympathy, appreciation, and attention.

"The Freak Show" opens with a subtle allusion to an earlier poem, "Making a Living" (1971). In "Making a Living," Sexton's speaker compares the plight of the confessional poet to that of the biblical character, Jonah:

Jonah made his living
inside the belly
Mine comes from the exact same place.

Jonah, like the speaker of "The Letting Down of the Hair" and the confessional poet, gains his insights from introspection. In putting himself on display, though, he compromises his right to privacy:

Jonah opened the door of his stateroom
and said, "Here I am!" and the whale liked this
and thought to take him in.

Caught in the whale's/audience's grasp, the subject's response is to perform according to its expectations, to attempt appeasement by acting out the confessional role. Thus, in the third stanza, Jonah interrogates his familial origins, strips off his clothes (metaphorically, peels back the layers to reveal his naked self), and scrutinizes his fate for financial gain. "This is my death" he proclaims, "and it will profit me to understand it."

Crucially, if paradoxically, it is this naked revelation which leads to the speaker's rejection by his audience. Jonah's performance renders him unpalatable: "At this point the whale / vomited him back out into the sea." His self-exposure is poison or anathema to his host—notwithstanding that it is this self-revelation ("Here I am!") which first attracted the whale to him. In "Live," Sexton explicitly complains about the antipathy of her audience to the revelations in her work, revelations which must, surely, come as little surprise:

People don't like to be told
that you're sick
and then be forced
to watch
you
come
down with the hammer.

Yet in "Making a Living," even the experience of vulnerability and rejection is grist to the mill for the confessional poet/Jonah. Neither can help but turn experience to account—in the figurative and in the commercial sense, recalling once again the line "it will profit me to understand it" in stanza four: "Then he told the news media / The strange details of his death." Yet ultimately, the subject's manipulation of the media/audience turns into his exploitation by them.[5] The subject becomes their object:

And they hammered him up in the marketplace
and sold him and sold him and sold him.
My death the same.

The audience which creates the "story" also assumes the power to bring it to an end. Implicit in these insistent repetitions ("sold him and sold him and sold him") is the three-times betrayal of Christ by Peter. What these lines also suggest is that there is no real closure in confession. Each confession is accompanied by some para- or extratextual experience or commentary. After the confessional "event," there are perpetual repercussions which sustain the confession, seemingly endlessly. The penitent is not permitted to walk away from the confession for, having shared it, he or she becomes the object of everyone else's hermeneutic endeavors.

"The Freak Show" draws on and develops the insights of "Making a Living." The essay begins: "One way poets make a living, make it by their own wits . . . is by giving readings." The essay is dramatic and thus, perhaps, deceptive in its description of Sexton's sudden rejection of this way of life: "On January 4, 1973, I stopped giving readings, and believe me, I needed the money." Indeed, and this is a point to which I shall return, the stance of victim adopted in the essay is as much a performance as the poetry readings which are its ostensible subject. The poet, Mona Van Duyn, indicates as much in a letter to the *American Poetry Review*, in which she complains about Sexton's article. She objects to Sexton's dramatization of her plight, and to her presentation of herself as a martyr to "the public's cruel and insatiable demand": "When some of us must give up readings, temporarily or permanently, we do so without regarding this as a tragic deprivation to the world" (39–40).[6]

Sexton's rhetorical flourish is continued in the second paragraph, where she asks: "What's in it for the poet? Money, applause, adulation, . . . an audience," before cynically remarking: "Don't kid yourself." Sexton implies that there is, in fact, nothing in it for the poet, and that the advantages are all to the audience:

You are the freak. You are the actor, the clown, the oddball. Some people come to see what you look like, what you have on, what your voice sounds like. Some people secretly hope your voice will tremble (that gives an extra kick). Some people hope you will do something audacious; in other words (and I admit to my greatest fears) that you vomit on the stage or go blind, hysterically blind or actually blind.

Sexton again makes her point by dramatizing it, illustrating her argument by reference to imagined theatrical or spectacular events. "Once," she declares, in suspenseful, storytelling mode, "I cried after I read a poem." She continues: "I had never read this poem before an audience and I had no idea it would move me so. I was embarrassed to cry. I had to go off stage and get my pocketbook, which had a Kleenex in it, so that I might blow my nose." This revelation of distress and embarrassment is merely an attenuation or repetition ("and sold him and sold him and sold him") of the confessional moment. As I have suggested, the apparently genuine and pitiable revelation is itself an act, a dramatic play for sympathy. For, some ten years earlier Sexton had offered as a measure of a strong poem precisely this capacity to move the speaker/performer to tears:

> The final test of a poem often comes during a public reading. I have almost always read this poem during a "reading" and yet its impact upon me remains strong and utterly personal. I get caught up in it all over again. By the time I get to the last verse my voice begins to break.... Because "Some Foreign Letters" still puts a lump in my throat, I know that it is my unconscious favorite. ("Comment" 17)

Sexton complains that people have willingly witnessed the spectacle of her emotional response to a poem. Yet it is arguable that this emotional response has been knowingly performed or offered up to the audience (tears are delivered on cue, as though from a script); first, by the repeated reading of a poem which is calculated to achieve certain effects, and second, by this essay's dramatic representation of the original trauma. There is a further level of performance within the article in that Sexton relates the story of her lecture agency's cynical dramatization and promotion of her stage reputation. In order to ensure further interest in her work, they speak "proudly of my presentation to their clients thusly: 'It's a great show! Really a pow! She cries every time right on stage!'" Sexton complains of her lecture agency that they "exploit your soul" and, more generally, that "somehow in this poetry biz, as one of my students calls it, we are asked to make a show of it." This, although persuasive in its confirmation of the commodification of experience, is disingenuous given that the exploitation is mutual. Mona Van Duyn makes a similar point, arguing that "most of us do not hire agents to sell us as performers, but if we did we would not publicly profess, as Ms. Sexton does, horror and shock at our agent's praise of us as performers" (40).

Sexton concedes, though, that there is some attraction in the spectacle of the "famous" poet reading, or, more specifically, in the famous poet spectacularly failing. As she admits:

> I remember being a fledgling poet and going to hear the famous poets read.... There was a sneaky, unconscious underground part of me that wanted the poet to be a little weird.... We want the big names to act a little alien, a little crazy.

The metaphor of acting ("to act a little alien") indicates an understanding that what we see is ineluctably a performance or masquerade. Maintaining the role of awestruck, "fledgling poet," Sexton recalls an anecdote about an Auden reading: "I have also been told of W. H. Auden coming on stage absent mindedly in his carpet slippers." Yet this anecdote, reported at one remove, is itself a masquerade, a dramatic reinterpretation of events calculated to achieve particular effects. It attempts modestly and misleadingly to distinguish between vulnerable, exploited "I" and the "famous poets" about whom she claims only tangential knowledge. In fact, Sexton had had direct and less benign experience of seeing Auden read. In 1967, as Sexton's then biographer and companion reports, Sexton was scheduled to appear at the same event as Auden:

> At the International Poetry Festival in London, she stood up to W. H. Auden and WON! It was a cut-throat evening. Poets from the world over competed for two minutes of reading time: ... Mr. Auden sent an emissary to Ms. Sexton. Auden, in his wrinkles and carpet slippers, held the honored anchor-end of the evening. Mr. Auden requested that Ms. Sexton cut short her reading of "The Double Image" so that Mr. Auden might be at home at 10.00 p.m. as was his custom. Ms. Sexton sent back word that she would be pleased to assist Mr. Auden by exchanging places on the program so that Mr. Auden could be at home

according to his custom. Mr. Auden left for home at 10.45 p.m. (Ames, "Remembering" 113)[7]

Clearly, it does not suit the thrust of Sexton's argument in "The Freak Show" to confess to such eagerness to read in public. Neither does it suit her presentation of herself as vulnerable and innocent party to reveal the assertiveness evidenced in her dealings with Auden. Moreover, in reiterating the image of Auden as carpet-slippered eccentric, Sexton may be said to be collaborating in the same kind of voyeuristic stereotyping (Auden always wears slippers) as she attacks in respect of popular images of herself (Sexton always cries).

Sexton's "script" is interesting because of the way in which it draws on, and indeed enters into a dramatic dialogue with, Auden's 1963 poem "On the Circuit." "The Freak Show" is an ironic and calculated interpretation of Auden's poem, modestly claiming dissociation, while modeling itself on, and subtly reinforcing the similarity of, their experiences. "On the Circuit," like "The Freak Show," begins with the poet/performer flying toward the destination for the reading and contemplating his imminent fate. Auden's speaker, like Sexton's, figures himself as the vulnerable victim of his lecture agency, "predestined" to fulfill their "unfathomable will." Auden uses similar religious idiom to Sexton. His management's "unfathomable will" is a pastiche of the will of God. So too, his poetry is described as "my gospel of the Muse," although unlike God, he is allowed no day of rest (he travels "daily, seven days a week"). For Auden, as for Sexton, the reading tour will be unmemorable:

> Unless some singular event
> Should intervene to save the place,
> A truly asinine remark,
> A soul-bewitching face.

Here, encapsulated, are all of the events which form the subject of "The Freak Show": the singular event (the disaster of the precisely evoked "January 4, 1973" reading), the "truly asinine remark" (Sexton complains about audiences who call out "Whatever you do, Annie, baby, we're with you"), and the "soul-bewitching face." The single redeeming element of Sexton's disastrous "final" reading is the presence of "an understanding sister," the sympathetic professor, Janet Beeler. Sexton, like Auden, finds the domestic arrangements for such trips "utter hell." She complains about the "badly burned hamburger" she was served in "the student bistro, a barn-like place, our table on top of a hot but fake fireplace" where she had to shout to be heard. The description replicates Auden's distaste for

> The radio in students' cars,
> Muzac at breakfast, or—dear God!—
> Girl-organists in bars.

More importantly, Auden expresses a sardonic anxiety about the availability of alcohol: "*What will there be to drink?*" This is a concern which Sexton foregrounds, admitting that on the occasion of her fateful last reading she "guzzled down the double vodkas. . . . I was drinking too fast and I was scared." Elsewhere, in making arrangements for readings, Sexton is precise about her needs. In a letter of 22 May 1974 she insists: "I have only one requirement and that is the need for a lot of vodka (don't bother with such niceties as limes, tonic water, etc.)" (HRHRC). Auden and Sexton are not alone in privileging alcohol as a cause for concern. As Lori Rotskoff has shown, alcohol consumption in post–World War II America was at the heart of changing notions of public and private life. It had contradictory significations, suggesting on the one hand a healthy social conformism and on the other a dangerously pathological corruption: "Alcoholism, understood as pathology, came to represent a host of other anxieties and problems permeating mid-twentieth-century social and cultural life" (211).

Sexton's choice of the title "The Freak Show," and the reference within the article to the poet as "freak," as "*nothing* but the freak," and as "a kind of expensive freak" anticipates the idiom of criticism directed towards present-day confessional talk shows (*The Oprah Winfrey Show* and *The Jerry Springer Show*, for example). Jane Shattuc notes the "outcry against the new talk shows as 'freak shows,' 'geek shows,' or, in the words of the *New York Post*, 'sicko circuses.'" She quotes a talk-show guest who "likens the shows to the nineteenth-century freak-show circuses but declares: 'What's different now is that we, as freaks, are doing the speaking. It isn't the barker telling our story for us'" (140, 93).

This, surely, is the point to be made about Sexton's article. Indeed, it constitutes one of the paradoxes and anxieties inherent in it and in confessional performance more generally. The "freak"/performer is complicit in, even solicits, her own exploitation. Like Jonah, she proclaims, "Here I am!" Her complaint about confessional performance is simply a sequel, a further confessional performance inviting the exact same voyeuristic attention as the original. "Look at me," Sexton declares, look at me suffering as people look at me—a mise-en-abyme—which sees her locked in the endlessly reflecting mirrors of the confessional role.

PART 3

*

True words

6

Language

"Language fails," writes Sexton: "Oh! There is no translating"; "no language is perfect"; "be careful of words"; "the words aren't good enough."[1] As these comments indicate, Sexton's is a poetry which is deeply and persistently exercised by the problem of language. Yet hers is also a poetics which is predicated on exploring "the possibilities of the word," one which boldly declares, "I am in love with words."[2] Her writing is engaged in an act of attrition and / or courtship with a language which is not a passive medium or vehicle for the expression of prelinguistic emotion but is autonomous, material, and elusive, and demands scrutiny in its own right. This interest in language is sustained throughout Sexton's writing: from the early and unpublished poem "The Thought Disease," which contemplates the concrete properties of language, to the sporadic sequence "Letters to Dr. Y.," which problematizes discursive linguistic practices, such as "the talking cure," to the fairy-tale poems of *Transformations*, which indicate the potential fictionality of language. Sexton's preoccupation is apparent, finally, in the late poems of *The Awful Rowing Toward God* (prepared for publication by Sexton, but appearing posthumously in 1975), which foreground the heterogeneity of language. As she explains in her penultimate Crawshaw lecture, what motivated her to start writing was not any compulsion to confess, but rather a "strange unconscious excitement over words" (Crawshaw [9]).

Poems such as these are challenging to the reader. They are characterized by apparent incomprehensibility, frustrating aporias, an irreducibility to coherence, and a general resistance to being rendered (in the sense both of being "represented" and "reduced") in accordance with the paradigmatic concerns of confessionalism. This is particularly true of the later poems (for example, those in *The Awful Rowing Toward God*), which have tended to be regarded as afterthoughts or aberrations, as atypical of Sexton's poetry, and even as unworthy of publication. As Kate Green comments, They seem "inaccessible . . . closed, like a code though full of energy. The language emanates from an inner place that stammers and does not articulate" (376–77). In short, these poems seem to give us no clues, their code remains uncracked, the key is hidden. Yet this, I will argue, represents their fascination. Far from being "inaccessible," they give us access to the condition of language as Sexton finds it. Our own inability to comprehend the language simply replicates hers. The difficulty of the late poems is a symptom and self-conscious exemplification of one of her main subjects—the profound impossibilities of the word.

A critical reluctance actively to consider the language of Sexton's poetry may, in part, be explained by the general historical tendency to read confessional poetry for its subject matter rather than its form—for "what the poet has to say" rather than "how he says it," as Robert Phillips puts it (xiii–xiv). As we saw in part one, the language of confessional poetry is regarded as passive, transitive, and mimetic, as simultaneously expressive and referential. Yet it is clear from Sexton's work that there are no such certainties. Language is rarely, if ever, accurate or transparent, but rather, as psychoanalysis has shown, is characterized by strategies of displacement and condensation and fraught with ambiguity and contradiction.

Such a persistent and quizzical concern with language has precedents, for example, in the work of Gertrude Stein, William Carlos Williams, and Wallace Stevens. Confessional poetry's debt to such forebears has been recognized by a diverse range of critics, from Kenneth Rexroth and Peter Brooker to Marjorie Perloff. Rexroth identifies in "almost all the poets of this generation . . . from Anne Sexton to Ed Sanders" a "reaffirmation of the anti-literary, no-nonsense aesthetic that goes back to Imagism and Literary Cubism" (67). Brooker cites Charles Olson's influence in reorienting the American poetic tradition away from European aesthetics and "along the axis of Ezra Pound—William Carlos Williams—Louis Zukofsky" (7–8) while Perloff proposes "a family tree that goes [from Pound] by way of Williams to Black Mountain, the Objectivists, and the confessional poets" (*Poetic* 121). Certainly the significance of this lineage merits scrutiny and offers a fruitful way of understanding Sexton's sense of the material and aural qualities of poetic language. It would be wrong, however, to dissociate Sexton's poetics from the concerns of literary high modernism or to suggest, as Gregory Orr does, that she rejects high modernism's "grand and inhuman schemes" (652). As this chapter will show, Sexton learns from both the American experimental model identified above and from the hugely influential work of T. S. Eliot, referencing his work numerous times, and constructing—in the image of *The Waste Land*—her own "grand . . . scheme," "Hurry Up Please It's Time."

Sexton's unpublished 1960 poem "The Thought Disease" toys with the same kinds of concerns as had exercised Stein, Williams, and Stevens.[3] The title itself tacitly invokes Williams's point, made in "A Sort of a Song" and "Paterson," that there are (or should be) "no ideas / but in things." It posits that immediacy of perception is preferable to the "disease" of contemplative thought. Thus, it also brings to mind the search in Wallace Stevens's "An Ordinary Evening in New Haven" for

> The poem of pure reality, untouched
> By trope or deviation, straight to the word,
> Straight to the transfixing object.

As Sexton avers in the 29 September 1967 entry in her "Journal of a Living Experiment," "It's the most important part of writing . . . being concrete, being specific."

"The Thought Disease" contemplates the physical properties of language, here represented by the alphabetical symbols on the typewriter. In this respect, Sexton may be said to go one stage further than Stein who, as William Carlos Williams describes it, has "gone systematically to work smashing every connotation that words have ever had, in order to get them back clean" (*Selected* 163). The poem breaks language down, not simply into words and sounds, but into its individual component letters and, thereafter, proceeds to play with the multiple possibilities which each discrete letter suggests:

> Taking them separately, I see the legs
> of children, pigs, chickens, a bald head,
> boards to walk over, sticks bent by hands.

Sexton, like Pound, is interested in the possibilities of the ideogram. The signification of the letters of the alphabet is to be understood pictorially rather than semantically. The poem contemplates the resonance of a selection of letters in turn (beginning with "a, you are a world of your own / with an umbrella over your head"), each time addressing their concrete, physical properties rather than their linguistic suggestiveness (although elsewhere, Sexton describes language as concrete and aural: "A poem is spoken. A poem has to be spoken. I like it on the page, I like to see the stops of the lines" [Packard 47]). In lines which subtly allude to the interest in palindromes and mirror images evident elsewhere in Sexton's work, the poem explains: "b and d is a fat [pudgy] nine month old baby / looking [sitting] in front of a mirror." Finally, and significantly, given the anxiety which Sexton expresses in other poems about the commercialization of poetry and the commodification of language, the poem contemplates "s": "that snake, that swan, / with a knife you are money." In other words, with a strike or line through its heart, "s" is physically transformed into the dollar sign ($). "The Thought Disease," like the other poems I discuss in this chapter, is difficult to assimilate within conventional confessional frameworks. It might best be read with an eye to the insights of modernism; that is, by attending to its allusiveness, its tensions, and its wit.

This is evident, too, in Sexton's "Hurry Up Please It's Time," which takes its title from, indeed writes back to, Eliot's *The Waste Land*. Sexton works in a mode ostensibly poles apart from the impersonalism of Eliot's aesthetic. However, there is evidence in her writing (for example in "Sweeney," "Gods," and even in "A Little Uncomplicated Hymn," discussed in the next chapter, with its Prufrockian exemplification of the impossibility of saying just what it means) of sustained engagement with his work.

"Hurry Up Please It's Time" was written in 1972 and published in the 1974 *The Death Notebooks*. The poem is divided into six sections of varying lengths, against *The Waste Land*'s five, as though to claim the last word in a critical dialogue. It makes sophisticated and purposive use of multiple personae, self-reflexively contemplates questions about memory, language, and subjectivity and juxtaposes private introspection and public display. It dramatizes an urgent quest not for an answer to the questions posed in the opening lines ("What is death, I ask. / What is life, you ask") but for an appropriate discourse in which to contemplate them. The idiom changes repeatedly throughout the poem: from the simple and childlike (the appeal to the mother in section four, and the nursery rhyme rhythms and allusions throughout) to the learned and contemplative ("learning to talk is a complex business"). The narration shifts tenses, moving from the present ("This is the rainy season") to the past ("Once upon a time we were all born") to anticipation of the future ("One noon as you walk out to the mailbox / He'll snatch you up"). The many different voices of the poem are shifting and elusive. They oscillate between the interrogatory and the declamatory, the defensive and the assertive, the reverential ("Forgive us, Father, for we know not") and the irreverent ("I am God, la de dah"). The poem is allusive, combining the popular, the contemporary, the emphatically, and purposefully American (as, for example, in section two: "Peanut butter is the American food / We all eat it, being patriotic") with the mythological, spiritual, and transcendent.

The first two lines foreground the dialogic or discursive nature of confessional poetry; the fact that, for the confession to be realized, there must be an "I" and a "you," a penitent and a confessor. These lines also make explicit the concerns about the meaning of life and death which remain implicit in Eliot's poem: "What is death, I ask. / What is life, you ask." The insistence and juxtaposition of the opening antitheses ("death" and "life") invite us to anticipate a further one. We expect to find the verb "ask" completed with "answer" ("What is death, I ask. / What is life, you answer"), and we are disconcerted when we realize—particularly at such an early stage—that there may not be any answers. This introduces a primary uncertainty, one which persists throughout and even motivates the whole poem. It dispels any confidence which we might have in the power of poetry, or language, to convey meaning.

Sexton's poem gestures repeatedly to Eliot's. An important point of connection is the tacit allusion to the Sibyl of Cumae (the subject of the epigraph to *The Waste Land*). Eliot's epigraph derives from the mythological story of the Sibyl of Ovid's *Metamorphoses* who, granted a wish by Apollo, asked for prolonged life, but neglected to ask for continued youthfulness. Eliot quotes a witness of the Sibyl's plight: "For indeed I myself have seen, with my own eyes, the Sibyl hanging in a bottle at Cumae, and when those boys would say to her: 'Sibyl, what do you want?' she replied, 'I want to die'" (Ferguson 1236 n. 9). Sexton's speaker's insistent opening question, "What is death?" evidences a preoccupation with death rather than an interest in life and thus, places her firmly on the side of the Sibyl; she assumes her voice, her longing for annihilation. Like her, she is caught and objectified by the gaze of her audience and resorts to what seems to be the only comprehensible language—the language of the body:

> I give them both my buttocks,
> my two wheels rolling off toward Nirvana.
> They are as neat as a wallet,
> opening and closing on their coins,

the quarters, the nickels,
straight into the crapper.

The rhetoric of tne poem becomes defensive here, as though anticipating criticism of such self-display and testing the limits of confessional discourse. How far can the speaker go before the audience ("executioner"/Eliot?) tires of her?

Why shouldn't I pull down my pants
and moon at the executioner
as well as paste raisins on my breasts?
Why shouldn't I pull down my pants
and show my little cunny to Tom
and Albert? They wee-wee funny.
I wee-wee like a squaw.
I have ink but no pen.

The repetition of "Why shouldn't I" in lines nine and twelve indicates that the speaker is aware of her transgression, that she is testing the boundaries of what is acceptable for women, especially for women writers (hence "ink" and "pen"). The scatological imagery ("wee-wee") indicates, among other things, the speaker's own ambivalence about her writing, an ambivalence perhaps born of the incorporation of others' repeated condemnation. Notwithstanding the lack (absence, and also loss, in the Lacanian sense) of the penis or power, the speaker still wishes, in a supreme effort of will and physical energy, to make her mark or to retaliate against the regime which would leave her pen(is)-less: "Still / I dream that I can piss in God's eye."

The shifting, and thus foregrounding, of gender ("I dream I'm a boy") and, most importantly, the allusion in the section quoted above to the "raisins" and the "breasts" invoke two other figures from Eliot's poem. First, Mr. Eugenides ("unshaven, with a pocket full of currants") and, thereafter, Tiresias ("old man" with "wrinkled female breasts," whose presence immediately succeeds Mr. Eugenides's in Eliot's poem). In "Hurry Up Please," Sexton's speaker, like Tiresias, experiments with these different gender positions. She exploits archetypal metaphors for women's (personal) and men's (impersonal) writing. Yet this is only in order to draw attention, by contrast, to what unites the sexes:

I have swallowed an orange, being woman.
You have swallowed a ruler, being man.
Yet waiting to die we are the same thing.

Section five of the poem confronts a fundamental question for confessionalism: How can personal, individual experience be brought to bear? How can it be made meaningful in the public world? Conversely, it asks how ordinary, shared, communal life can continue in the face of private suffering. The reproduction of the species ("People copulate / entering each other's blood") and the maintenance of routine function, it is suggested, as a panacea or strategy of displacement in order to ensure that the public is distracted from the terrifying vulnerability of the individual:

It doesn't matter if there are wars,
the business of life continues
unless you're the one that gets it.

Notwithstanding this personal—and also political—crisis, the poem insists that everyday life can and must continue. There are shades here of Sexton's "To a Friend Whose Work Has Come to Triumph," itself a contemplation of Auden's "Musée des Beaux Arts," where suffering "takes place / While someone else is eating or opening a window or just walking dully along."

Sexton's subject in "Hurry Up Please" is, as the poem reaches its climax, still seeking an answer. This represents a triumph of hope over experience, given the rebuttal of the poem's opening lines. At the end of the penultimate section:

Ms. Dog stands on the shore
and the sea keeps rocking in
and she wants to talk to God.

Her position replicates that of Eliot's speaker in *The Waste Land*:

I sat upon the shore
Fishing, with the arid plain behind me
Shall I at least set my lands in order?

However, the increasing urgency of Ms. Dog's quest is signified by her "stand[ing] on the shore" while Eliot's speaker sits, and by her determination (she "wants") while Eliot's speaker exhibits only passive hesitancy ("shall I?").

The sixth and final section attempts to bring together the multiple strands of the earlier sections by contemplating, or interrogating, the single characteristic which unites them: their identity as language. Like Eliot in "East Coker" and "Burnt Norton," Sexton is concerned with the nature, origins, and capacity of language: concerned with the processes by which it constructs rather than reflects meaning. The section begins:

> Learning to talk is a complex business.
> My daughter's first word was *utta*,
> meaning button.

The poem asks questions about language acquisition, problematizes the received relationship between thought and language, experience and its expression, and raises the possibility that language precedes and dominates the speaker:

> Before there are words
> do you dream?
> In utero
> do you dream?
> Who taught you to suck?
> And how come?

Sexton's questions about language are, in part, questions about origins, and this takes us back to the beginning of the poem. The specific connection with the opening section is reinforced by the half-rhymes of "*utta*," "button," and "utero," which invoke the "buttocks" of section one—a noun which figures again in the next stanza of this final section as though to reinforce the syntactical and figurative connection. Paradoxically, and highly significantly, the passage which expresses this uncertainty and anxiety is itself an exemplification of the way in which writing might succeed. The chain of signification ("*utta*," "button," "utero," "buttocks") and subsequent artful rhymes, associations, and oppositions ("*help*" / "hello," "crow" / "know," "beautiful" versus "ugly") emphasize contradiction by means of their own internal coherence.

The awful consequence of this linguistic stalemate is that the subject's plaintive cry seems incomprehensible:

Is the cry saying something?
Does it mean *help*?
Or hello?
The cry of a gull is beautiful
and the cry of a crow is ugly
but what I want to know
is whether they mean the same thing.

Sexton's questions exemplify the modern crisis of faith in the structure and power of language. What does come first: thought ("dream[s]") or "words"? Do two distinct cries, uttered in different contexts, "mean the same thing"?

Her poem asks, finally, for an end to the clearly futile questioning with which it opened. It advocates, instead of inquiry, acquiescence:

It is only known that they are here to worship,
to worship the terror of the rain,
the mud and all its people,
the body itself.

Yet in a complex and seemingly paradoxical move, we find that what Sexton is in fact advocating is a continuation of that questioning, albeit one which is undertaken for its own sake rather than in order to divine any answers: "But more than that, / To worship the question itself." In a supreme metaphor for Sexton's poetics, it is the process of looking which is more important than any possible resolution.

The text finally closes in on itself, even diminishing typographically on the page as it gradually loses the orchestra of images and voices which has reverberated throughout until only "Ms. Dog" remains. Her "shantih shantih shantih," or "peace which passeth understanding" (to quote from *The Waste Land*) derives from a reconciliation with uncertainty, with not knowing the answers:

Bring a flashlight, Ms. Dog,
and look in every corner of the brain
and ask and ask and ask
until the kingdom,
however queer,
will come.

In addition to the precedents to be found in twentieth-century poetry such as this, there are theoretical precursors to Sexton's problematization of language. For example, several of her poems (such as "Telephone," discussed below) confirm some of the insights of Saussurean linguistics. Moreover, her poetry may be said to anticipate more recent poststructuralist accounts of language and postmodernist poetic practice. In order for us to obtain a clear understanding of Sexton's interrogation of language, it is necessary to situate her work within the context of burgeoning contemporary debates within the field. Marjorie Perloff's complaint about "reductive" readings of the post-modern poetry of Susan Howe and Lorine Niedecker and about the critical inability to do justice to the linguistic and metalinguistic complexity of the texts is surely applicable to readings of Sexton's work:

> I take it that poetry is, first and foremost, the language art. In the wake of deconstruction, one would think it no longer necessary to repeat the truism that the verbal signifier is not equivalent to its signifieds. But the current wave of ideologically motivated criticism has ushered in a curious form of backsliding. When, on the one hand, we talk theory, we continue to talk of "difference" and "erasure," of "decenteredness" and "supplementarity." When, on the other, we engage in practical criticism, whether of poetry or of prose, we read texts as if language were a mere conduit to a truth beyond it. (*Poetic* 36, 51)

Central to Sexton's poetry about language, and to her problematization of previously accepted beliefs about its communicative and referential potential, is the understanding that there is no essential or intrinsic relationship between language and referent, signs and the things that they name. Easthope and Thompson describe in more detail the approach taken by Perloff. They summarize the roots of Sexton's understanding that language creates and organizes our world, rather than simply reflecting some prelinguistic actuality:

> It would be hard to exaggerate the importance . . . of the linguistic distinction introduced by Ferdinand de Saussure between the word as signifier or shaped sound and the word as signified or meaning. At this point "reality" as the referent to which words may (or may not) refer becomes a secondary or derivative effect on human discourse, ceasing

to be available as a foundation on which certain knowledge can be based. (*Contemporary* vii–viii)

This unsettling of hitherto accepted certainties about language, and thereby about truth and referentiality, paves the way for a profound and comprehensive reorientation of critical perspective on Sexton's writing.[4]

Saussure's opening contention, in the first part of his *Course in General Linguistics*, that "Some people regard language, when reduced to its elements, as a naming-process only—a list of words each corresponding to the thing that it names"— illustrates the view of language characteristic of much earlier Sexton criticism. As Saussure explains:

> This conception is open to criticism at several points. It assumes that ready-made ideas exist before words. . . . It lets us assume that the linking of a name and a thing is a very simple operation—an assumption that is anything but true. (65)

"Telephone," from the posthumous volume *Words for Dr. Y.*, dispels such an assumption, demonstrating that words do not necessarily correspond to the things which they seem to delineate. The "Telephone" of the title does not, in fact, designate a telephone, but rather a telephone book: "Take a red book called TELEPHONE, / size eight by four. There it sits." The object bears the label "TELEPHONE" but the label, taken literally, is misleading. Sexton exploits, to startling effect, Saussure's understanding that "the choice of the signifier . . . actually has no natural connection with the signified" (69). There is a purposive disjunction here. The signifier "telephone" seems to suggest the signified (a telephone) but in fact signifies a different thought concept (a telephone book), thus creating a distinct and meaningful, but unexpected, sign. "Telephone" signifies either and both concepts. Similarly, the aural pun on "red" and "read" (a "red" book which is "read") draws attention to the potential ambivalence of language or, as Sexton puts it in an earlier poem, "Letter Written During a January Northeaster" (1962), to the "possibilities of the word." The effect of this is to highlight the unpredictability of language, the absence of referentiality, and the fact that, as Saussure argues, "language is not a mechanism created and arranged with a view to the concepts to be expressed" (85).

Later in the poem, it transpires that the noncoincidence of the signifier "telephone" with its apparent signified is not the only misnaming:

Yet some of these names are counterfeit.
There beside *Frigidaire* and *Dictaphone*,
there beside Max and Fred and Peggy and John,
beside Eric of Seattle and Snook of Saskatchewan
are all the dear dead names. The ink lies.
Hello! Hello! Goodbye. And then excise.

The telephone book names, and so revivifies, the deceased. The continued inclusion of "all the dear dead names" implies that they are still alive, still contactable. Yet, as the speaker concludes, this impression is erroneous ("some of these names are counterfeit"), serving only to prove that "the ink lies." If we read "ink" as a metonym for language generally, we can see that what is being proposed is that once one sign (perhaps the misleading "Telephone" of the title) has proved fallacious, then the value of all and any signs, of the confessional poem, and of language itself, is cast into doubt. In her *Hudson Review* interview, Sexton comments: "People lie to themselves so much—postmarks lie, even gravestones lie" (Marx 76). Karen Jackson Ford reads Sylvia Plath's "landmark" poem "Words Heard by Accident" in a similar way: "It is not simply confessional," Ford argues, "but uses the excruciating vividness and immediacy of the confessional mode to depict the material force of language" (121). Here Plath encounters "the brute materiality of language—its fierce potency and oppressive weight, its perniciousness and ineluctability" (128).

The physical, elusive, and combative nature of language is evident in the "Letters to Dr. Y." sequence of poems. The sequence is riddled with metaphors and metonyms for writing: "voice," "breath," "books," "cry," "words," "names," "read," "asks," "sings," "said," "truth," "tongue," "says," "answer," "sign." That these issues are of primary concern in this group of poems, written sporadically over a period of ten years from 1960 to 1970, provides further grounds for challenging the orthodoxy that it is only in Sexton's later poems that such complex linguistic questions are raised. Language (metonymically represented by the "Letters" of the title) ostensibly signifies communication—it is referential and functional and offers the key to understanding. Yet it is also potentially "disorderly," vicious, private, querulous, deceitful, and incomprehensible.

Diana Hume George reads "Letters to Dr. Y." as a direct account of that "ritualized human relationship unique to our time and our social structures, that between a healer of the mind and his or her patient"; while Caroline Hall concludes that "therapy itself is the theme" of the poems (*Oedipus* 147; Hall 162). However, although it is apparent from the outset that the therapeutic situation provides the background to the sequence, it is the discursive nature of this healing or "therapy"—its identity as the "talking cure"—which is isolated and put to the test. The poem indicates that language hinders, confuses, and obfuscates its own articulation, preventing "free" association, not only in the therapeutic arena but more generally.

The sequence takes the form of a series of letters addressed by the speaker to her doctor/therapist, interspersed with remembered dialogue between the two. The opening lines of the first of the "Letters to Dr. Y." ("February 16, 1960") confirms the implication of the sequence title that language (here represented by the doctor's voice) is a means of connection. Moreover, language is represented as a physical necessity, as the source of energy and life:

> Dr. Y.
> I need a thin hot wire,
> your Rescue Inc. voice
> to stretch me out,
> to keep me from going underfoot.

These lines alone contain multiple and sophisticated references to language in its broadest sense. The first line with its aural pun on "Y" (why?) may be read either as a mark of the doctor's own interrogative stance or as an instance of the speaker's own questioning of the addressee: "Doctor, why . . .?" In the manuscript drafts, the sequence is entitled: "Letters to Doctor Why—1958–1968." The "thin hot wire" is a metonym for intense or heated telephone conversation which, like in Plath's "Words Heard," conveys the sense of language as charged and powerful. In addition, if we read "hot wire" as a verb we find connotations of forced entry or access gained illicitly without a key. Thus the hot wire of the doctor's voice provides an entry into the subject's unconscious. The third line, like the first, features aural puns on "Rescue Inc." (the doctor's voice stands in for the emergency services and is actively "rescuing"). Moreover, it may be argued that the doctor's voice, by keeping the speaker alive, is rescuing her writing (or "ink" ["Inc."]). It should also be said that in all of these possible readings, it is the materiality of language, its physical presence, which is emphasized.

Language is denaturalized. It is figured as volatile, anarchistic, and prohibitive. It seeks to control the speaker rather than to liberate her. At issue is inhibition (hence the "cop car") rather than expression:

Death,
I need your hot breath,
my index finger in the flame,
two cretins standing at my ears,
listening for the cop car.

The rhetoric of violence and attrition is characteristic of Sexton's writing about language. In her *Hudson Review* interview, Sexton describes her writing in similar terms: "What you're doing is hunting for what you mean, what you're trying to say. You don't know when you start. . . . You're always fighting to find out what it is you want to say" (Marx 73). To another interviewer, she explains: "It's just like a runner getting into training or a fighter hitting a punch bag" (Weeks 115). Again, the "free association" of the psychotherapeutic situation is problematized, and shown to be enacted under conditions of prohibition and restraint. These metaphors of "fighting," "hunting," and, later in the same interview, of "struggling," suggest that language is the enemy. It is the quarry to be caught or the predator to be escaped. It is alien and separate, it is watchful or needs to be watched. Sexton pictures herself as "fighting" or "hunting" for a meaning which is always one step beyond her, which is evasive, uncontainable, and thus inexpressible. Similar rhetoric is found in Eliot's poetry. "East Coker," for example, with its militaristic metaphors ("raid," "squads," "conquer," "strength and submission," and "fight") regrets that "one has only learnt to get the better of words."

The second poem of the "Letters to Dr. Y." sequence ("June 6, 1960,") pursues many of these ideas. It self-reflexively comments on the Faustian situation of the confessional poet: "I have words for you, Dr. Y., / words for sale." "June 6, 1960," bears comparison with Sylvia Plath's "Lady Lazarus." Both poems open with a sense of personal bravado: Sexton's defiant, "I have words for you, Dr. Y.," like Plath's provocative, "I have done it again," wields words like weapons. Both poems use similar devices of enumeration as a way of identifying and controlling the multiplicity and weight of the traumas to which each speaker has been exposed. Images of violence dominate both:

Words right now, alive in the head,
heavy and pressing as in a crowd.

Pushing for headroom, elbowing,
knowing their rights.

While in Plath's poem it is the audience which proves murderously voyeuristic, in Sexton's, it is the language. We find a similar situation in Sexton's
"Demon," where the speaker becomes the victim and object of surveillance by
language or "the public voyeury eyes / of my typewriter keys."

In "June 6, 1960," the addressee (Dr. Y.) demands coherence and progression, asking four times "And where is the order?" Yet the words themselves
resist such control, reveling in their own profusion:

A disorderly display of words,
one after the other.
It's a huge gathering ball of words,
not a snowball, but an old string ball,
one from the rag bag.

A later poem, "Flee on Your Donkey" (first written in 1962 and revised in
1965), regrets the loss of this fruitful linguistic chaos: "Disorder is not what
it was. / I have lost the trick of it!" Emily Dickinson's poetry, for example
Poem 937, uses similar metaphors of wool, yarn, thread, knitting, and sewing,
to connote both the dissolution of meaning and a self-conscious attempt to
ravel it back into coherent order (Ford 69–70).

Oppressed by the Doctor/addressee's insistent demands, the speaker tries
to define, and thus contain, the words. The metaphors of the snowball and
string bag may be read as an attempt to impose order by way of establishing some meaningful (metaphorical) equivalence. In a vain attempt at appeasement, the speaker tries to conform to Dr. Y.'s request by enumerating
the qualities of language, although the veiled allusion to Hamlet's despairing "Words, words, words" (II.ii.191) in the first line quoted here implies the
speaker's own sense of meaninglessness:

Words, words, words,
piled up one on another,
making a kind of weight of themselves.
    1. each less than a pound
    2. each less than a stick of butter
    3. one the size of a roasted peanut, light and wrinkled

> 4. another one, a slim precise girl, a sunflower seed
> 5. one, as small as my thumb, a beach stone in the hand
> 6. and there is always that one, the toad. The toad
> has many brothers.

Geoffrey Hartman notices the "obtruding irrelevance of number" in many of Sexton's poems, and suggests that this "adds to the sharpness, evoking as in love-songs or magic rimes . . . the action of fate, its absurd yet demonically just jackpot" ("On To Bedlam" 120). I would add that this poem's speaker is victim of its unpredictability and its accumulative power. In Saussure's terms, "Language is a system of interdependent terms" (Sexton's words, "piled up one on another / Making a kind of weight of themselves") within which "the value of each term results solely from the simultaneous presence of the others" (114). In "June 6, 1960," these "words, words, words" cannot direct the reader to any prior order or transcendent truth. Their meaning is self-relational and shifting, never fixed, always potentially disordered. One can only ascertain order by reference to other "words" in the system; language signifies by a process of metaphorical and metonymical equivalence.

Language is potentially threatening or punitive, posing a particular threat to the female speaker who fights for a voice within this alien, masculine register. The speaker responds to the questioning refrain, "And where is the order? You will ask," with a list of

> Words waiting, angry, masculine,
> with their fists in a knot.
> Words right now, alive in the head,
> heavy and pressing as in a crowd.
> Pushing for headroom, elbowing,
> knowing their rights.

The final stanza of "June 6, 1960," isolates—at first in the form of a metaphor—one particular word; the unnamed, elusive word which, were it to be captured, might prove to be the truth or meaning which patient (speaker) and doctor (addressee) alike seek:

> A word, a sunflower seed.
> One we would surely overlook.
> So easily lost, a dead bee.

The figure of the bee is used consistently in Sexton's poems about language as a metaphor with which to encapsulate the simultaneously functional and destructive, purposive and erratic nature of language. In addition, "Bee" is the nickname which the poet James Wright bestowed on Sexton at around this time when the two were involved in a relationship (Middlebrook *Biography* 128–34). That Sexton uses the same signifier ("Bee") for her writing self and for language is deeply telling.

The sense of language's autonomous, alien, evasive, potentially aggressive indeterminacy—the principle subject of "Letters to Dr. Y."—is developed and intensified in *The Awful Rowing Toward God*. Like "Letters," this volume features multiple metonyms for writing. Almost every one of the thirty-nine poems in the volume foregrounds images of writing, language, or poetry. "Story" figures repeatedly, as do "say," "song," "speak," and "speeches" (and their metonyms "tongues" and "mouth"); "write," "writers," and "words in my hand" (and the metonyms "fingers" and "hands"); and "lines," "typewriter," "naming," and "Logos."

The poems in *The Awful Rowing Toward God* expose the failure of words to deliver what is expected of them. They exemplify the impermanence of the printed word, the transience of language, and the absence of referentiality. The volume's opening poem, "Rowing," draws instant attention to its own textuality: "A story, a story! / (Let it go. Let it come)." This is a writing which is to make its own way in the world independent of any authorial control. The poem conveys, in waves of cumulative lines (punctuated with the refrains "I grew, I grew" and "I am rowing, I am rowing," which emphasize the repetitive and ceaseless nature of the task), the futility of trying to use language as a route to truth or meaning. "Rowing" or, metaphorically, writing gets one nowhere: "But I am rowing, I am rowing, / though the wind pushes me back."[5]

Similarly, the third poem in the volume, "The Children," opens: "The children are all crying in their pens / and the surf carries their cries away." Again, within the economy of Sexton's references to language, "pens" may be read both as a reference to children's playpens and as a metaphor for writing. The confessional poet is infantilized and shown to be engaged in a futile and transitory endeavor; writing "on the wings of an elf / who then dissolves." A similar image is used in the same volume in "Jesus, the Actor, Plays the Holy Ghost" in order to suggest the fragility and temporality of written words which "crumble like men's ashes." The poem refutes the assumption that words are there to be worked, that language is a plastic and passive medium. Language (metonymically represented in numerous poems in this volume and elsewhere by the image of a typewriter) is far from subordinate and malleable. Instead it is mechanistic, domineering, autonomous, and, above all, dissociated from the author. It is self-willed and responsible for generating its own meaning. In this model, the supposedly originating author becomes the tool of the machine. As Sexton explicitly stated on submitting the manuscript of *The Awful Rowing Toward God* to her agent: "It's a bit 'odd' but after all, I didn't do it, the typewriter did" (*Letters* 403). This contradicts Charles Olson's view of the way ahead for contemporary poetry. He perceives the typewriter to be in the service of the poet: as the "personal and instantaneous recorder of the poets' work." Sexton does not share this perception. For her, the typewriter is the source, not the "recorder" of or vehicle for the writing (Olson 155). In "Frenzy," it is the typewriter and not some prior originating "author" which is responsible for the poem:

> I am, each day,
> typing out the God
> my typewriter believes in.

A similar dissociation of self from text appears in the chilling, somber, even abject 1974 poem "The Big Boots of Pain." This depicts the speaker at the moment of realization that the typewriter or, by extension, language is disloyal. Writing is not acquiescent (it cannot be "worked"), instead it is alien and antagonistic:

> One learns not to blab about all this
> except to yourself or the typewriter keys
> who tell no one until they get brave
> and crawl off onto the printed page.

In her 1966 television interview, Sexton complains that the typewriter obstructs free expression. She plays a recording of the music of Villa Llobos at full volume, and explains:

> In there is something I've lost and I just can't get it out of this damned typewriter. . . . I feel like words are phoney compared to music . . . If it would come out of my fingers somehow, . . . something in that and I

don't know what it is; would come out, but I don't know. It never really has properly.

She describes her sense of the abject failure of words to evoke the experience suggested by the music (an indication, perhaps, of the irreconcilability of the symbolic and semiotic orders). As she speaks, she angrily gestures towards the keys of the typewriter which stands on the desk beside her: "Can I put into words what that feels, that music feels like? It's a terribly difficult thing but it moves me, if it moves me, I'm already moved see I'm working with these clumsy horrible things."

Sexton proceeds to distinguish between listening to music (which is a purely aural act) and creating the poem (which is first visual, and only secondarily aural): "Hear, I don't hear, I watch; then I see my, my . . . ear is so tuned to what I see that I know without thinking." The aural origins of Sexton's writing have been well documented, but this physical, concrete dimension of her poetic practice—the importance of the physical properties of the words as they appear on the page—has not hitherto been recognized.[6] Certainly, it exemplifies that connection with the objectivists and, for example, with Robert Creeley, which Perloff has inferred. However, it also sets Sexton apart from some of the key principles of Olson's projective verse which Perloff also proposes as a precursor. Whereas, for Olson, it is "the breath, the breathing as distinguished from the hearing" which is important, one might argue that, for Sexton, it is "the sight as distinguished from the hearing." For Olson, "That verse will only do in which a poet manages to register both the acquisitions of his ear and the pressures of his breath" (149). For Sexton, it is the acquisitions of her eye which are primary.

To return to the motif of the typewriter as metonym for writing, the implication that it is watchful, uncooperative, and potentially judgmental is demonstrated in a number of poems. "The Room of My Life" is dominated by the vast, solid, omniscient typewriter: "the forty-eight keys of the typewriter / each an eyeball that is never shut." The typewriter's surveillance suggests, first, that the speaker in this room / life is under constant scrutiny. Second, it confirms that meaning derives from the machine rather than from its operator. The typewriter is personified, yet the contradictory effect of this is to reinforce the mechanistic features of language. Interestingly, Sexton had engrossed the typescript of her unpublished poem "The Thought Disease" with the words "Fix this." It is possible to read this early (1960) poem as a draft of "The Room of My Life" (written in January 1973). In both poems, the typewriter, and the letters, phonemes, and words which it represents, are defamiliarized.

"The Room of My Life" offers a description of the physical and figurative space from which the writing emerges. The poem exploits, by taking literally, the process by which the confessional writer lays herself bare. It invites the readers in, such that they can more effectively scrutinize and understand what is going on inside. This space, the scene of writing, is predominantly a place of disorder and uncertainty: "In the room of my life / the objects keep changing." The typewriter, as we have seen, is on guard, watching its owner's and user's every move. The books are in cutthroat but essentially trivial competition with each other ("the books, each a contestant in a beauty contest"). The writer's chair swallows up and destroys any creature which sits on it, exuding murderous intent: "the black chair, a dog coffin made of Naugahyde." There are objects everywhere waiting to trip up, ensnare, or injure the speaker/writer:

> The sockets on the wall
> waiting like a cave of bees,
> the gold rug
> a conversation of heels and toes,
> the fireplace
> a knife waiting for someone to pick it up.

Even the windows represent a vicious threat, driving "the trees like nails into my heart." Similarly, the lights in this room are destructive and vindictive ("the lights / poking at me"). The poem closes with the dreadful sense that even in the writer's supposedly sacrosanct study, and even when writing about what she knows best ("my life"), she is ultimately subject to and victim of a deceitful and malicious language. The objects with which she has crowded her room and her life have assumed an independent life of their own, "compelled" not by her inner trauma, but by language:

> Nothing is just what it seems to be.
> My objects dream and wear new costumes,
> compelled to, it seems, by all the words in my hands
> and the sea that bangs in my throat.

The typewriter functions both as the autonomous source of writing and as a demanding and judgmental vehicle of surveillance. The specific allusions in "The Room of My Life," "Is It True?" and elsewhere to typewriter keys are thus particularly significant. First, the implicit association of "lock" with "key" sustains the impression of the typewriter's controlling and prohibitive function. Second, the motif of the typewriter's keys acknowledges and then interrogates orthodox assumptions about language's propensity to open the door, or give access, to meaning and truth. In a letter to Tillie Olsen dated 2 October 1965, Sexton implicitly makes this connection (the metaphor of "spring[ing] outward" suggesting the action of springing, or breaking, a lock):

> I hate to work by hand, hate my hand. I'm not too friendly with the typewriter either these days . . . no poems . . . a silence like a snail growing inward . . . whereas typewriter keys should/could spring outward. (HRHRC)[7]

The metaphor indicates a frustration (hence the emphasis on what the "typewriter keys should/could" do) with language's inability, or refusal, to free the subject.

In *Transformations*, too, the image of the key is employed in order to explore the possibilities and/or limitations of language and to test whether words can indeed deliver such a liberating release. Throughout the volume, questions about language, about the roles of teller and listener, about speech and silence, and discursive and linguistic power, are foregrounded. The prefatory poem, "The Gold Key," by means of its emphasis on metonymies of writing (speaking, arms, book, mouth, story), introduces the predominant theme of the whole volume:

> The speaker in this case
> is a middle-aged witch, me—
> tangled on my two great arms,
> my face in a book
> and my mouth wide,
> ready to tell you a story or two.

The point is not simply that the usually vilified witch has assumed the position of subject, but that she has assumed a voice. It is not her presence, even at center stage, which is significant, it is the fact that she speaks. Roland Barthes makes a similar point of the psychoanalytic situation: "If psychoanalysis is condemned, it is not because it thinks but because it speaks; if one could confine it to being a purely medical practice and immobilize the patient . . . they would worry about it as little as they do about acupuncture" (*Criticism* 43).

In *Transformations*, the speaker/witch highlights the significance of "the key." She speaks directly to her audience ("I have come to remind you") who are at once the individuals named in the poem and the wider readership ("all of you"), and she is at pains to emphasize their shared desire for knowledge and understanding. We all want to own the key that "should/could" give access to the truth: "We must have the answers." And although one child ("let me present to you this boy") is selected to find and use the key to this case, there is a marked insistence on the fact that his role is symbolic of "each" of us: "I mean you. / I mean me." Of course, the key belongs in a lock (the lithograph illustrations which accompany the original volume of *Transformations* emphasize this implicit connection by depicting, in close-up, an eye peering through a keyhole).[8] Together these images represent a metaphor for language—for the necessary link between signifier and signified, word and referent, poem and truth.

Yet the point is made that the key offers only possibilities, not answers, suggestions rather than solutions. When the boy, on everybody's behalf, "turns the key," the result is mystification rather than clarity:

> Presto!
> It opens this book of odd tales
> which transform the Brothers Grimm.
> Transform?
> As if an enlarged paper clip
> could be a piece of sculpture.
> (And it could.)

Thus Sexton foregrounds issues of interpretation, and highlights the indeterminacy of writing and the arbitrariness of the sign.

In subsequent poems in the collection, we find similar doubts about the potential of language to act as the key to insight or understanding. In "Rumpelstiltskin" the one-time miller's daughter (now queen) is faced with the task of finding the dwarf's real name in order to avoid losing her child to him. She must find the (nominal) key to his identity in order to achieve freedom.

So long as Rumpelstiltskin retains secret possession of the name, he has the power. Control seems to transfer from Rumpelstiltskin when she discovers, or unlocks, his secret: "The queen was delighted. / She had the name!" Yet the nominal key fails to provide the insight which it promises. Although deprived of his name, Rumpelstiltskin lives on: "one part soft as a woman, / one part a barbed hook." The name can never be understood as providing a single, transcendent answer or truth. All that it can do is give access to yet another linguistic door to be opened, to a further sequence of complex signs.

As we have seen, use of the key brings its own risks. It is possible to see these poems as palimpsests of the Pandora's box myth and of the fairy tale "Bluebeard," with its prohibition against unlocking the door which obscures Bluebeard's murderous secrets. "Locked Doors" (from *The Awful Rowing Toward God*) develops some of these themes. Here, what lies behind the locked doors can only be imagined:

> There is a locked room up there
> with an iron door that can't be opened.
> It has all your bad dreams in it.
> It is hell.

The scene is reminiscent of Bluebeard's castle: a place of cruelty where physical contact is prohibited or punished ("The people inside have no water / and are never allowed to touch"). This is a place of repression—"They are mute / They do not cry help"—and finally, of death: "Their hearts are covered with grubs." The speaker (and, metaphorically, the confessional poet) attempts to reach the imprisoned, the repressed, and the unresponsive through language to unlock the "iron door" of their prison and their repression. Yet her efforts are futile. Again, the ability and will to wield the key does not guarantee that communication will be established. The key which promises access and insight is rusty; it is imperfect, marked, and ineffective. In Perrault's "Bluebeard," the key is tainted with blood (red, like the rust in Sexton's poem), and this is seen as a sign of the wife's treachery and unworthiness. "Locked Doors" concludes with the speaker's profound sense of her own unworthiness, of the inadequacy of her own key (language) to perform the task asked of it. She would like to open doors, to reach people, and to "hold each fallen one in my arms / but I cannot, I cannot."

That language may be volatile, erratic, self-possessed is confirmed in the recurrent metaphor, mentioned briefly earlier, of the word as "bee" and of language as "bee-like." Middlebrook notes that one of the side effects of Thorazine (the medication which Sexton was prescribed to control her manic episodes) was a sensation akin to bees stinging the skin. She comments that the drug also had sedative properties, and produced a distinct decline in Sexton's linguistic and poetic capacities (*Biography* 221–32). One might go further and posit a connection between this prescription and metaphors in Sexton's poetry of bees as belligerent and linguistically damaging. For Sexton, the bee is simultaneously violent and destructive, useful and susceptible to domestication. The bee offers a sophisticated metaphor for inspiration and burn-out, volatility and vulnerability, desire and necessity. In addition to her own experience with Thorazine, it is arguable that coming some eight years after the publication of Plath's *Ariel* (with its sequence of bee poems), Sexton also had her writing in mind.[9]

In Sexton's 1973 poem "Words," the image of the swarming insects emphasizes the cumulative power of words, their unpredictability, and volatility. They are likely to swarm out of control, and under their own direction, at any moment:

> Be careful of words,
> even the miraculous ones.
> For the miraculous we do our best,
> sometimes they swarm like insects.

This bears comparison with Plath's "Words" which opens with threatening "axes" and, more importantly, with her "The Arrival of the Bee Box" which draws specific attention to the force of the bees as a community and uses explicitly linguistic images. Listening to the bees trapped in the box, Plath's speaker exclaims:

> The unintelligible syllables.
> It is like a Roman mob,
> Small, taken one by one, but my god, together!

The performative power of language (its ability to make things happen, or work miracles) is acknowledged, but is also subject to a caution. While performative, it also forces the speaker to perform; she must do justice to, or do her best for, the "miraculous" words.

Yet Sexton's poem also offers an important recognition of the potential beneficence of language, what it might be able to do if only its powers could be harnessed, or one's own antipathy and fear (Plath's "my god, together!") could be quashed. For although sometimes these words "swarm like insects," at other times they "leave not a sting but a kiss." Words offer extremes of pleasure and pain interchangeably. The potential of language is described in disconcertingly erotic ways: Words may leave "a kiss," may be "as good as fingers" or "as trusty as a rock / you stick your bottom on." The speaker's relationship with language is, then, a sexual or even masochistic one. In spite of the bruising received at the hands of demonic and unpredictable language, "Yet I am in love with words." In images of innocence, fertility, and organic growth, which are again sexualized—(the lap, the legs, the passionate face)—words are revered in language which echoes that of a love poem:

> They are doves falling out of the ceiling.
> They are six holy oranges sitting in my lap.
> They are the trees, the legs of summer,
> and the sun, its passionate face.

This recalls the distinctly sexual connotations of, for example, Plath's "The Bee Meeting" with its bridelike veil, its flowers, and its witnesses to the "wedding" and defloration of the virgin bride. Similarly, in Sexton's poem "Frenzy," the speaker masochistically calls to the bees, sacrificing herself in order to acquire the inspiration which they proffer.

However, the attempt in "Words" to use language in order to evoke plenitude, abundance, and contentment spills over or exceeds its own limits. The glimpse of the fertile possibilities of language ("six holy oranges," the sun's "passionate face") is snatched away. The epiphany is momentary, and we are left with a more rudimentary confession about the inadequacy of words:

> Yet often they fail me.
> I have so much I want to say,
> so many images, words, proverbs, etc.
> But the words aren't good enough,
> the wrong ones kiss me.
> Sometimes I fly like an eagle
> but with the wings of a wren.

The abbreviating device "etc." paradoxically expresses its own failure of articulation, demonstrating that the words are indeed not "good enough." Their limitations are displayed in the monotonous monosyllables of the lines, "the wrong ones kiss me" and "but with the wings of a wren." The poem closes with a reiteration of the speaker's responsibility towards, and subservience to, language:

> But I try to take care
> and be gentle to them.
> Words and eggs must be handled with care.
> Once broken they are impossible
> things to repair.

The connotations of this superficially simplistic truism (emphasized by the rhyme of "care" and "repair") are many. First, the lines offer a caution against breaking one's word: Eggs, like oranges, signify creativity and in their fragility offer a reminder of the writer's responsibility. Second, there is a latent recognition of that implied connection (language to referent, text to truth) which sustains the speaker's faith in the language being used and the reader's trust in the text's authenticity. These could, it is suggested, be shattered at any time. Thus, crucially, the permanence, truthfulness, and referentiality of language are once more cast into doubt.

Notwithstanding the promise of its title, Sexton's "Love Song" (written in 1963, some ten years earlier than "Words") is already exercised by the potentially destructive nature, first of language, and then by extension, of the writing self. It questions how, if at all, one can translate "love" into "song" or experience into poetry:

> I was
> the girl of the chain letter,
> the girl full of talk of coffins and keyholes,
> the one of the telephone bills,
> the wrinkled photo and the lost connections.

The writing self is out of control, victim of a language which like a "chain letter" seems to have taken on a life of its own. There is no key, not even truly a "keyhole," but only "talk of one." This is the scene of "lost connections" (the image echoes the closing line of Lowell's "Memories of West Street and Lepke"). Language fails, and we are left with abstraction, ellipsis, aporia.

The vicious and precise imagery of parts of this poem indicate language's performative potential. As J. L. Austin proposes: "The issuing of the utterance is the performing of an action" (6–7). The implicit or explicit statement, "I confess," may, arguably, be read as a performative in Austin's sense that: "To say something is to do something" (12); however, it is also arguable that the ostensible performatives uttered by Sexton ("I confess," "I lie," and similar others) fail or, in Austin's terms, are "unhappy" (14). A performative may be regarded as "unhappy" if the procedure is not executed by all parties (in the case of a confession, by penitent and confessor), or, where the speaker's intention or commitment fails, or where the action, having been uttered, is not completed in practice (15, 40, 45–46).

The speaker in "Love Song" refers to herself in the third person, as though to dissociate herself from the violence of the language. She describes: "an old red hook in her mouth, / the mouth that kept bleeding." Language is self-lacerating just as it describes self-laceration. Similarly, in "The Dead Heart," it is the performative force of the single word "EVIL" (significantly, in form and effect, a reversal of the imperative to "LIVE") which kills the speaker's heart, and thus metaphorically the writing. The word is capitalized for emphasis and as though to reinforce its status as a command, its performative responsibility:

How did it die?
I called it EVIL
I said to it, your poems stink like vomit.
I didn't stay to hear the last sentence.
It died on the word EVIL.
I did it with my tongue.

To return to "Love Song," however, there is a shift in tone after this moment of abjection (the bleeding mouth, the desolate soul). The poem slows down, and the violence gives way to acquiescence, to a cessation of hostilities. The speaker abandons her struggle against writing and gives way to its fumbling uncertainty: "and then she'd be as safe as / as delicate as . . ." As the repetitions and ellipses indicate, the (chain) letter is left open, since closure and meaning cannot be forced. In the final section of "Love Song," there is a profound sense of relief attendant on the decision to accept language's intrinsic indeterminacy. Not to have to continue the doomed struggle to reduce language to a single, fixed meaning is, paradoxically, the way to comprehend it. In "Love Song," as in "A Little Uncomplicated Hymn," all that can be expressed is the impossibility of expression. As the former concludes:

Oh! There is no translating
that ocean,
that music,
that theater,
that field of ponies.

It is in the sequence of poems "O Ye Tongues," which closes *The Death Notebooks* that questions about language, and specifically about translation, come to the fore. As a number of critics have noted, the sequence of ten distinct "Psalms" which makes up the group is loosely based on the eighteenth-century English poet Christopher Smart's *Jubilate Agno*, and indeed "Christopher" figures in the poem as the brother/companion of the speaker.[10] Sexton's sequence features many of the same metaphors and metonyms for writing as have been discussed thus far (bees, typewriters, locks, "ink," and the "print on the page," for example). "O Ye Tongues," like previous poems, depicts writing as a magical act (the line, "we swallow magic and we deliver Anne," from the "Fourth Psalm" confirms the importance of linguistic "tricks" in Sexton's poetics). It also implies, as we saw earlier, that the persona "Anne" is performatively produced, or conjured up, by the magic of writing. The writing self is a fragmented or dissociated self which can only be represented (or translated) by the figure of synecdoche (in the "Eighth Psalm," by her "ten long fingers").

The sequence represents a final attempt to understand and control language, to apprehend or reach some reconciliation with it such that it can productively be used and meaning brought to bear, or such that experience and thought can be translated. It attempts to exploit the performative potential of language, appropriating—even preempting—the Word of God, or Logos: "Let there be a God." Stan Smith describes a similar figure in Eliot's "Mr. Eliot's Sunday Morning Service" as "an originary statement about origins" (*Origins* 120). This is, of course, a bold, even heretical, step. The speaker simultaneously undermines the notion of God's preeminence (significantly, she summons "a" not "the" God) and confirms it by appropriating his powerful idiom. Throughout the ten Psalms of "O Ye Tongues," Sexton's protagonist may be seen commanding, praising and appealing to God, assuming authority over his creation ("Let there be seasons") and the right to give benediction ("Bless with the locust"). As though to demonstrate the power of language (or of Logos), the scope of "O Ye Tongues" ranges from the private, personal, and confessional ("For I shat and Christopher smiled") to the public, impersonal, and shared ("For America is a land of Commies and Prohibitionists"). Sexton's poem is a provocative song of praise, appeal, and explanation which, regardless of its defiant posture, culminates, in the final Psalm, with a recognition of the inevitable failure and limitations of language.

"O Ye Tongues" attempts to "translate" Christopher Smart's "translation" of the Psalms (*Jubilate Agno*). Patricia Meyer Spacks concludes of Smart's writing:

> Smart, the translator of Horace, working in the asylum on his version— a sort of translation—of the Psalms and of the parables, finds in his efforts with language the promise of his salvation. For there is no doubt in his mind that language in general, poetry in particular, exists—like all the natural creation—to praise the Lord. (*Poetry* 142–43)

Yet Sexton's attempt (and arguably Smart's pretext) is doomed to failure. By the tenth and final psalm, the speaker has realized that, the ambition of her opening lines notwithstanding, she cannot "translate the language"—that is, the primary, originary Word of God. As J. Hillis Miller has suggested in his study of religious and secular parables, "The Word . . . is demonstrably untranslatable. . . . The failure of translation is the result of the absence of any adequate original in any humanly comprehensible language" (*Tropes* 144). There is no effective signifying system, and the attempt to appropriate the ultimate (Logos) has failed. The only language open to her is predicated on silence: "For I am placing fist over fist on rock and plunging into the altitude of words. The silence of words." This insight is, I would argue, crucial to an understanding of the confessional project. Although we may be beguiled by the frankness and ostensible authenticity of confessional revelation, it is precisely in that which cannot be said, that which remains unstated, silent, untranslated (and untranslatable), that truth may reside. There is, indeed, in the words of "Love Song," "no translating."

Patricia Meyer Spacks draws attention to Christopher Smart's punning on the word "translation":

> Let Libni rejoice with the Redshank, who
>   Migrates not but is translated to the
> Upper regions.
> For I have translated in the charity, which

> makes things better & I shall be trans-
> lated myself at the last
>   (qtd. in Spacks, *Poetry* 142).

She suggests that "the double meaning of *translate* [to represent in another language, and to "convey to heaven without death" (*Shorter Oxford English Dictionary*)] provides a way of expressing the power of language" (*Poetry* 142). In Sexton's "O Ye Tongues," translation—or, more properly, its failure—expresses the ineffectiveness of language, its inability to convey experience or subjectivity. The poem's closing lines ("For God was as large as a sunlamp and laughed his heat at us and therefore we did not cringe at the death hole") return us, inescapably, to the beginning of the poem with its parody of the first, generative, logocentric act: "Let there be a God as large as a sunlamp to laugh his heat / at you." Like "Hurry Up Please," "O Ye Tongues" finally abandons hope of finding a resolution. It surrenders to the condition of living in uncertainty, rather than persisting with a desperate and doomed attempt to find and tell a truth which is ever evasive, ever indefinable, ever untranslatable.

7

Truth and lies

Sexton's poetry demonstrates a stance or series of stances towards truth of some complexity and ambiguity. She essays a number of sometimes contradictory positions with respect to the possibility or desirability of capturing and conveying truth, often situating the voice of the poem in a middle ground between telling all (confessing) and telling nothing (hiding). She deals in paradoxes—that she is lying about lying, that poetic artifice is necessary to evoke truth—and in antitheses (truth versus lies, volubility versus silence); in whole truths; partial truths; truths whispered, disguised, or denied. Thus "A Little Uncomplicated Hymn" (1965), in spite of the promise and express aim of its title, is concerned with a complicated truth which patently cannot be conveyed in poetry. "Live" (1966) foregrounds the "perjury of the soul" and proclaims "an outright lie." "The Errand" (1972) dramatizes the act of "double crossing," advocates deceit ("let us deceive with words") and celebrates masquerade ("decades of disguises"). The important 1973 poem "Is It True?" the main focus of this chapter, poses a question which it is unable to understand and incapable of answering.

More important in Sexton's poetry than speaking the truth, is speaking about truth. Paradoxically, the frequency, loquacity and persistence with which Sexton does this acts to obscure truth as an essence. The prominence of the question of truth in her writing has a similar effect to the "discourse on sex" which Foucault has identified as central to post-Enlightenment Western culture:

> By speaking about it [sex] so much, by discovering it multiplied, partitioned off, and specified precisely where one had placed it, what one was seeking essentially was simply to conceal sex: a screen-discourse, a dispersion-avoidance. (*History* 53)

Similarly in Sexton, the ostentatious foregrounding of truth serves to conceal it. Her work is engaged not in "a battle on behalf of the truth, but . . . a battle about the status of the truth." It asks not "what is the truth?" but "what is truth?" ("Truth" 74). It is important to note that the debate about, or appeal to, truth is carried out not only in the poems but also in paratextual comments (interviews, lectures, and other authorial explanations) and extratextual clarifications and interpretations offered by others, for example, by Sexton's daughter. Thus truth is endlessly displaced, endlessly attenuated, and seemingly impossible to determine. My own intention in drawing on paratexts such as these is not to position them as evidence of the truth behind the poems, but to indicate how layered or splintered, and thus how undecidable, this is.

As we will see, Sexton sidesteps questions about the truth status of the events or experience apparently at the source of the poems and works hard to displace her own responsibility for it. Like Emily Dickinson, she seems to aim to "tell all the truth but tell it slant" (Poem 1129). As she explains in an interview: "In some ways as you see me now, I am a lie. The crystal truth is in my poetry" (Weeks 115). However, even this seemingly crystal-clear explanation is a guise. First, crystal is notoriously vulnerable to flaws (this being the metaphor at the heart of F. Scott Fitzgerald's "The Cut-Glass Bowl," of Henry James's *The Golden Bowl*, and of Sexton's own "For John Who Begs Me Not to Enquire Further"). In Sexton's personal copy of *The Golden Bowl*, she has underlined Amerigo's words: "If I'm crystal I'm delighted that I'm a perfect one, for I believe they sometimes have cracks and flaws—in which case they're to be had very cheap!" (HRHRC). Second, in claiming that the "crystal truth" is contained in the poetry, Sexton indicates that truth is a product of perception. That is, she acknowledges the role of the reader/observer in espying the truth through the glass. Her use of the metaphor also indicates that the truth is not, perhaps, "in" the poetry, but is refracted outside of it—displaced onto, and only comprehensible as part of, a public, discursive domain.

Sexton's repeated insistence that the truth originates in the text—"the crystal truth is in my poetry" and "to really get to the truth of something is the poem, not the poet" (Marx 74)—indicates the futility of looking beyond the writing for evidence of its authenticity. In Marjorie Perloff's terms, it rejects the option of reading the poetic text as though it were "a mere conduit to a truth" (*Poetic* 51). There is, Sexton suggests, no identifiable reference to prior actuality: The text generates and represents its own truth. One effect of this is that it permits the poems to authorize or validate their own truths, to sidestep extratextual validation. In a 23 August 1965 letter to a reader who wished to know more about the poems, Sexton explains: "I feel that each poem is its own song and deserves its own voice. More than anything else I ask of each poem that it not be boring and that it be, somehow, true to itself" (HRHRC).

There is something quite complex and quite evasive taking place here. Sexton's claims about the self-referential truthfulness of her texts are clearly belied by the dense para- and extratextual frameworks which surround them. I draw here on Gerard Genette's definition of the paratext, that is: all of those "accompanying productions" (interviews, letters, diaries, prefaces and so on) which "surround a work and, to a greater or lesser degree, clarify or modify its significance" (1, 7). These processes of para- and extratextual validation and accreditation are crucial to the text's apparent authenticity. However, in a further twist (which we should by now recognize as characteristic of Sexton's discourse on truth), even these paratexts may be said to refer to or validate only themselves. Moreover, they are invariably contradictory. As Sexton explains in one of her Crawshaw lectures "I like to lie. I like to confess. I like to hide" (Crawshaw [1] 2). Each paratext potentially possesses its own paratexts and all or any of these may offer a distinct and contradictory version of the truth ostensibly being validated. Each constructs a new metatruth about the truth of the poem, and none finally, or with any authority, identifies a prior, pretextual truth. The context is itself textual. There is no ultimate truth which will validate the poem but only a tissue of other discourses which are open to readerly interpretation and which generate and validate what we understand to be the truth.

In Sexton's comments about her work, a preexisting script or version of events can frequently be identified to which she refers in order to complete or validate the truth of the text. A number of these comments acquire their authority not by proximity or reference to some prior truth but by repetition. In several interviews, Sexton rehearses a story about the authenticity which she perceived in W. D. Snodgrass's "Heart's Needle" and about the way in which her reading of that poem galvanized her into reclaiming her estranged infant daughter. This experience, she explains, motivated the poems "The Double Image" and "Unknown Girl in a Maternity Ward" (Marx 75–79; Kevles 89).

Her admission, in these interviews, that the actual truth (sacrificed for the sake of the poem's dramatic truth) is that she had two daughters, not just the one who features in the poem, and that the reconciliation with her infant daughter which forms the resolution of "The Double Image" was unsatisfactory and brief, seems only to extend the confessional moment. It is a mock confidence to the interviewer and readership which serves to prolong the poem's closure.

Yet the success of these confessions (poetic and paratextual) is undercut in two ways. The first is by the glimpse of a less evocative and dramatic situation, a further unconfessed truth about the experience in question. This can be read in Sexton's reference to "The Double Image" in her lecture notes, where a sense of anger, shame, and distress emerges in the fractured language and dissolving sense of her comments:

> Sounds nice, doesn't it? Poetic. That I should write such a poem and get my daughter. Truth was she went back in three days, crying for her Nana, not me the mother, the never remembered, the not often enough, the not teach me the word for Mama, the not put me on the toidy [sic] seat, the not feed me the cereal. (Crawshaw [1] 7)

The other is in the extratextual contradiction to these glib statements subsequently offered by the poet's eldest, and here forgotten, daughter Linda. Linda Sexton describes her own disturbing memories of the relationship in quite a different way (*Searching* 14). She accuses her mother, in omitting to mention her either in the poems or her later explanation of their sources, of denying the truth of the real and terrible situation into which she was expelled—a period of neglect with allegedly abusive relatives. From this, one could argue that Sexton's omission of an older daughter was not for the sake of dramatic coherence, but because the truth behind that child's experience was too awful to confess. Similarly, Linda Sexton reveals that her mother's seemingly vulnerable admission that she was not well enough to take care of her daughter when they were first temporarily reunited masks a more mundane and less sympathetic truth, one which she only discovered many years later:

> I saw that she had actually come home after a brief hospitalization of a few weeks. She spent the remainder of the time I was in Scituate [the

six months while Linda was with the relatives] at home: keeping her
appointments with her analyst, lunching with friends, having her hair
done. She slept in her own bed and wandered through her own house.
(*Searching* 25)

My point here is not to judge any one of these versions of past events to be
more credible than any of the others, but to demonstrate that the "true" experiences which the poet suggests are at the root of the poem are terminally
undecidable. The attempt to isolate and finalize the truth is doomed to failure, and is the subject of endless reiteration and reinterpretation. The apparent truth of the poem is shown to be a falsehood by means of the additional
insights afforded by the extratextual commentary, and truth itself is thus deferred beyond the text. This is an evasive strategy by which the subject avoids
speaking honestly and displaces the responsibility onto another. Truth, then,
is not sought out, but sidestepped.

Sexton's paratexts, like the poems which they ostensibly validate, are characterized by contradiction and casuistry. Her supposedly sincere confessions,
or perhaps metaconfessions, about the truth-status of the poems are as evasive
and dissembling as the poems themselves. Clearly, Sexton is conscious of this:
"It rather pleases me in a quizzical fashion to do this because then I don't have
to really admit to anything" (Heyen 137). In her apparent explication of the
referentiality (or truth-value) of "Some Foreign Letters," she declares that
the poem "is a mixture of truth and lies. I don't feel like confessing which is
which. When I wrote it I attempted to make all of it 'true.' It remains true
for me to this day" ("Comment" 16). Here, she uses confident, frank rhetoric to persuade us that she is confiding something—giving the key to the
poem—whereas, in fact, she is giving nothing away. Similar statements include the equivocal: "Many of my poems are true, line by line, altering a few
facts" (so, in other words, they are not "true"); the evasive: "Each poem has
its own truth" (thus denying any connection with actuality); and the artful:
"I don't adhere to literal facts. . . . I make them up" (Kevles 103). Moreover,
in her insistence that "Some Foreign Letters" remains "true *for me*," Sexton
concedes an important point about the subjective nature of truth, thereby
disputing the kind of reading which would see the confessional text as offering a transcendent truth for all people and all time.

It is apparent that, in statements such as these, Sexton is toying with the classic contradictions which fuel any discourse about truth. This is seen most clearly in her 1965 *Hudson Review* interview. Asked about her earlier comment that "All poets lie," Sexton explains:

> I think maybe it's an evasion of mine. It's a very easy thing to say, "All poets lie." It depends on what you want to call the truth, you see, and it's also a way of getting out of the literal fact of a poem. You can say there is truth in this, but it might not be the truth of my experience. Then again, if you say that you lie, you can get away with telling the awful truth. That's why it's an evasion. (Marx 75)

This is an example of the Cretan Liar Paradox: If "all poets lie," then this poet must be lying. If she is lying, how can we credit her assertion that some poems depict "the awful truth," or that behind her lie, there is a truth? The consequence of this paradoxical truth-game is to question the possibility or reliability of any claim to authenticity or referentiality. Thom Gunn comments on this paradox: "It may well be that she is most credible when she fictionalizes her experience" ("On All" 126). The reader in such a case is wrong-footed, unable to identify the most truthful texts and unsure whether those which appear most truthful are, in fact, simply the most successful fakes. In her 1966 television interview, Sexton admits "I faked it up with the truth."

It is the reader, though, who is crucial to the establishment of the truth. In a draft introduction to her work written for the Poetry Book Society (commissioned on its recommendation of Sexton's 1964 *Selected Poems*, published only in the United Kingdom), Sexton acknowledges the debt: "Many of them [the poems] are true. Others are about lives I haven't led. Yet I keep thinking . . . someone has to believe them! I hope someone will" (HRHRC). The 16 June 1967 entry in her (aborted) "Journal of a Living Experiment" (the diary which she was required to keep as part of her participation in the Teachers and Writers Collaborative) explains:

> I also know something about moments in time, the sense of a good, right, clear moment. Confusion getting rinsed off. I call these moments Truth. But actually they are moments of understanding in people I'm with or in the books of what is alive. (HRHRC)

Hence truth is to be found in the text ("in the books") or in the process of reading ("moments of understanding in people") rather than in some prior and authenticating authorial experience. Thus Sexton shrugs off the role of truth-finder and teller, and assumes instead that of innocent listener. She reads other people's critiques "to see where the truth might lie" and explains that "I am told that my poetry is the work of a victim, of the passive sufferer, of the crucified man. And I put that thought in my mouth and taste it and find it surprising but true" (Crawshaw [9] 1–2).

Throughout her work, Sexton draws attention to the strategies and techniques by which "truth" might be produced in the sense both of brought forth and of created. For example, she insists repeatedly on the importance of strict poetic form as a means of capturing and displaying it. Her draft introduction for the Poetry Book Society explains:

> If you care about form, about half are in form of some sort. But form, for me, is a trick to deceive myself, not you but me. When I am finished with this trickery, I often hide it so that no one can see that I had my back to the wall all the time. Who, after all, wants to be caught doing an acrostic while they thought they were really telling all? What I mean to say is that some poems are too difficult to write without controls of some sort. (HRHRC)

Truth, then, will only emerge as a consequence of a nexus of prohibitions. It is inextricably connected with power. Sexton's "Journal of A Living Experiment," mentioned on a number of occasions above, although eventually discontinued, is the only one of her prose diaries to be sustained for more than a few days. This, I would venture, is because it was written under the kind of strict imperatives, controls, and time constraints she here describes. Truth is difficult of access, evasive, shifting and needs to be trapped or beguiled by the "trickery" of form; only then can it be isolated and revealed. In an interview with Patricia Marx, apropos these comments, Sexton explains:

> I think all form is a trick to get at the truth. Sometimes in my hardest poems, the ones that are difficult to write, I might make an impossible scheme, a syllabic count that is so involved, that it then allows me to be truthful. . . . But you can see how I say this not to deceive you but to deceive me. I deceive myself saying to myself you can't do it, and then if I can get it, then I have deceived myself, then I can change it and do what I want. I can even change it and rearrange it so no one can see my trick. (80)

Sexton's repeated explanations of the importance of these formal tricks as a way of accessing truth may in themselves, as a close reading of her syntax suggests, be a trick or deception. Specifically, "I say this" proclaims the possibility that what she "says" is not true. Hers is a problematic assertion, not least because it is clear that, notwithstanding her insistence that she is the one beguiled by this technique, we too, as readers of the putatively authentic truth, are affected and even served by the strategy. As J. D. McClatchy points out, the tricks "serve as a method of conviction for both poet and reader" (256).

Most importantly, as I have indicated, Sexton's explanation of the importance of "tricks," controls, and constraints in the representation of truth should be understood as an acknowledgment of the importance of such procedures in constructing truth. As Foucault argues, truth is "produced only by virtue of multiple forms of constraint": "'Truth' is to be understood as a system of ordered procedures for the production, regulation, distribution, circulation, and operation of statements" ("Truth" 72, 74).

An equally effective strategy is Sexton's insertion of "made-up" facts to add verisimilitude to her text. Specific and intimate details are incorporated in the poems in order to seduce the reader into believing that they are seeing true, lived experience. As Jean-Jacques Rousseau explains of his own *Confessions*: "It is not enough for my story to be truthful, it must be detailed as well" (169). In Sexton's case as, arguably in Rousseau's, such details are synthetic. They are consciously added to give the impression of authenticity: "I don't adhere to literal facts all the time; I make them up whenever needed. Concrete examples give a verisimilitude" (Kevles 329). The simulation of "real life" is a strategy of dissimulation. Verisimilitude is not truth, it is like truth. To adopt Julia Kristeva's words, there is a "semblance of truth which is at work in the discourse of art" (220). Roland Barthes refers to Aristotle's understanding of verisimilitude as not necessarily what is, or even what once was, but what is possible (*Criticism* 34)—a distinction which is replicated in Julia Kristeva's notion of the "plausible" (220, 217). The truth is that which the reader can be persuaded to believe. The credible is that which can be read with credulity. The wealth of personal and specific details, the use of the intimate, first-person voice which appears to be confiding difficult and deeply felt secrets, and the personal address to significant others or to the reader—all characteristics of Sexton's work—contribute to the impression of verisimilitude.

Equally, Sexton makes use of narrative chronology to give the impression of "honest precision." As McClatchy proposes, "the poems . . . have a kind of chronicle effect on readers, as one keeps track volume by volume" (251, 252). Narrative coherence is established within and between poems and collections. For example, the "story" of Sexton's relationship with her parents is sustained throughout *All My Pretty Ones* and beyond; the "story" of her friend Ruth informs "With Mercy for the Greedy" and "The Letting Down of the Hair." A further effect of this cumulative chronology is that the poems are not only permitted to validate (to be "true to") themselves, but to validate, or authenticate, each other. Thus the details of "A Little Uncomplicated Hymn" seem to authorize the truth of "The Double Image." The sequences of poems in Robert Lowell's *The Dolphin* and Ted Hughes's *Birthday Letters* arguably work in the same way.

Sexton wants both to give the impression of truthfulness (I use the word "impression" advisedly in order to indicate both a semblance and an imprint or mark) and to dissociate herself from overly credulous readings. It is noteworthy that the verbs which we have available to us in this context (produce, establish, find) unavoidably work in two ways; they are themselves dissembling, or "double crossing." It is the equivocation which seems inescapably to accompany any discussion of truth which is one of Sexton's most persistent, and important, subjects.

Such is the case in the 1972 poem "The Errand." Apparently addressed to a fellow poet, it takes as its subject the deceitful and prevaricating nature of the ostensibly truthful confession. It also alludes to the pressure on the confessional poet to continue to produce the truth, hence the poem's dogged and weary opening line: "I've been going right on, page by page." "The Errand" conjures up images of disguise, veiled truth, and misdirection to describe the two poets' work: "two hunger-mongers throwing a myth in and out, / double-crossing our lives with doubt." The image of "double-crossing" is a frank recognition both of the potentially deceitful nature of the confession, and of the status of the paratextual comments which supposedly clarify, but merely obfuscate, the difference between truth and lies. The image of "hunger-mongers" suggests a traffic in, fascination with and exploitation of need and is particularly pertinent to the confessional role.

The perceived obsessions of the confessional poet are catalogued. These include hedonistic and practical means of self-destruction ("cognac and razor blades"), medical and psychiatric relationships ("my shrink" and "some doctor") and religious concerns ("The Cross" and "that eggless man"). The truth is vulnerable to manipulation and division: "But then I've told my readers what I think / and scrubbed out the remainder with my shrink." It is shifting and evasive (it "won't settle" and is described in terms of "escapades" and "barriers"). The role of the poet is revealed to be just a disguise, masking uncertainty:

> Let us be folk of the literary set,
> let us deceive with words the critics regret,
> let us dog down the streets for each invitation,
> typing out our lives like a Singer sewing sublimation . . .

The very specific image of the "Singer sewing sublimation" alludes to the costume or material camouflage adopted by the confessional poet (the pun, too, is on poetry as song). The simple rhyming couplets which constitute the basic form of the poem may be read as a mocking demonstration of the ease with which the "literary set" may be joined, and supposedly authentic and meaningful texts produced. Yet the jumble of experiences and images on which such "delicate" sublimations draw is itself shown in all its emergent and excessive power.

The penultimate stanza sees the return of the repressed objects which had been veiled by the earlier sublimations, brought back to life in all of their violent, sexual excess:

> They were spanked alive by some doctor of folly,
> given a horn or a dish to get by with, by golly,
> exploding with blood in this errand called life,
> dumb with snow and elbows, rubber man, a mother wife . . .

However, neither the poetic sublimations, nor the final garbled and energetic effort to retain a voice, can fight off the real truth which is the inevitable and impending fact of death: "because this errand we're on goes to one store." The "decades of disguises" are obsolete. The desperate attempt to evoke day-to-day life, to create verisimilitude, fails:

> the shopkeeper plants his boot in our eyes,
> and unties our bone and is finished with the case,
> and turns to the next customer, forgetting our face
> or how we knelt at the yellow bulb with sighs
> like moth wings for a short while in a small place.

This may be read as a reference to the vicissitudes of the literary marketplace which threatens a metaphorical death, as well as a literal one. The quiet and monosyllabic words of the final line of the poem offer a simple and grave acknowledgment of the weakness and insignificance of the poet's words and thus of the truths apparently revealed. Although earlier referred to as "stones," we see them now as fragile, vulnerable things.

It is important to recognize that although all forms of confession seem to promise truth, they may not be able to deliver. According to Foucault, the Western technique of confession produces "a literature ordered according to the infinite task of extracting from the depths of oneself in between the words, a truth which the very form of confession holds out like a shimmering mirage" (*History* 59). Thus the truth of the text may be found, if at all, neither in its utterances nor in any pretextual experience, but in its own silences, gaps, elisions, and aporia:

> Silence itself—the things one declines to say, or is forbidden to name, the discretion that is required between different speakers—is less the absolute limit of discourse, the other side from which it is separated by a strict boundary, than an element that functions alongside the things said, with them and in relation to them within all-over strategies. (*History* 27)

Thus the lying and hiding that Sexton declares to be at the heart of her confessions may, paradoxically, be the means of establishing their truth.

Sexton's iconic 1965 poem "A Little Uncomplicated Hymn" asks how voice and silence work together to present a truth. It explores the competing pressures under which the confessional poet labors (tell all versus tell nothing) and provokes questions about the speaker's degree of activity or passivity (is she evading truth, or is it escaping her?). The initial tone of the poem is controlled and confident, declaiming the speaker's intended voice and subject. Yet it quickly becomes uncertain. There is a tentative and self-conscious recognition (shown by the use of the past tense, "I wanted" and "there was," and emphasized by the enjambment of the title and first line) of the failure of representation, of what the poem cannot be:

A LITTLE UNCOMPLICATED HYMN
for Joy

is what I wanted to write.
There *was* such a song!

The poem bears comparison with William Carlos Williams's line "I wanted to write a poem" in his "January Morning."

Having alerted us to the failure of the poem on the terms anticipated by its title, Sexton's speaker teases the reader with a catalogue of what might have been:

> There was such a song!
> A song for your kneebones,
> a song for your ribs,
>
> . . .
>
> a song for your dress-up high heels,
> your fire-red skate board.

There is an energy and a conscious creativeness in this summary of what the poet had wanted to write, with its lively images and Whitmanesque anaphora ("a song for your"). This is a celebration of the poet's power to evoke the body, the mind, and the potential of her daughter. In the second stanza, however, the pace is slowed, and the paean becomes "a song for your night." The lines are longer, the vowels heavier ("spooned," "moving," "mumbling"). The syntax is more complex, demanding greater concentration from the reader. In the first stanza, the speaker deftly conjures up a wealth of dancing images; in the second, she is powerless: "I cannot undo." The refrain "a song for" appears infrequently. It can no longer communicate on its own terms and, instead, must be followed by a lengthy explication as though the literary convention (the poetic "song") has malfunctioned or proved inadequate for evoking the desired truth.

The speaker attempts to appropriate the power of naming, in stanza five declaring, "I named you Joy" but then being forced to concede the limits of her power. In naming the child "Joy," as she confesses, she has told only a partial truth:

> I named
> all things you are . . .
> except the ditch
> where I left you once.

In stanza six again the speaker tries to attach a word to her child, and to make it a meaningful representation: "Joy, I call you." But again, she must admit that she has failed; her own words cannot counter the child's: "'Why was I shut in the cellar?'"

In a later stanza, the speaker insists on the failure of her project, taking us full circle back to the opening of the poem:

> And I can only say
> a little uncomplicated hymn
> is what I wanted to write
> and yet I find only your name

The speaker is in a passive position, used by, and at the mercy of, language. She has failed to represent adequately the truth of the daughter's experience or of the mother/daughter relationship, has failed to provide the "little uncomplicated hymn" promised in the title, and has delivered, instead, only confusion, silence, and misunderstanding:

> There *was* such a song,
> but it's bruised.
> It's not mine.

The image of the bruise encapsulates the speaker's experience of telling the truth as one of suffering and loss. The poem closes with a reprise of her original optimistic intentions, and with an inevitable acceptance of the inability of the form to represent the subject, of the literary work to reflect reality, or of the writer to convey the truth. Of this vast, complex and spirited exercise, "just one" truth—evoked in simple, monosyllabic words—remains:

> I found just one.
>
> you were mine
> and I lent you out.
>
> I look for uncomplicated hymns
> but love has none.

The typographical gaps on the page reinforce the void between the "hymn"/poem and the complex emotion which it seeks to represent. Foucault's truth "in between the words" is embodied in the spaces between the lines. The aporia here exemplifies Kristeva's point that truth is that which is not and cannot be expressed; it is the "unspoken of the spoken," something beyond the grasp of orthodox truth-discourses: " the unspoken in all discourse . . . whatever remains unsatisfied, repressed, new, eccentric, incomprehensible, that which disturbs the mutual understanding of the established powers" (153, 156). J. M. Coetzee makes a similar point in "Confession and Double Thoughts": "The 'unconscious' truth slips out in strange associations, false rationalizations, gaps, contradictions" (257).

What are we to make of the best endeavors of the confessional poet when the truth escapes representation other than by means of the concentration of these few simple words and the silence which surrounds them? Ironically, we are left with a confessional voice which resists the lure of the dramatically and visibly poetic to offer an uncomplicated hymn which says all there is to say, while acknowledging that confession cannot express the truth of the complex relationship between the speaker and her child. We should note, however, that the speaker has disclaimed ownership of such a truth ("There was such a song / . . . It's not mine"). The truth which emerges at the end of this poem does so in spite of the best intentions of the poet (as the past tense of the opening line suggests, the poet's wishes, or what she "wanted to write," are irrelevant). The silences and omissions in the poem indicate a paradoxical truth about the unrepresentability of truth which cannot be told. In insisting that the text cannot do justice to the truth, the poem tells its own form of truth:

> I wanted to write her a little uncomplicated hymn. I spent a year try-
> ing. Stops and starts, fumbles. . . . I wanted to write it and I couldn't,
> perhaps because of my own guilt. So as it goes, I wrote it honestly an
> anti-hymn, very complicated. You can't always write the way you want
> to. (Crawshaw [10] 12)

There is an analogy here with the psychotherapeutic situation. Although it is common to read confession as a form of therapy or talking cure, it is obvious that there are some truths which avoid exposure. The fact that psychotherapy and confession might seek the truth is no guarantee of the success of either: "you can't always write the way you want to"; one can't always say what one means.

Sexton's long poem, "Is It True?" written in 1973, brings to the fore the doubts and uncertainties about truth which everywhere characterize her writing. Most importantly it questions the accuracy and efficacy of any de-piction or representation of truth, including, crucially, its own representations. Like "Little Uncomplicated Hymn," it problematizes the process by which "truth" is translated into words, symbols, song. "Is It True?" which, in part, questions the truth of God, should be seen as problematizing a Western epistemology which sees Logos as the ultimate guarantor of truth.[1] Yet it is a poem of profound uncertainty. It does not declare the referent of the "it" of the title. It asks a question, yet is uncertain what it is asking, unsure where to look, and doubtful about the possibility of finding an answer.

The poem opens with the image of a carpenter occasionally glancing up to heaven, as though for reassurance as he goes about his daily work:

Once more
the sun roaming on the carpenter's back
as he puts joist to sill
and then occasionally he looks to the sky
as even the hen when it drinks
looks toward heaven.

Ostensibly, this image indicates that all creative acts are in service of a greater good, or in the service of God, and that his blessing is sought. Yet such an epistemology is undermined by the resonance in Sexton's poetry of the image of the carpenter as death-seeker or suicide (as, for example, in "Wanting to Die" where "suicides have a special language. / Like carpenters they want to know *which tools*"). Thus, this carpenter is not seeking a blessing, but rather glancing upwards in fear of retribution. So, too, the image of the hen represents all creatures' subservience to divine will and, more bathetically—and certainly more in keeping with Sexton's style—a nursery-rhyme "Chicken Licken" frightened that the sky is going to fall. In either case (and by metaphorical extension, in the case of the poet herself), we have a vulnerable subject who is unsure and who is seeking evidence of God's presence and of the extent of his power.

The speaker, like the hen and carpenter of the opening lines, seeks approval or reassurance. Although the "sun" (God/Logos/light) shines frequently on the supplicant, the speaker has only "once" sought him out and praised him:

Once in Rome I knelt in front of the Pope
as he waved from his high window.
It was because of a pain in my bowels.

The deflation from the formal syntax of "as even the hen" in line five to the anecdotal "Once in Rome" to the scatological ("my bowels") establishes a tension which sustains the poem between reverence and irreverence, the spirit and the body, faith and skepticism, and truth and falsehood. The sacred and the profane coexist—a juxtaposition which provokes the first of many wondering exclamations throughout the poem: "Perhaps it is true." Israel, it seems, is still "the promised land" in spite of the excesses of twentieth-century commercialism: "Now even the promised land of / Israel has a Hilton."

The point of these geographically and culturally incongruous images (from Rome to Israel to the United States; Catholicism to the Hare Krishna movement) is to indicate the lengths to which the speaker will go to find truth. Yet the facility with which one place or creed replaces another is evidence of a profound moral and spiritual dissatisfaction: an inability to find truth in any of these "promised lands." In a letter to Louis Untermeyer, written on 3 April 1963 some ten years before "Is It True?" and thanking him for his support of her application for her traveling fellowship, Sexton quotes some lines from Emerson about the futility of such a journey:

> "Traveling is a fool's paradise. . . . At home I dream that at Naples, at Rome, I can be intoxicated with beauty, and lose my sadness. I pack my trunk, embrace my friends, embark on the sea, and at last wake up in Naples, and there beside me is the stern Fact, the sad self, unrelenting, identical, that I fled from. I seek the Vatican, and the palaces. I affect to be intoxicated with sights and suggestions, but I am not intoxicated. My giant goes with me wherever I go." (HRHRC)

Further, the textual guides—the map and the Bible—which would conventionally permit one to find the literal and figurative path to truth are shown to have failed: "I have lost my map / and Jesus has squeezed out of the Gideon."

Later (stanza ten), the speaker abandons these physical and spiritual routes to truth, concentrating on secular sources closer to home. She focuses on the literal, the practical and the mundane, as though, as a last resort, to test the truth value of the real world ("typewriters," "skillets," "shoes"). This recalls "The Errand," where the most tantalizing of material objects proves unable to disguise the truth of imminent death. None of these resources can satisfy her desire for understanding, hence the repeated, plaintive cries ("Is it true? /

Is it true?") which punctuate the poem. Again, there is a profound self-consciousness about her own failure as a writer, either to find or—an important distinction—to convey the truth.

In stanza five, the speaker turns to a priest and tries to represent the despicable nature of her own identity. Yet in spite of the apparent frankness of her explanation, this priest/confessor, is unable to understand or see the truth of her condition:

> When I tell the priest I am evil
> he asks for a definition of the word.
> Do you mean sin? he asks.

It transpires that the meaning of evil, like the meaning of truth, does not inhere in the term itself, but can only be signified by reference to what it does not mean:

> Sin, hell! I reply.
> I've committed every one.
> What I mean is evil,
> (not meaning to be, you understand,
> just something I ate).

The speaker is able to define truth only by reference to its conventional antithesis, to lying: "Evil is maybe lying to God. / Or better, lying to love." Put simply: If one lies, one betrays the truth, and thus deserves the label "evil." Yet the priest does not understand. Throughout the poem, the primary barrier to the realization and representation of truth is the failure of interpretation, specifically on the part of those ascribed (in Foucault's phrase) a "hermeneutic function." The priest (standing in here for the audience, judge, or psychiatrist) is charged with the acceptance and interpretation of the confession, and when he fails in his duty, truth cannot be realized. Here, in spite of the speaker's attempt at a clear definition, the priest/confessor "shakes his head. / He doesn't comprehend." Crucially, the priest can only "comprehend" if he is permitted to witness the physical dramatization of the truth. Action speaks louder than words; the body signifies where language does not. What the priest and the avaricious confessional audience want to see here, like in "The Letting Down of the Hair" or "Talking to Sheep," is physical evidence, relics, the embodiment, or performance of the truth:

> But the priest understands
> when I tell him that I want to
> pour gasoline over my evil body
> and light it.

The auditor's inability to understand the truth impacts on the speaker's own ability to comprehend it. In stanza seven, she is forced into the position of interrogating herself, addressing herself in the second person in a manner reminiscent of Berryman's *Dream Songs*: "Ms. Dog, / why is you evil?"

Stanza eight conveys the desperation of this search for truth. It invokes, while mocking, the psychotherapeutic practice of looking to the past and to past parenting for the roots of present trauma: "Maybe my mother cut the God out of me / when I was two in my playpen." The speaker envisions herself as suffering in a waste land of uncertainty (the image replicates the central metaphor of "Hurry Up Please It's Time," written one year earlier). She is in a wilderness of her own making: "All is hay that died from too much rain, / my stinky tears." "Stinky tears" evokes the same sense of abjection, shame, and worthlessness as attended the reference to the queer-smelling confession in "Talking to Sheep." There is a self-consciousness here about the easy, glib, but nevertheless inaccurate, representations of truth in this and other texts. In "The Black Art" (published in 1962), for example, the act of confession is an excessive gesture: "There is too much food and no one left over / to eat up all the weird abundance." In "Cigarettes and Whiskey and Wild, Wild Women" (1974), the speaker comes to realize that her identity as a "woman of excess, of zeal and greed" has distanced her from, rather than brought her into proximity with, the truth which she seeks.

In "Is It True?" "need is not quite belief." The desperate lengths to which the truth-seeker is prepared to go are no indication of her eventual success. However, there is no mistaking the profundity of her desire for spiritual nourishment:

> A starving man doesn't ask what the meal is.
> I would eat a tomato, or a fire bird or music.
> I would eat a moth soaked in vinegar.

Regardless of the speaker's avowed lack of interest in asking questions, a fundamental and persistent uncertainty about the nature and origin of truth remains. Paradoxically, the speaker's doubts about the existence of God are expressed in the repeated invocation of His word (signifying either a deep cynicism or the vestiges of belief): the reference to the "wilderness" in stanza eight, quoted earlier, draws on the book of Isaiah, as does the allusion to wood in stanza nine.[2]

The mood shifts in stanza ten from one of anxiety and despair to one of hope and optimism—although the benedictions ("Bless all, . . . / Bless also") which figure throughout this stanza have the effect of a talisman rather than a credo. The leap of faith signified by the attempt to offer a blessing is always grounded, and thereby spoiled, by the persistent uncertainty about whether "it" is true. This stanza, I would argue, offers a veiled but nevertheless effective refutation of the notion that the confessional poet serves merely as a mirror of or "conduit" (Marjorie Perloff's term) to truth. Here, in an exemplification of Sexton's intention, quoted earlier, to "make all of it true," it is tools, artifice, the process of construction which are praised ("Bless all useful objects"). The speaker twice valorizes the cooked over the raw ("the mattress I cook my dreams upon" and "the skillet, / black and oil soaked"), thus refuting Lowell's distinction between the two and indicating that truth may be found in the former rather than the latter (Hamilton 277).

The end of the stanza returns to the persistent and still unanswerable question posed in the poem's title. Coming straight after this confident and self-reflexive examination of the text's own processes, it tables the possibility that "it" (certainty about anything) is not true and thereby undermines its own processes of inquiry and exposition. Yet even in the face of evidence of the absence of God, or truth, the speaker still clings to the vestiges of belief:

> If religion were a dream, someone said,
> then it were still a dream worth dreaming.
> True! True!
> I whisper to my wood walls.

"Whispering" is a way of partially revealing the truth without declaiming it in full. Sexton uses whispering as a trope to suggest deceit, ambivalence, and reticence or the barely perceptible truth hidden behind the declamatory surface. In "The Passion of the Mad Rabbit," for example, or "The Letting Down of the Hair," the truth is to be found not in the frank and forceful confessions but in whispered asides and confidences. Whispering, as a metaphor for writing, signifies a quiet, latent truth waiting to be told. It also signifies, in the fact that the whisper must not publicly be heard, secrecy, shame, and fear of punishment.

Crucially, the speaker foregrounds her own inability to tell the truth. Stanza fifteen declares: "My tongue is slit / It cannot eat." This projects an image of self as liar (she has a slit or forked tongue) who is therefore not worthy of God's truth. Her tongue is slit because, as we know from stanza eight, this is the part of the body which the mother sliced open "to take the God out of me." If God is not in her tongue, she does not have the power to describe, invoke, commune with, or even receive him. Significantly, this loss is figured as a physical phenomenon akin to the autotomy and synecdoche which we have seen elsewhere. The only way in which Sexton is able to write about herself, and her own relation to confessional writing, is in terms of the casting-off of parts of the self, in terms of fracture, loss, or incompletion.

"Is It True?" emphasizes the barriers to representation and explication. It is frank in its acknowledgment of the difficulties of communicating truth, even if truth were first to be found. It is impossible for the speaker (penitent) to make the reader (confessor) comprehend: "Do you understand? / Can you read my hieroglyphics?" The reference to the hieroglyphics both invokes Ezra Pound's championing of the ideogram as an effective signifying system and brings to mind the earlier section of the poem where the priest is incapable of understanding language but can interpret gestures (Pound *ABC*). "Hieroglyphics" also makes self-deprecating reference to the text's own impenetrability, to the barriers which inevitably attend the evocation and interpretation, the finding and telling of truth. The onus is firmly placed on the reader—"Can you read?"—to decipher the truth of the text. The 29 September 1967 entry in Sexton's "Journal of a Living Experiment," while reflecting on the experience of teaching poetry, contemplates such a conundrum. The errors in the syntax unwittingly exemplify the very barriers it describes:

> It was the poet's job is to write so their understood [*sic*]. . . . Poems shouldn't be hieroglyphics. They should be explicit . . . easily understandable . . . moving. Not that you shouldn't read a poem twice. . . . Not that I wanted them to guess what I meant, but I wanted them to guess what the poem said. I kept referring to the text. (HRHRC)

There is a profound anxiety here about the apparent incomprehensibility and thus unavoidable failure of the confession.

The poem returns, finally, to the problematic exchange between penitent and priest. The failure to tell the truth is matched by the audience's failure to hear it:

When I tell the priest I am full
of bowel movement, right into the fingers,
he shrugs. To him shit is good.
To me, to my mother, it was poison
and the poison was all of me
in the nose, in the ears, in the lungs.
That's why language fails.
Because to one, shit is a feeder of plants,
to another the evil that permeates them.

In a letter of 29 May 1974 addressed to J. D. McClatchy in response to his comments on "Is It True?" Sexton explains: "As it so happens, in the bio-graphical/confessional truth of it all, it was both first a priest then a psychia-trist. Neither liked the 'evil' until I made it into a metaphorical truth-telling, shit driven explanation" (HRHRC). Sexton's comments encapsulate the am-bivalent position of the confessional speaker. She is applauded by the "priest" for her purgative or therapeutic act (for the "gift" of the faeces), yet she is con-demned by her culture for her sordid revelations, and she is simultaneously seized by her own anxiety about, and revulsion towards, her emissions. The "metaphorical truth-telling, shit driven explanation" attempts to bring these polarized positions into proximity (yoking "shit" and "good," "poison" and nutrition). It emphasizes the latent contiguity, even identity, between them. The "metaphorical truth-telling, shit driven explanation" (the poem) offers itself as a paradigm of the process by which truth is a product of reading, of interpretation. "Shit" is, in one context or for one reader, a metaphor for evil; in another context or for another reader, it is a metaphor for good. The image of the "muck funnel" in Plath's "Words Heard" similarly connotes both waste and fertility (Ford 131).

Finally, in a supreme metaphor for confessional process, the speaker is forced to concede: "I can only imagine it is true." Truth can never be found or "told," instead it must be approached and suggested in metaphor, fictional-ized or "imagine[d]." It cannot even be played out on the speaker's body for this, too, has betrayed her: "Maybe my evil body is done with." In a manner which entirely exemplifies the larger points made by "Is It True?" the final section of the poem is susceptible to at least two major and contradictory interpretations. From one perspective, it suggests that there is a pretextual truth which will, inevitably and finally, emerge. Truth will out, and will sidestep any attempts to capture it, showing itself only when the speaker has given up the search (rather like in "A Little Uncomplicated Hymn" where it is on abandoning the attempt to capture her daughter's experience that the truth surfaces). In other words, the poem does answer in the affirmative its own questions: It finds "truth," and it offers us a truthful representation. Alternatively, the answer or truth, such as it is, is that the question is insoluble. There is no glorious epiphany, only a mechanical gesture. There is no sense of resolution, only tenacity, persistence:

> For I look up,
> and in a blaze of butter is
> Christ,
>
> . . . .
> . . . who lives on, lives on
> like the wings of an Atlantic seagull.
> Though he has stopped flying,
> the wings go on flapping
> despite it all,
> despite it all.

Sexton's personal library holds a heavily annotated copy of a book entitled *Helping Your Child to Understand Death*. Sexton has underlined one particular line—"the mystery is harder to bear than the reality"—and has inscribed "always" in the margin. This seems to me to signify both the question and the answer of "Is It True?" It invokes the condition of indeterminacy, the absence of closure and the inevitable continuation of the ceaseless quest to find the awful unknown. Just as "Is It True?" refuses to declare what "it" is, the poem exemplifies the impossibility of ascertaining whether "it" is true. Neither the question nor the answer can ever be resolved.

Marjorie Perloff sees as characteristic of modern poetry the eventual realization of "some sort of epiphany, a moment of insight or vision with which the poem closes" (*Dance* 156–57). Yet as we have seen in "Is It True?," "Hurry Up Please It's Time," "A Little Uncomplicated Hymn" and, before that, in "For John Who Begs Me Not to Enquire Further" and "An Obsessive Combination," this is not a characteristic of Sexton's work. Rather, her poetry features an—arguably postmodernist—tendency towards equivocation and indeterminacy, towards provisionality, uncertainty and evasion. Sexton's reluctance to conclude her writing on a resounding, authoritative and thus normative and reassuring note is sign of a refusal to concede to totalization, and of a wish to keep multiple interpretative possibilities open. The unanswered and unanswerable questions of "Is It True?" and "Hurry Up Please," the multifaceted bowl of "For John" and the many-pointed star of "An Obsessive Combination," alongside similar tropes, indicate that insight is always complex and elusive. This contradicts received perceptions of confessional writing which is conventionally conceived as predicated on the desire to find and reveal the truth, to reach closure and to deliver catharsis. Sexton's poetry represents, to return to Linda Hutcheon, "a questioning of commonly accepted values of our culture (closure, teleology, and subjectivity), a questioning that is totally dependent upon that which it interrogates. This is perhaps the most basic formulation possible of the paradox of the postmodern" (*Poetics* 42).

Sexton's writing exemplifies what John Cage has proposed as the way forward for postmodernism: "The situation must be yes-and-no not either-or" (qtd. in Perloff, *Dance* 183). In the terms of these poems, it must be I-and-you ("For John") and RATS-and-STAR ("An Obsessive Combination"). Looking back to "Her Kind," it must be light-and-dark, order-and-disorder, life-and-death, being-and-nothingness. The right reserved in her poetry is the right to appropriate the middle ground, the medial space between the outside and the inside and the public and the private (equally, between lies and truth, obfuscation and confession, artifice and authenticity). As Irving Weinman, a student with Sexton in Lowell's writing class, confirms: "She was not an either/or poet."[3]

Although Sexton has been labeled as a confessional poet, it is only by rethinking what confession signifies and entails and by conceding its discursiveness, contingency, and finally its indeterminacy that we can begin fully to understand her place in the mode and in the tradition of modern American poetry more generally. As this book has shown, the relationships between subject, experience, and representation are far more complex in Sexton's work than a superficial reading might reveal, and none of these elements can be comprehended without giving a degree of attention to other key factors in the construction of the meaning of the confession: namely, the role of the recipient, reader, or confessor and the specific historical and cultural contexts in which the work is generated.

Most important of all to the reassessment of Sexton's work I have proposed is the profound self-consciousness with which Sexton approaches the field. It is the process of confession, rather than the product, which is the sustained concern of her writing. This attentiveness to process can be identified both in Sexton's persistent paratextual commentaries on the mode and, more subtly and yet more strikingly at the detailed level of the poetic text. It is with the limitations of this process that Sexton finally, particularly in the late poems discussed in the last part of this book, reaches some kind of accommodation.

Appendix

"The Thought Disease"

Overhead the books are noisy.
I try to write.
The wallpaper is old,
the color of soured wine.
Thirty unwashed window panes
smoke in the weak March light.
Underneath,
the typewriter keys are beige thumbs.
I write at my mother'd [*sic*] desk,
but the words are mine.
Also, I have died here twice,
but that was ~~last~~ [illegible] year,
a poison that I tried.

This year, I've been watching
~~the alphabet, that nesting bunch~~
my words, that nesting bunch of
figures popping out of my thumbs.
Taking them separately, I see the legs
of children, pigs, chickens, a bald head,
boards to walk over, sticks bent by hands.

These dear families . . .
a, you are a world of your own

with an umbrella over you [*sic*] head;
b and d is a fat pudgy mine [*sic*] month old baby
looking in front of a mirror;
c, is shell, cup handle and coat hook,
is the eye of a lobster;
h is chair and j is barbless hook;
l is a flag on a golf course;
m is a radiator and n is a gravestone
and o, old o, old god, is a shout
from the end of a long pipe;
p pokes out like a muscle and is
the nose of a clown while q is a fat nine
and forgetting the others who also
resemble the others I see s,
that snake, that swan,
with a knife you are money.
    Unpublished typescript (HRHRC)

Notes

Chapter 1. The confessional mode

1. Sexton's daughter recalls that "the most poignant image I have of the difficulties she endured as an artist was my discovery, on the evening of her suicide, that she still carried in her wallet a clipping of the ax-job James Dickey had done" (Linda Gray Sexton, *Searching* 96).

2. John Diamond's *C: Because Cowards Get Cancer Too*, for example, is praised as a "brave and brilliant book" (*Times Literary Supplement* 9 Oct. 1998: 29). Such epithets are parodied to brilliant effect in Bel Littlejohn's spoof confession *Hug Me While I Weep for I Weep for the World* which she describes as "a brave book, brave and intimate" before declaring "My stark, painful, almost unbearable reminiscences are out: enjoy."

3. As Sexton explains the poem was written after she had had an (illegal) abortion: "When I came back from the abortion, I wrote my friend Ruth who lived in Japan about what I had done. Her reply was religious, and she sent me her dog bitten cross" (Crawshaw [9] 16).

4. Equally, one can detect similarities between Sexton's drafts and Plath's later "Lady Lazarus." The rhythms, rhyme, and bravura tone of the July 1959 draft of "Witch" are distinctive and, surely, provide a model for the resounding end rhymes of Plath's poem. "Witch" closes: "Who see me here / this ragged apparition / in their own air / see a wicked appetite / if they dare" (Middlebrook, *Biography* 114).

Chapter 2. Narcissism

1. Middlebrook speculates that "An Obsessive Combination" was written during August 1958 (*Biography* 124). However, as Sexton studied Hopkins's poetry during her time as a student in Robert Lowell's writing class (September 1958 to 1959), it is arguable that her poem originates at least one month later. On Lowell and Hopkins, see Hamilton 78 and Lowell, *Collected Prose* 167–70.

2. The mother's portrait is perceived as "a cave of a mirror" and "a stony head of death." Sexton's linking of the mirror and the cave is profoundly significant, paralleling Echo's retreat to the "caves" in Ovid's story.

3. Sexton's poem was probably critiqued in one of Robert Lowell's Boston University workshops in the spring of 1959. Plath audited the class from 24 February 1959; in her *Journal* entry for the next day she uses the image of a "bell jar." One month later (29 March 1959) the seeds of the plot of the novel are recorded in Plath's *Journal*. The "bell jar" motif had been used once before by Plath (July 1952) to describe the ennui of the summer vacations. Sexton's poem's inverted glass bowl may have prompted Plath to revisit the metaphor. Arguably, Sexton's use of the image in this exploration of writing, gender, and subjectivity offered Plath exactly the figure she needed to represent Esther Greenwood's mixed sense of vulnerability and visibility.

Chapter 3. Suburbia

1. My argument is informed, in part, by recent work in the field of cultural geography. As Edward Soja notes, "As we approach the fin de siècle, there is a growing awareness of the simultaneity and interwoven complexity of the social, the historical, and the spatial, their inseparability and interdependence" (3).

2. W. H. Auden in his "Foreword" to McGinley's *Times Three* rather overlooks the critical edge in these poems, asserting that "Phyllis McGinley needs no puff. Her poems are known and loved by tens of thousands. They call for no learned exegesis" (ix).

3. See Marianne Moore on Lowell's "Boston-in-its-glory residence" (qtd. in Hamilton 23).

4. Sexton later gave her annotated copy to her daughter who describes the "scribbled notes across the pages—notes that showed her identification with the problems Friedan described" (Linda Gray Sexton, *Searching* 98).

5. See http://teachingamericanhistory.org/library/index.asp?document=176.

6. As Tracy Brain has shown in relation to the poetry of Sylvia Plath, the 1950s and '60s saw an "emergent environmentalism" with Rachel Carson (author of *The Silent Spring* [1962]) as its figurehead (85).

7. The My Lai Massacre took place in Vietnam in March 1968. Up to 500 villagers were murdered, there was an immediate cover-up. The platoon commander was not charged until September 1969 and it was another two months before the U.S. public became aware of the scandal via journalist Seymour Hersh's exposés on November 12 and 20. See Oliver.

Chapter 4. Autobiography

1. Sexton claimed in a letter to her English publisher that "My family tree goes back to William Brewster who came over here on the Mayflower" (*Letters* 271).

2. Ted Hughes's "Your Paris" from *Birthday Letters* makes a similar point (36).

3. Amputation may signify punishment—a just retribution for the autobiographer who seeks to see and know too much (like Actaeon whose curiosity is punished by dismemberment by his own hounds). See Brooks 115.

4. This reciprocity of touch confirms that the confession is a two-way process. It is not just that the speaker "touches" or affects her audience; as Sexton explains in her interview with Barbara Kevles: "I want them to feel as if they were touching me" (329).

Chapter 5. Performance

1. From a letter of 16 March 1960, in which Sexton refers to having sent a story called "Hair" to her friend Ruth Soter, it is clear that the narrative existed in some form at this date. However, Soter died in 1964, and the story closes with contemplation of her death, thus, it appears that "The Letting Down of the Hair" was completed after this time (*Letters* 102).

2. Sexton may have obtained this image from a journalist who described her as "the loveliest recluse since Emily Dickinson" (Kenny).

3. Asked about the benefits brought by her fellowship to Radcliffe College, Sexton exclaimed: "It got me this room" (her house was extended with the benefit of her grant). Interview with Martha White. Audiotape (July 1963). Radcliffe Institute for Independent Study Archives.

4. Middlebrook records that in Sexton's first interview with her psychiatrist in 1956, she had "told him that she thought her only talent might be for prostitution: She could help men feel sexually powerful" (*Biography* 42). Maxine Kumin likens Sexton's reading style to "pimping" in "Kumin on Kumin and Sexton: An Interview" (2).

5. Ironically, after her death, Sexton's executors were accused of the posthumous exploitation of her writing, or the "crass capitalization on her saleable reputation as a personality, which is a disservice to her value as a poet" (Rev. of *Words for Dr. Y.*).

6. Sexton kept a cutting of Van Duyn's letter, and drafted a poetic reply: "Open Letter to Mona Van Duyn" (HRHRC).

7. Charles Osborne, Auden's biographer and the organizer of the event, remembers differently: "Wystan came and read his poems, and amused the audience by being visibly impatient with the American poet Anne Sexton, whose reading of her confessional verse went on and on. Before the evening was over he had reduced her to tears" (320).

Chapter 6. Language

1. Respectively, "Is It True?" "Love Song," "Is It True?" and "Words" (last two quotations).

2. "Letter Written During a January Northeaster" and "Words."

3. "The Thought Disease," unpublished typescript, HRHRC (quotations in square brackets indicate manuscript amendments to the original text). See Appendix.

4. Although Sexton does not acknowledge a debt to Saussure, and there is no evidence of her having encountered his work (the second edition of his *Course in General Linguistics* was translated and published in New York in 1959), I think it justifiable to suggest that her problematization of language, her demonstration of the two-sided and arbitrary nature of the sign, and her denial of the referentiality of language, echo and exemplify his thought.

5. See William Shurr for a discussion of the parallels with Emily Dickinson's "rowing" metaphors.

6. See Maxine Kumin "A Friendship Remembered" and "A Nurturing Relationship."

7. Sexton emphasized the importance to her writing of her acquaintance with Tillie Olsen in her interview with Martha White of the Radcliffe Institute for Independent Study: "Hearing Tillie's seminar probably changed my writing as much as anything... the whole theory of failure and how you can waste yourself." Radcliffe Institute for Independent Study Archives.

8. See "A Reminiscence" by Barbara Swan (the book's illustrator).

9. Sylvia Plath wrote to Sexton about "keeping bees and raising potatoes." Letter to Anne Sexton, 21 August 1962, HRHRC. In "The Bar Fly Ought to Sing," Sexton recalls: "Sylvia wrote of one child, keeping bees, another child, my poems" (10).

10. Sexton was introduced to Smart's *Jubilate Agno* in 1967. Anne Sexton, Letter to Nathaniel Tarn, 13 September 1967, HRHRC.

Chapter 7. Truth and lies

1. As Jacques Derrida argues, if language is deconstructed then so, exponentially, is truth. If it is understood that writing "no longer issues from a logos" what follows is "the de-sedimentation, the de-construction, of all the significations that have their source in that of the logos. Particularly the signification of truth" (10).

2. The biblical source is Isaiah 40:20. So, too, the question posed in stanza eleven ("If all this can be / then why am I in this country of black mud?") evokes Isaiah 34: 9–10 and the devastation of the land of Edom. See Morton 26.

3. Interview with the author, November 1992.

Bibliography

Primary sources: Sexton works

Sexton, Anne. *A Self-Portrait in Letters*. Ed. Linda Gray Sexton and Lois Ames. Boston: Houghton Mifflin, 1977.

———. "All God's Children Need Radios." In Colburn, ed., *No Evil Star*, 23–32.

———. *All My Pretty Ones*. Boston: Houghton Mifflin, 1962.

———. *The Awful Rowing Toward God*. Boston: Houghton Mifflin, 1975.

———. "The Bar Fly Ought to Sing." In Colburn, ed., *No Evil Star*, 6–13.

———. *The Book of Folly*. Boston: Houghton Mifflin, 1972.

———. "Comment on 'Some Foreign Letters.'" In Colburn, ed., *No Evil Star*, 14–17.

———. *The Complete Poems: Anne Sexton*. Boston: Houghton Mifflin, 1981.

———. "Dancing the Jig." *New World Writing* 16 (1960): 146–53.

———. *The Death Notebooks*. Boston: Houghton Mifflin, 1974.

———. *45 Mercy Street*. Boston: Houghton Mifflin, 1976.

———. "The Freak Show." *American Poetry Review* (May/June 1973): 38–40. Rpt. in Colburn, ed., *No Evil Star*, 33–38.

———. "The Letting Down of the Hair." A Story by Anne Sexton. *Atlantic Monthly* (March 1972): 40–43.

———. *Live or Die*. Boston: Houghton Mifflin, 1966.

———. *Love Poems*. Boston: Houghton Mifflin, 1969.

———. *Selected Poems*. Oxford: Oxford University Press, 1964.

———. *Selected Poems of Anne Sexton*. Ed. Diane Wood Middlebrook and Diana Hume George. Boston: Houghton Mifflin, 1988.

———. *Transformations*. Boston: Houghton Mifflin, 1971.

———. *Words for Dr. Y.: Uncollected Poems with Three Stories*. Ed. Linda Gray Sexton. Boston: Houghton Mifflin, 1978.

Interviews and recordings

Ames, Lois. "Anne Sexton: From 'Bedlam' to Broadway." Interview with Anne Sexton. *Boston Herald Sunday Traveler Book Guide* 12 October 1969: 1, 2–16.

Balliro, Charles. "Interview with Anne Sexton." *Fiction* (ca. June 1974): 5, 12–13.

Fitz Gerald, Gregory. "Interview with Anne Sexton." In Colburn, ed., *No Evil Star*, 180–206.

Heyen, William, and Al Poulin. "Interview with Anne Sexton." In Colburn, ed., *No Evil Star*, 130–57.

Inglis, Ruth. "Anne Sexton and Her Poetry." Interview. *Nova* (ca. October/November 1966): 113–17, 125.

Kevles, Barbara. "Interview with Anne Sexton." *The Paris Review Interviews: Women Writers at Work*. Ed. George Plimpton. New York: Random House, 1981.

Macbeth, George. *Interview with Anne Sexton.* 20 January 1968. BBC Third Programme. London: National Sound Archive, British Library.

Marx, Patricia. "Interview with Anne Sexton." In Colburn, ed., *No Evil Star*, 70–82.

Moore, Harry. "Interview with Anne Sexton." In Colburn, ed., *No Evil Star*, 41–69.

Sexton, Anne. *Anne Sexton.* National Educational Television (outtakes). 1 March 1966. American Poetry Archive. San Francisco State University.

———. "Craft Interview with William Packard." In McClatchy, ed., 42–47.

Sexton, Anne, and Maxine Kumin. "Seminar on poetry." 13 February 1967. Audiotape. Radcliffe Institute for Independent Study Archives, Harvard University.

Showalter, Elaine, and Carol Smith. "A Nurturing Relationship: A Conversation with Anne Sexton and Maxine Kumin, April 15 1974." *Women's Studies* 4 (1976): 115–36.

Weeks, Brigitte. "Interview with Anne Sexton." In Colburn, ed., *No Evil Star*, 112–18.

White, Martha. "Interview with Anne Sexton." July 1963. Audiotape. Radcliffe Institute for Independent Study Archives, Harvard University.

Secondary sources

Adams, Timothy Dow. *Light Writing and Life Writing: Photography in Autobiography.* Chapel Hill: University of North Carolina Press, 2000.

Adorno, Theodor W. *Prisms.* Trans. Samuel and Shierry Weber. London: Spearman, 1967.

Altman, Janet. *Epistolarity: Approaches to a Form.* Columbus: Ohio State University Press, 1982.

Alvarez, Al. "Beyond All This Fiddle." *Times Literary Supplement.* 23 March 1967: 229–32.

———. *Beyond All This Fiddle.* London: Allen Lane/Penguin, 1968.

Ames, Lois. "Remembering Anne." In McClatchy, ed., 111–14.

Ashley, Kathleen, Leigh Gilmore, and Gerald Peters, eds. *Autobiography and Postmodernism.* Amherst: University of Massachusetts Press, 1994.

Auden, W. H. *Selected Poems.* Ed. Edward Mendelson. London: Faber and Faber, 1979.

Austin, J. L. *How To Do Things with Words.* Ed. J. O. Urmson. London: Oxford University Press, 1962.

Axelrod, Steven G. *Sylvia Plath: The Wound and the Cure of Words.* Baltimore: Johns Hopkins University Press, 1992.

Badia, Janet. "The Bell Jar and other prose." *The Cambridge Companion to Sylvia Plath*. Ed. Jo Gill. Cambridge: Cambridge University Press, 2006. 124–38.

Barthes, Roland. *Camera Lucida*. Trans. Richard Howard. London: Fontana, 1984.

———. *Criticism and Truth*. Trans. and ed. Katrine Pilcher-Keuneman. London: Athlone Press, 1987.

Beech, Christopher, ed. *Artifice and Indeterminacy: An Anthology of New Poetics*. Tuscaloosa: University of Alabama Press, 1998.

Berman, Jeffrey. *The Talking Cure: Literary Representations of Psychoanalysis*. New York: New York University Press, 1987.

Berryman, John. *The Dream Songs*. London: Faber and Faber, 1990.

Bishop, Elizabeth. *One Art: Letters*. Ed. Robert Giroux. New York: Farrar Straus Giroux, 1994.

Bixler, Frances, ed. *Original Essays on the Poetry of Anne Sexton*. N.p.: University of Central Arkansas Press, 1988.

Bogan, Louise. *What the Woman Lived: Selected Letters of Louise Bogan 1920–1970*. Ed. Ruth Limmer. New York: Harcourt Brace Jovanovich, 1973.

Bordo, Susan. "The Body and the Reproduction of Femininity: A Feminist Appropriation of Foucault." *Gender/Body/Knowledge: Feminist Reconstructions of Being and Knowing*. Ed. Susan Bordo and Alison M. Jagger. New Brunswick, N.J.: Rutgers University Press, 1992. 13–33.

Boyers, Robert, ed. *Contemporary Poetry in America: Essays and Interviews*. New York: Schocken, 1974.

———. "Live or Die: The Achievement of Anne Sexton." In McClatchy, ed., 204–15.

Brain, Tracy. *The Other Sylvia Plath*. London: Longman, 2001.

Britzolakis, Christina. *Sylvia Plath and the Theatre of Mourning*. Oxford: Clarendon Press, 1999.

Brooker, Peter, ed. *Modernism/Postmodernism*. London: Longman, 1992.

Brooks, Peter. *Body Work: Objects of Desire in Modern Narrative*. Cambridge, Mass.: Harvard University Press, 1993.

Brunner, Edward. *Cold War Poetry*. Urbana: University of Illinois Press, 2001.

Bryant, Marsha. "Ariel's Kitchen: *Ladies Home Journal* and the Domestic Surreal." *The Unraveling Archive: Essays on Sylvia Plath*. Ed. Anita Plath Helle. Ann Arbor: University of Michigan Press, forthcoming. 269–95.

Ciardi, John, ed. *Mid-Century American Poets*. New York: Twayne, 1950.

Coetzee, J. M. *Doubling the Point: Essays and Interviews*. Ed. David Attwell. Cambridge, Mass.: Harvard University Press, 1992.

Colburn, Steven E., ed. *Anne Sexton: Telling the Tale*. Ann Arbor: University of Michigan Press, 1988.

———. *No Evil Star: Selected Essays, Interviews and Prose—Anne Sexton*. Ann Arbor: University of Michigan Press, 1985.

Comentale, Edward. "Thesmophoria: Suffragettes, Sympathetic Magic, and H. D.'s Ritual Poetics." *Modernism/Modernity* 8.3 (2001): 471–92.

Costello, Bonnie. *Marianne Moore: Imaginary Possessions.* Cambridge, Mass.: Harvard University Press, 1981.

Cowan, Ruth Schwartz. *More Work for Mother: The Ironies of Household Technology from the Open Hearth to the Microwave.* New York: Basic Books, 1983.

Cox, C. B., and A. R. Jones. "After the Tranquillized Fifties: Notes on Sylvia Plath and James Baldwin." *Critical Quarterly* 6.2 (1964): 107–22.

Dante Alighieri. *The Inferno: Dante's Immortal Drama of a Journey through Hell.* Trans. John Ciardi. New York: Penguin, 1954.

Davidson, Michael. "'Skewed by Design': From Act to Speech Act in Language Writing." In Beech, ed., 70–76.

Davie, Donald. "'Beyond All This Fiddle': A Rejoinder to A. Alvarez." *Times Literary Supplement.* 25 May 1967: 472.

de Man, Paul. *Allegories of Reading: Figural Language in Rousseau, Nietzsche, Rilke and Proust.* New Haven: Yale University Press, 1979.

Derrida, Jacques. *Of Grammatology.* Corrected edition. Trans. Gayatri Chakravorty Spivak. Baltimore: Johns Hopkins University Press, 1998.

Diamond, John. *C: Because Cowards Get Cancer Too.* London: Vermilion, 1998.

Dickey, James. "Five First Books." *Poetry* 97 (1961): 316–20.

———. "On *All My Pretty Ones.*" In Colburn, ed., *Telling the Tale* 106.

Dickinson, Emily. *The Complete Poems.* Ed. Thomas H. Johnson. London: Faber and Faber, 1975.

Dobriner, William M. *Class in Suburbia.* Englewood Cliffs, N.J.: Prentice Hall, 1963.

DuPlessis, Rachel Blau. *Genders, Races, and Religious Cultures in Modern American Poetry 1908–1934.* Cambridge: Cambridge University Press, 2001.

Eakin, Paul John. *Fictions in Autobiography: Studies in the Art of Self-Invention.* Princeton, N.J.: Princeton University Press, 1985.

Easthope, Antony. *Poetry as Discourse.* London: Methuen, 1983.

Easthope, Antony, and John O. Thompson, eds. *Contemporary Poetry Meets Modern Theory.* Hemel Hempstead, UK: Harvester Wheatsheaf, 1991.

Egan, Susanna. *Mirror Talk: Genres of Crisis in Contemporary Autobiography.* Chapel Hill: University of North Carolina Press, 1999.

Eliot, T. S. *Collected Poems 1909–1962.* London: Faber and Faber, 1974.

———. "Tradition and the Individual Talent." *The Sacred Wood: Essays on Poetry and Criticism.* 1920. London: Faber, 1997. 39–49.

———. *The Waste Land and Other Poems.* London: Faber and Faber, 1940.

Felman, Shoshana, and Dori Laub, eds. *Testimony: Crises of Witnessing in Literature, Psychoanalysis, and History.* New York: Routledge, 1992.

Felski, Rita. "On Confession." In Smith and Watson, eds., 83–95.

Ferguson, Margaret, Mary Jo Salter, and Jon Stallworthy, eds. *The Norton Anthology of Poetry.* 4th ed. New York: Norton, 1996.

Fischer, Michael M. J. "Autobiographical Voices and Mosaic Memory: Experimental Sondages in the (Post)modern World." In Ashley, Gilmore, and Peters, eds., 79–129.

Fitzgerald, F. Scott. "The Cut-Glass Bowl." *Flappers and Philosophers*. New York: Washington Square Press, 1996.

Ford, Karen Jackson. *Gender and the Poetics of Excess: Moments of Brocade*. Jackson: University of Mississippi Press, 1997.

Foucault, Michel. *The History of Sexuality. Volume I: An Introduction*. Harmondsworth, UK: Peregrine, 1981.

———. "Truth and Power." *The Foucault Reader: An Introduction to Foucault's Thought*. Ed. Paul Rabinow. Harmondsworth, UK: Penguin, 1986. 51–75.

Freud, Sigmund. "An Autobiographical Study." Trans. James Strachey. London: Hogarth Press/Institute of Psychoanalysis, 1948.

———. "Case Histories: Fraulein Anna O." *Studies on Hysteria*. Penguin Freud Library (PFL), Vol. 3. Ed. Angela Richards. Trans. James and Alix Strachey. Harmondsworth, UK: Pelican, 1974. 73–102.

———. *Civilization, Society and Religion: Group Psychology, Civilization and its Discontents and Other Works*. PFL, Vol. 12. Ed. Albert Dickson. Trans. James Strachey. Harmondsworth, UK: Pelican, 1985.

———. *On Metapsychology: The Theory of Psychoanalysis*. PFL, Vol. 11. Ed. Angela Richards. Trans. James Strachey. Harmondsworth, UK: Pelican, 1984.

———. "The Uncanny." *Art and Literature*. PFL, Vol. 14. Ed. and trans. James Strachey. Harmondsworth, UK: Penguin, 1985. 335–76.

Friedan, Betty. *The Feminine Mystique*. Harmondsworth, UK: Penguin, 1965.

Furst, Arthur. *Anne Sexton: The Last Summer*. New York: St. Martin's, 2000.

Genette, Gerard. *Paratexts: Thresholds of Interpretation*. Trans. Jane E. Lewin. Cambridge: Cambridge University Press, 1997.

George, Diana Hume. *Oedipus Anne: The Poetry of Anne Sexton*. Urbana: University of Illinois Press, 1987.

———. ed. *Sexton: Selected Criticism*. Urbana: University of Illinois Press, 1988.

Gill, Jo. "Anne Sexton and Confessional Poetics." *Review of English Studies*. New Series, 55, no. 220 (2004) 424–45.

Gilmore, Leigh. *Autobiographics: A Feminist Theory of Women's Self-Representation*. Ithaca, N.Y.: Cornell University Press, 1994.

———. *The Limits of Autobiography: Trauma and Testimony*. Ithaca, N.Y.: Cornell University Press, 2001.

Goodwin, James. "Narcissus and Autobiography." *Genre* 12 (1979): 69–92.

Gordon, Richard E., Katherine K. Gordon, and Max Gunther. *The Split-Level Trap*. New York: Bernard Geis, 1960.

Graham, David, and Susan Sontag, eds. *After Confession: Poetry as Autobiography*. St. Paul, Minn.: Gray Wolf Press, 2001.

Green, Barbara. *Spectacular Confessions: Autobiography, Performative Activism and the Sites of Suffrage*. Basingstoke, UK: Palgrave Macmillan, 1997.

Green, Kate. "Inventory of Loss." In Colburn, ed., *Telling the Tale*, 376–80.

Grimm, Jacob and Wilhelm. *Grimm's Fairy Tales*. 1823. Harmondsworth, UK: Penguin, 1995.

Gunn, Thom. "On *All My Pretty Ones*." In McClatchy, ed., 124–26.

Hall, Caroline King Barnard. *Anne Sexton*. Boston: G. K. Hall, 1989.

Hall, Donald, ed. *Contemporary American Poetry*. 2nd ed. Harmondsworth, UK: Penguin, 1972.

Hamilton, Ian. *Robert Lowell: A Biography*. London: Faber and Faber, 1983.

Harris, Judith. "Breaking the Code of Silence: Ideology and Women's Confessional Poetry." In Graham and Sontag, eds., 254–68.

Hartman, Geoffrey. "On *To Bedlam and Part Way Back*." In McClatchy, ed., 118–21.

———. *Beyond Formalism: Literary Essays 1958–1970*. New Haven: Yale University Press, 1970.

H. D. *Selected Poems*. Ed. Louis L. Martz. Manchester, UK: Carcanet, 1997.

Henke, Suzette. *Shattered Subjects: Trauma and Testimony in Women's Life-Writing*. Basingstoke, UK: Macmillan, 2000.

Hoffman, Steven K. "Impersonal Personalism: The Making of a Confessional Poetic." *English Literary History* 45 (1978): 687–709.

Hopkins, Gerard Manley. *Poems of Gerard Manley Hopkins*. 4th ed. Ed. W. H. Gardner and N. H. Mackenzie. London: Oxford University Press, 1967.

Howard, Richard. *Alone With America: The Art of Poetry in the United States Since 1950*. London: Thames and Hudson, 1970.

Howe, Susan. *My Emily Dickinson*. Berkeley, Calif.: North Atlantic Books, 1985.

Hutcheon, Linda. *Narcissistic Narrative: The Metafictional Paradox*. London: Methuen, 1984.

———. *A Poetics of Postmodernism*. London: Routledge, 1988.

James, Henry. *The Golden Bowl*. 1904. Harmondsworth, UK: Penguin, 1987.

Jay, Paul. "Posing: Autobiography and the Subject of Photography." Ashley, Gilmore, and Peters, eds., 191–210.

Jones, A. R. "Necessity and Freedom: The Poetry of Robert Lowell, Sylvia Plath and Anne Sexton." *Critical Quarterly* 7.1 (1965): 11–30.

Juhasz, Suzanne. *Naked and Fiery Forms: Modern American Poetry by Women, a New Tradition*. New York: Harper and Row, 1976.

———. "Seeking the Exit or the Home: Poetry and Salvation in the Career of Anne Sexton." *Shakespeare's Sisters, Feminist Essays on Women Poets*. Ed. Sandra M. Gilbert and Susan Gubar. Bloomington: Indiana University Press, 1979.

Kammer, Jeanne. "The Witch's Life: Confession and Control in the Poetry of Anne Sexton." In Colburn, ed., *Telling the Tale* 125–34.

Keats, John. *The Crack in the Picture Window*. Boston: Houghton Mifflin, 1956.

Kenny, Herbert A. "Commitment Necessary to Be a Poet." *Boston Sunday Globe*, 19 May 1963.

Kristeva, Julia. *The Kristeva Reader*. Ed. Toril Moi. Trans. Seán Hand. Oxford: Blackwell, 1986.

Kumin, Maxine. "A Friendship Remembered." In McClatchy, ed., 103–10.

———. Interview by Enid Shomer. *Massachusetts Review* 37 (1996–97): 531–55.

———. "Kumin on Kumin and Sexton: An Interview." Interview by Diana Hume George. *Poesis* 6, no. 2 (1985): 1–18.

Lacan, Jacques. *Écrits: A Selection*. Trans. Alan Sheridan. London: Tavistock/Routledge, 1977.

———. *The Four Fundamental Concepts of Psychoanalysis*. Ed. Jacques-Alain Miller. Trans. Alan Sheridan. Harmondsworth, UK: Penguin, 1979.

Lang, Candace. "Autobiography in the Aftermath of Romanticism." *Diacritics* 12 (1982): 2–16.

Lasch, Christopher. *The Culture of Narcissism: American Life in an Age of Diminishing Expectations*. London: Norton, 1991.

Lerner, Laurence. "What is Confessional Poetry?" *Critical Quarterly* 29, no. 2 (1987): 46–66.

Levertov, Denise. "Biography and the Poet." *Ohio Review* 48 (1992): 7–18.

Littlejohn, Bel. "Now You Can Read my True Searing Story." *Guardian*, 24 Oct. 1997: 19.

Lowell, Amy. *Selected Poems of Amy Lowell*. Boston: Houghton Mifflin, 1928.

Lowell, Robert. *Collected Prose: Robert Lowell*. Ed. and Intro. Robert Giroux. London: Faber and Faber, 1987.

———. *Life Studies*. London: Faber and Faber, 1959.

Lucie-Smith, Edward. "A Murderous Art?" *Critical Quarterly* 6, no. 4 (1964): 355–63.

Luedtke, Janet. "'Something Special for Someone': Anne Sexton's Fan Letters from Women." In Oliphant, ed., 165–89.

McCabe, Jane. "'A Woman Who Writes': A Feminist Approach to the Early Poetry of Anne Sexton." In McClatchy, ed., 216–43.

McClatchy, J. D., ed. *Anne Sexton: The Artist and Her Critics*. Bloomington: Indiana University Press, 1978.

———. "Anne Sexton: Somehow to Endure." In McClatchy, ed., 245–90.

McDonnell, Thomas P. "Light in a Dark Journey." In Wagner-Martin, ed., 40–44.

McGinley, Phyllis. *Times Three: Selected Verse from Three Decades with Seventy New Poems*. Foreword W. H. Auden. New York: Viking, 1960.

May, Elaine Tyler. *Homeward Bound: American Families in the Cold War Era*. Revd. ed. New York: Basic Books, 1999.

Middlebrook, Diane Wood. *Anne Sexton: A Biography*. London: Virago, 1991.

Miller, J. Hillis. *Theory Now and Then*. Hemel Hempstead, UK: Harvester Wheatsheaf, 1991.

———. *Tropes, Parables, Performatives: Essays on Twentieth-Century Literature*. Hemel Hempstead, UK: Harvester Wheatsheaf, 1990.

Miller, Jonathan. *On Reflection*. London: National Gallery Publications, 1998.

Mills, Ralph J. Jr. "Anne Sexton." In Colburn, ed., *Telling the Tale* 110–24.

Moi, Toril. "Representations of Patriarchy: Sexuality and Epistemology in Freud's 'Dora.'" In *Dora's Case: Freud, Hysteria, Feminism*. Ed. Charles Bernheimer and Claire Kahane. Virago: London, 1985. 183–97.

Mood, John. "'A Bird Full of Bones': Anne Sexton—A Visit and a Reading." *Chicago Review* 23, no. 4 (1972): 107–23.

Morton, Richard Everett. *Anne Sexton's Poetry of Redemption: The Chronology of a Pilgrimage.* Lampeter, UK: Edwin Mellen Press, 1989.

Mulvey, Laura. "Visual Pleasure and Narrative Cinema." *Screen* 16, no. 3 (1975): 6–18.

Mumford, Lewis. *The City in History: Its Origins, Its Transformations and Its Prospects.* London: Secker and Warburg, 1961.

Nelson, Deborah. *Pursuing Privacy in Cold War America.* New York: Columbia University Press, 2002.

Oates, Joyce Carol. "On *The Awful Rowing Toward God.*" In McClatchy, ed., 168–72.

Olds, Sharon. *Strike Sparks: Selected Poems 1980–2002.* New York: Knopf, 2004.

Oliphant, Dave, ed. *Rossetti to Sexton: Six Women Poets at Texas.* Austin: Harry Ransom Humanities Research Center/University of Texas at Austin Press, 1992.

Oliver, Kendrick. *The My Lai Massacre in American History and Memory.* Manchester, UK: Manchester University Press. 2006.

Olney, James, ed. *Autobiography: Essays Theoretical and Critical.* Princeton: Princeton University Press, 1980.

Olson, Charles. "Projective Verse." *The Poetics of the New American Poetry.* Ed. Donald Allen and Warren Tallman. New York: Grove, 1973. 147–58.

Orr, Gregory. "The Postconfessional Lyric." *The Columbia History of American Poetry.* Ed. Jay Parini and Brett C. Millier. New York: Columbia University Press, 1993. 650–73.

Orr, Peter. *The Poet Speaks.* London: Routledge and Kegan Paul, 1967.

Osborne, Charles. *W. H. Auden: The Life of a Poet.* London: Eyre Methuen, 1980.

Ostriker, Alicia. "The Nerves of a Midwife: Contemporary American Women's Poetry." *Parnassus: Poetry in Review* (1977): 69–87.

———. *Stealing the Language: The Emergence of Women's Poetry in America.* London: Women's Press, 1987.

Ovid. *The Metamorphoses of Ovid.* Trans. Mary M. Innes. Harmondsworth, UK: Penguin, 1955.

Paglia, Camille. *Sexual Personae: Art and Decadence from Nefertiti to Emily Dickinson.* New Haven: Yale University Press, 1990.

Peel, Robin. *Writing Back: Sylvia Plath and Cold War Politics.* Madison, Wisc.: Farleigh Dickinson University Press, 2002.

Perloff, Marjorie. "The Changing Face of Common Intercourse: Talk Poetry, Talk Show, and the Scene of Writing." In Beech, ed., 77–106.

———. *The Dance of the Intellect: Studies in the Poetry of the Pound Tradition.* Cambridge: Cambridge University Press, 1985.

———. *Poetic License: Essays on Modernist and Postmodernist Lyric.* Evanston, Ill.: Northwestern University Press, 1990.

Phillips, Robert. *The Confessional Poets.* Carbondale: Southern Illinois University Press, 1973.

Plath, Sylvia. *Ariel.* London: Faber and Faber, 1965.

———. *The Bell Jar*. London: Faber and Faber, 1966.

———. *Collected Poems*. Ed. Ted Hughes. London: Faber and Faber, 1981.

———. *The Journals of Sylvia Plath: 1950–1962*. Ed. Karen V. Kukil. London: Faber and Faber, 2000.

———. *Letters Home: Correspondence 1950–1963*. Ed. Aurelia Schober Plath. London: Faber, 1978.

Plato. *The Republic*. 2nd ed. Trans. Desmond Lee. Harmondsworth, UK: Penguin, 1974.

Pound, Ezra. *ABC of Reading*. New York: New Directions, 1960.

Pritchard, William H., "The Anne Sexton Show." *Hudson Review* 31, no. 2 (1978): 387–92.

Rahv, Philip. "The Cult of Experience in American Writing." *Partisan Review* 7 (1940): 412–24.

Rees-Jones, Deryn. "Consorting with Angels: Anne Sexton and the art of confession." *Women: A Cultural Review* 10, no. 3 (1999): 283–96.

Reeve, F. D. "Inadequate Memory and the Adequate Imagination." *American Poetry Review* 32, no. 3 (2003): 11–13.

Reik, Theodor. *The Compulsion to Confess: On the Psychoanalysis of Crime and Punishment*. New York: Grove, 1959.

Rexroth, Kenneth. "The New American Poets." *Harper's Magazine* 230, no. 1381 (1965): 65–71.

Rich, Adrienne. *On Lies, Secrets and Silence: Selected Prose 1966–1978*. London: Virago, 1980.

Rose, Jacqueline. *The Haunting of Sylvia Plath*. London: Virago, 1991.

———. *States of Fantasy*. Oxford: Clarendon Press, 1996.

———. *On Not Being Able to Sleep: Psychoanalysis and the Modern World*. London: Chatto and Windus, 2003.

Rosenthal, M. L. *The New Poets: American and British Poetry Since World War Two*. New York: Oxford University Press, 1967.

———. "Poetry as Confession." *The Nation* 189 (1959): 154–55.

Rotskoff, Lori. *Love on the Rocks: Men, Women and Alcohol in Post-World War Two America*. Chapel Hill: University of North Carolina Press. 2002.

Rousseau, Jean-Jacques. *The Confessions of Jean-Jacques Rousseau*. Trans. J. M. Cohen. Harmondsworth, UK: Penguin, 1953.

Rukeyser, Muriel. "On *The Book of Folly*." In McClatchy, ed., 154–61.

Russo, Mary. *The Female Grotesque: Risk, Excess and Modernity*. London and New York: Routledge, 1994.

de Saussure, Ferdinand. *Course in General Linguistics*. Ed. Charles Bally, Albert Sechehaye, and Albert Riedlinger. Trans. Wade Baskin. New York: McGraw-Hill, 1966.

Sennett, Richard. *The Fall of Public Man*. New York: Norton, 1974.

Severin, Laura. *Stevie Smith's Resistant Antics*. Madison: University of Wisconsin Press, 1997.

Sexton, Linda Gray. *Searching for Mercy Street: My Journey Back to my Mother, Anne Sexton*. Boston: Little Brown, 1994.

Shattuc, Jane M. *The Talking Cure: TV Talk Shows and Women*. New York: Routledge, 1997.

Shurr, William. "Mysticism and Suicide: Anne Sexton's Last Poetry." In Wagner-Martin, ed., 193–210.

Smith, Sidonie. *A Poetics of Women's Autobiography: Marginality and the Fictions of Self-Representation*. Bloomington: Indiana University Press, 1987.

———. "Performativity, Autobiographical Practice, Resistance." *Women, Autobiography, Theory: A Reader*. Ed. Sidonie Smith and Julia Watson. Madison: University of Wisconsin Press, 1998. 108–15.

Smith, Stan. *The Origins of Modernism: Eliot, Pound, Yeats and the Rhetorics of Renewal*. Hemel Hempstead, UK: Harvester Wheatsheaf, 1994.

Snodgrass, W. D. *Selected Poems: 1957–1987*. New York: Soho Press, 1987.

Soja, Edward. *Third Space: Journeys to Los Angeles and Other Real-And-Imagined Places*. Oxford: Blackwell, 1996.

Soper, Kerry. "From Swarthy Ape to Sympathetic Everyman and Subversive Trickster: The Development of the Irish Caricature in American Comic Strips between 1890 and 1920." *Journal of American Studies* 39, no. 2 (2005): 257–96.

Spacks, Patricia Meyer. "On 45 Mercy Street." In McClatchy, ed., 186–89.

———. *The Poetry of Vision: Five Eighteenth-Century Poets*. Cambridge, Mass.: Harvard University Press, 1967.

Spigel, Lynn. *Welcome to the Dreamhouse: Popular Media and Postwar Suburbs*. Durham, N.C.: Duke University Press, 2001.

Stein, Gertrude. *The Autobiography of Alice B. Toklas*. 1933. London: Arrow Books, 1960.

Stevens, Wallace. *The Collected Poems of Wallace Stevens*. London: Faber and Faber, 1945.

Stewart, Gwendolyn. *Anne Sexton*. Http://www.people.fas.harvard.edu/~gestewar/sexton.html.

Swan, Barbara. "A Reminiscence." In McClatchy, ed., 81–88.

Van Duyn, Mona. "Letter to American Poetry Review." *American Poetry Review* 2, no. 6 (1973): 39–40.

Von Hallberg, Robert. *American Poetry and Culture, 1945–1980*. Cambridge, Mass.: Harvard University Press, 1985.

Wagner, Erica. *Ariel's Gift: Ted Hughes, Sylvia Plath and the Story of "Birthday Letters."* London: Faber and Faber, 2000.

Wagner-Martin, Linda, ed. *Critical Essays on Anne Sexton*. Boston: G. K. Hall, 1989.

Williams, Polly. "Sexton in the Classroom." In McClatchy, ed., 96–101.

Williams, William Carlos. "A1 Pound." *Selected Essays*. New York: New Directions, 1969.

———. *The Collected Poems 1909–1939*. Ed. A. Walton Litz and Christopher MacGowan. Manchester, UK: Carcanet, 1987.

———. *I Wanted to Write A Poem: The Autobiography of the Works of a Poet*. Ed. Edith Heal. New York: New Directions, 1978.

Williamson, Alan. "Confession and Tragedy." *Poetry* 5, no. 142 (1983): 170–78.
———. "Stories about the Self I & II." In Graham and Sontag, eds., 51–70.
Woolf, Virginia. *Moments of Being*. St. Albans, UK: Triad/Panther, 1978.
———. *Orlando: A Biography*. 1928. London: Vintage, 1992.
———. *A Room of One's Own*. 1928. Harmondsworth, UK: Penguin, 1945.
Words for Dr. Y. Book review. *Choice* 16, no. 1 (1979): 81.
Wurtzel, Elizabeth. *Bitch*. London: Quartet, 1998.
Yezzi, David. "Confessional Poetry and the Artifice of Honesty." *New Criterion* 16 (June 1998). Available online at http://newcriterion.com/archives/16/06/hughes-yezzi/.

Index

Jo Gill is lecturer in twentieth-century literature at the University of Exeter. She has published on modern poetry in numerous journals, including *Review of English Studies* and *Twentieth-Century Literature*. She is the editor of *The Cambridge Companion to Sylvia Plath* (2006) and *Modern Confessional Writing: New Critical Essays* (2006).